PEOPLE CMM

Interpreting People CMM for Software Organizations

A Guide for Improving People Related and Work Force Practices

PEOPLE CMM

Interpreting People CMM for Software Organizations

A Guide for Improving People Related and Work Force Practices

Raghav S Nandyal

SITARA Technologies
Bangalore

Tata McGraw-Hill Publishing Company Limited

NEW DELHI

McGraw-Hill Offices

New Delhi New York St Louis San Francisco Auckland Bogotá Caracas
Kuala Lumpur Lisbon London Madrid Mexico City Milan Montreal
San Juan Santiago Singapore Sydney Tokyo Toronto

Tata McGraw-Hill

This edition can be exported from India only by the publishers,
Tata McGraw-Hill Publishing Company Limited

ISBN 0-07-048307-8

Published by Tata McGraw-Hill Publishing Company Limited
7 West Patel Nagar, New Delhi 110 008 and typeset in Gatineau at The Composers,
20/5 Old Market, West Patel Nagar, New Delhi 110 008 and text and cover printed at
SDR Printers, A-28, West Jyoti Nagar, Shahdara, Loni Road, Delhi 110 094

Cover Design: Mesmerizers, Bangalore

RZZYCRADDLCRC

The **McGraw-Hill** Companies

To

The memory of my noble parents

Veda and Dr Srinivasa Murthy,

pedagogues par excellence who taught me human values,
which are so very eternal

It is my greatest good fortune to be their son

Foreword

In 1998, I had the pleasure of introducing the People CMM to India in classes overflowing with professionals asking insightful questions. In the spring of 1999, I returned to teach the first People CMM Lead Assessor class in India to 10 exceptional candidate Lead Assessors. One member of that class struck me as a natural leader with an instinctive understanding of what we were trying to accomplish in the People CMM. It is rewarding to see Raghav Nandyal emerge as a leader and communicate his insights so effectively in this book.

Raghav has assisted many Indian companies in implementing the practices recommended in the People CMM. This book integrates his excellent grasp of the material with his growing experience in helping companies interpret the People CMM within the context of their culture, environment, and business strategy. As a result, this book is an excellent companion to the actual text of the People CMM, and should be used to help interpret the intent of the practices and process areas contained therein. More than just restating the practices, Raghav offers examples of methods and procedures that can be used to implement them. This is a practical book for practical people, who want to improve the capability of their organizations using practical methods.

This book is especially valuable for organizations transitioning from Version 1 to Version 2 of the People CMM. It compares the process areas and goals between the two versions and provides insights into what changed and why. It does not surprise me that this book is the best current source comparing the two versions of the People CMM, since Raghav was one of the heaviest contributors of comments and change requests during the international review process that preceded the completion of Version 2. Raghav's incisive comments influenced some of the toughest decisions regarding improvements in Version 2.

The strongest commitment to implementing the People CMM has emerged in India. India understands the competitive value of the great natural resource represented in its people. Indian companies understand that the day they can win business simply by having lower labor rates will ultimately pass. Indian companies understand that when this day passes they can still win consistently if the capability of their workforce exceeds than that of their competitors. Finally, Indian companies know that implementing improved workforce practices now, ahead of their international competitors, may make the barrier to entry against them too high, even as labor rate differences dissipate.

I have been impressed that Indian executives have a clear sense of their responsibility in building great organizations. They know that their job is as much about organizational development and capability as it is about business strategy and execution. In fact, they know that the former provides the most reliable foundation for the latter. In most of the world I get briefings about People CMM-related accomplishments and plans from the Human Resources Director. In India I get these briefings from the CEO, and their knowledge of the implemented practices is sophisticated. Raghav's book emerges from this culture, a culture committed to the development of people as a primary business strategy.

BILL CURTIS
Fort Worth, Texas
December 25, 2002

Prologue

"If you jump into the lake, you may or may not learn to swim. But you cannot help getting wet."

—Ancient wisdom

I have often wondered why individuals and organizations embark on any journey. Some do it—because they want to explore new avenues, some because they want to accompany another person, some to ensure that they are not left behind, and yet some do it because they really want to make the journey. Obviously, the last is the most compelling reason. If a horse is thirsty, making the horse drink is not an issue. If you point the horse to the water, it will drink on its own.

The most important question for any organization planning to begin the People CMM journey is: "Do we have a problem looking for a solution or do we have a solution like People CMM looking for a problem?" If it is the second question, I would urge them to look deeper within themselves before looking outward. Because, as the author emphasizes in the book, People CMM is not about getting a certification or an external seal of approval or keeping up with the Jones. It is about looking at yourself more clearly. People CMM is like a mirror that shows your reflection. What you change depends on what you want to and how much you want to.

Motivation precedes perception. Think about the thirsty horse. And motivation is provided by goals that are synchronous and congruent with organizational vision. If the organizational vision depends on people competencies, processes and participation, then People CMM has valuable insights to offer.

People CMM is not the responsibility of the Human Resources function alone. Everyone has a role to play in it—the sponsor, the manager and every employee. The Human Resources Development function can help in building competencies and offer specialized knowledge on People CMM. But it has to be leadership driven, supported by managers and experienced by the employees if it has to be pervasively institutionalized.

The good news about this book is that it has something for everyone.

- For leaders and managers, it provides an overview about the People CMM model. More important, it helps them to define what their expectations should be from the process.

- For the experts and those who want to know more about People CMM, it offers interpretation and clarity on a variety of issues. For instance, how a Process Area looks when it is at a level below or a level above, helps in making a final call while arriving at the People CMM level. The element of interpretation in People CMM becomes a lot more systematic and easy because of the guidance provided in this book.

- For an absolute novice or student, this book provides a fairly comprehensive understanding of the People CMM model.

At a personal level, my journey with People CMM began way back in 1999, when I attended the first introduction program by Dr Bill Curtis. I was amazed by what I heard because it seemed to offer so many insights to what we were grappling with. All of us at Wipro were looking at four important questions:

(a) How to set a direction for Human Resources and how to measure where we have reached?

(b) How to make our people processes world class?

(c) How to ensure that all our people processes are integrated on common criteria, and become the basis for recruitment, selection, performance management, promotion, compensation and development

(d) How do we develop and retain our leaders?

We found that the People CMM model had many insights to offer. I then went on to develop my People CMM knowledge through the Lead Assessors' Course. At Wipro, I evangelized the People CMM model and also participated as an Assessment Team Member for both the People CMM Level 5 assessments. (We had an external Lead Assessor for both these assessments.) Last year I finally became a SEI Certified Lead Assessor.

At an organizational level, once we began the journey, what really amazed us about People CMM is that we could see how the entire paradigm actually moves as we moved from one level to the other, I guess this is natural when you implement People CMM in all sincerity. Wipro was a firm believer in the importance of people. Some of the practices in Wipro, which were over two decades old were pioneering practices. But People CMM helped in bringing them together. In the book, *"The Road Less Travelled"*, the author Scott Peck describes how the natural force of entropy creates disorder from order. It is the force of evolution, which counteracts this, moves in an opposite direction to create a higher order. I consider People CMM as a force, like the evolutionary force, that helps organizations to become more ordered, harmonious and mature. People CMM can therefore be utilized as a very important change management model.

I have no doubt that this book by Raghav Nandyal, who has added to my own understanding of People CMM in a significant way, will be useful to you. I wish that a book like this was available when I began my own People CMM journey. Whether your organization pursues People CMM till the assessment at the highest level or not, it will certainly make you 'wet' and evoke an abiding interest in People CMM and more importantly, the spirit behind it.

Success with People CMM, like in anything else, depends on at least four important dimensions according to our sages:

(a) The quality of understanding provided by the author or the guru

(b) The motivation and dedication of the receiver of knowledge

(c) The contact and interaction with similar others pursuing the same goal

(d) The alchemy of time

By this book, the author has taken the first step. The next two steps depend on the reader. And finally, it takes time for the concept to sink in, for the processes to stabilize and for the benefits to become tangible and visible.

The greatest part of the entire journey is that the process will transform you as much as the result. There is really no destination when you get off. At People CMM Level 5, all you achieve is the capability for continuous improvement. And the only problem is that this continues forever.

RANJAN ACHARYA
Vice President-Corporate
Human Resources Development
Wipro Limited

Preface

The origins of this book lie in my exposure to the People Capability Maturity Model in November 1996 during a consulting assignment with a large multinational in South Korea. I was inclined to learn more about the effectiveness of a prescription-based approach for developing organizational culture. Since culture development and organizational transformation is so very inherent in the People CMM, I picked this model up more out of curiosity to understand how it might work in a culture that has deeply entrenched, hierarchy-driven value systems. Many noteworthy *chaebols* in South Korea are extremely successful businesses with revenues quoted in billions of dollars. If the People CMM advocates an empowered work culture, while a hierarchy-driven system can produce phenomenal financial success, should a successful system in one cultural setting, which may be hierarchy-driven and authoritarian in its ways, change its simple success formula—speed, marketing aggression, and overstretched goals? If empowered work culture is what the People CMM attempts to build, I was almost certain that the prescriptions of the People CMM would fail hopelessly in this cultural setting!

But then the critical question is—could they be *more* successful in a knowledge-intensive industry, such as software development, if only they learn the art of empowering individuals? I was, therefore, interested to conduct an in-depth study of the applicability of the People CMM vis-à-vis the many cultural influences that shape the destinies of a workforce, besides just having great practices. The results of my study and my interpretation of the People CMM are what you are holding in your hands. This was made possible due to the generous support and sponsorship of SITARA Technologies. Many of the implementation ideas contained in this book have their origins in the SITARA Process JewelBox™ [SITARA 2000] which is a repository and treasure-trove of global best practices that were engineered during my consulting engagements. The basis for many of these concepts and process designs come from the synthesis of improvements to the three systemic components of people–process–technology using SITARA's Universal Excellence Framework (UEF). UEF treats each improvement opportunity as an opportunity to improve the overall system and not just an isolated process or process component.

I am fortunate to be among the authorized People CMM Lead Assessors by the Software Engineering Institute, Carnegie Mellon University. I was also fortunate to be a coach and a People CMM advocate representing the sponsor for an Indian subsidiary of one of the very first commercial People CMM Level 2 companies in the world—Intelligroup Asia Pvt. Ltd. I have contributed as a reviewer of the People CMM version 2.0 and therefore understand both the distinctions and the limitations inherent in the model. The essence of this book, therefore, captures the multiple perspectives; that of a sponsor, reviewer, and a lead assessor, while interpreting the People CMM.

Topics covered in the book lay special emphasis on what the spirit and purpose behind a People CMM implementation ought to be rather than taking a view of a People CMM advocate. A broad range of ideas from the People CMM are integrated with my own learning of Virginia Satir's pioneering research on family therapy and Peter Senge's seminal work on learning organizations. After all, the People CMM is a compilation of the necessary practices that enable individuals to be more productive by searching for ways to compel personal mastery and at best competing with oneself to move this benchmark of performance up, continuously. The hunger for personal mastery is a prerequisite for what is called achievement motivation. And, this hunger must rest within every individual and cannot be extrinsically induced through the People CMM discipline.

Why this book at this time?

This book is being written at a time when the People CMM, first published as Version 1.0 in September 1995 and revised to become Version 2.0 in July 2001, seems to have stabilized and caught the attention of the industry. It is an attempt to interpret the practices of the People CMM with a clear emphasis on *how to achieve and realize* the People CMM discipline within an organization. While the People CMM version 2.0 is a prescription for *what is needed* by the model, this book is a supplement to the model itself describing *how to interpret the model*. The People CMM can be downloaded for free off the website of the Software Engineering Institute at Carnegie Mellon University (http://www.sei.cmu.edu) as a maturity model description with a reference of CMU/SEI-2001-MM-01.

How to use this book?

A superficial way to read this book is through a mere intellectual understanding. A deeper way is to connect to the feelings behind insights of the narration. This book is a suite of implementation ideas relevant to every individual in an organization. The emphasis is on interpretation. Since each chapter builds on what is presented earlier, I recommend you start at the beginning and read through the chapters in order. Topics are built to facilitate integration of learning as you progress in the understanding of the implementation of People CMM as a discipline. Relevance of the People CMM model to organizations, both big and small, is highlighted throughout the book. Many times it is tempting to beg, borrow, or steal process implementations from other organizations that have done them successfully. While I advocate these essential hallmarks of a learning organization to adapt imaginatively, borrow shamelessly, and imitate creatively, a good portion of the foundation for process improvement, however, has to be homegrown. As I will point out from time to time both overtly and covertly, 'the best common sense available in your organization to make the day-to-day changes necessary for optimal performance, is the best practice that is both relevant and applicable within your organizational context'. For instance, the best way to reduce attrition is to make sure that people are treated with dignity and honor and made to feel important as contributors to the canvas in the painting of organizational success. It is a lot easier to retain talent when individuals perceive a sense of fairplay and fairness. Just having flowery policies to reduce attrition will not work! When the birds begin to fly, that is a clear indication for the chief executive to take note.

The fundamental premise that is best made at the outset is that 'people are doing the best in the given circumstances; process improvement has to do with changing or improving these circumstances'. In order to avoid the temptation of biting more off the People CMM model than is practically possible to chew, it is necessary to emphasize that even after establishing an optimizing or a Level 5 process there is work to do! There is nothing like, you have arrived. So, taking measured steps to build robust processes and practices that have a lasting value is what a sponsor should make every attempt to demonstrate. In the context of People CMM, the word process means a set of defined activities, methods, and transformations that people create and use to continuously improve the organizational ability to manage workforce competency.

After all is said and done, we will come to conclude that having the right systems and processes in place is only a necessary condition, but not sufficient.

condition to operate at high maturity. And, having a well-defined process is nothing more than the best available common sense—the best practice that is probably the right response to the circumstances surrounding current time.

Copyright Permissions

Special permission to reproduce and adapt portions of People Capability Maturity Model® Version 1.0, CMU/SEI-95-MM-02, Overview of the People Capability Maturity Model® Version 1.1, CMU/SEI 95-MM-01, People Capability Maturity Model® Version 2.0, CMU/SEI-2001-MM-01 by Carnegie Mellon University, is granted by the Software Engineering Institute.

No Warranty. Any material furnished by Carnegie Mellon University and Software Engineering Institute material is furnished on an "as is" basis. Carnegie Mellon University makes no warranties of any kind, either expressed or implied as to any matter including, but not limited to, warranty of fitness for purpose or mechantability, exclusivity, or results obtained from use of the material. Carnegie Mellon University does not make any warranty of any kind with respect to freedom from patent, trademark, or copyright infringement.

Use of any trademarks in this book is not intended in any way to infringe on the rights of the trademark holder.

The author and publisher have taken care in the preparation of this book, but make no expressed or implied warranty of any kind and assume no responsibility for errors or omissions. No liability is assumed for incidental or consequential damages in connection with or arising out of the use of the information or program contained herein.

The following service marks and registered trademarks are used in this document.

Capability Maturity Model®   CMM Integration^SM   CMM®

CMMI^SM   IDEAL^SM

Capability Maturity Model and CMM are registered trademarks in the US Patent and Trademark Office. CMM Integration, CMMI; IDEAL; Personal Software Process, PSP; SCAMPI; SCAMPI Lead Assessor; SCE; and Team Software Process, TSP, are service marks of Carnegie Mellon University.

Special permission to reproduce and adapt portions of SITARA Process Jewelbox™ is granted by SITARA Technologies Pvt. Ltd. (India) and SITARA Technologies, Inc. (USA).

RAGHAV S NANDYAL

Acknowledgements

Much of the material in these pages represents the intellectual output of the numerous fertile minds with whom I had the good fortune to interact—directly and indirectly. Whatever the shortcomings of this book, they are mine; whatever its strengths, I owe it entirely to this large brain-trust. I wish to express my appreciation for their contributions. Unfortunately, they are so numerous as to be virtually unknowable. A few, however, have had direct impact upon this book and I would like to acknowledge them specifically.

First and foremost, Dr Bill Curtis, who has shaped the way I think about the People CMM to a great extent by accepting me as his student and encouraging me to write this book when I first told him about it. He also graciously accepted to write a foreword for this book. In true Indian tradition, I pay my respects to my teacher.

Had it not been for the willing sponsorship of the People CMM initiative at Intelligroup by Arjun Valluri, Chairman and CEO of Intelligroup, Inc., much of what I am writing today would still be a dream. My heartfelt thanks to him and my fellow professionals at Intelligroup Asia who made a big difference to the way I think and live in the defining moments of my life.

The persistent encouragement and support of Shailaja Nandyal, my co-founder at SITARA Technologies, made it easy for me to stir up the right thought process. Her requirement for this work product was that 'it should be a source of inspiration for any creative person who is compelled to be a process innovator rather than a mere process conformist'. Therefore, the vision for this book is to kindle an internal dialogue within you and offer you a range of possibilities and organizational contexts you might potentially encounter with the People CMM practices—worst case, at the planned level, and best case.

I would like to thank Ranjan Acharya, Vice President Corporate Human Resources Development of WIPRO Corporation for setting the right tone and pitch for this book in his Prologue. Actually, the vision for this book as stated above has its roots in a very profound discussion we had in Columbus, Ohio, comparing harmonics in music to the capability dimensions for a process area!

The comments of students taking SITARA's People CMM Model training, upon which this material is based, were of remarkable value. Finally, I wish to express my appreciation to my family whose patience and support by good-naturedly enduring the preoccupation of their family co-worker while this text was in preparation was instrumental in accomplishing this task. I must say, I have really enjoyed writing this book all the way. I would like to express my heartfelt thanks to R Chandra Sekhar, Nidhi Sharma and the production team at Tata McGraw-Hill for their excellent support.

This book is a mechanism to establish a learning community with its readers. There is much to learn from your experiences and wisdom. So, keep in touch!

RAGHAV S NANDYAL
raghav_nandyal@SITARATECH.com
November 13, 2002

Contents

Executive Decisions

WHAT EVERY SPONSOR SHOULD KNOW ABOUT PEOPLE CMM

What the People CMM is All About?

THE PEOPLE CMM is a well-documented set of practices that enables growing organizational workforce competencies. I have always believed that the word 'people' in the People CMM is a misnomer since it is not just a model for the human resource manager. It is more of a strategic management framework for building and growing organizational competencies. The People CMM practices help to retain, grow, and nurture competent individuals. It is a model for all managers as much as it is for the human resource (HR) manager, and more so for the chief executive officer (CEO).

Since culture development is inherent in the People CMM framework, when applied in the context of business goals, the People CMM helps to attract, develop, motivate, organize, and retain talented people. However, it must be emphasized that like any model which is only a depiction of an approximation of reality, the People CMM alone cannot solve all the problems within an organization. This is because, inherent in People CMM is a dimension, which addresses improving interpersonal skills and building workforce competencies; both of which require conscious effort and determination from every individual in the organization. The degree of detail and the intention behind the implementation of the People CMM determines the effectiveness of practices to a large extent.

At the core of the People CMM lies a framework to define workforce capability and practices, which help to continuously improve this capability. The whole organization can't get better overnight. But it can start getting better, piece by piece right away. Each operation can substantially and even dramatically improve. In order to make such improvements possible, it is required to abandon traditional management styles. The emphasis is on the word 'management', because from what I have observed, the majority of the problems are not process problems, but they are management problems.

The People CMM is structured as a staged model wherein such improvements happen through progressive, evolutionary steps. At level 2 or the *managed level* the process basically enables managers to sensitize themselves to the fundamental workforce issues to help create a management foundation across units. The focus of improvement is more tactical and less strategic at level 2. Managers take personal responsibility for managing and developing people reporting to them. In my consulting engagements with organizations, I find a rather disturbing trend that I will highlight here and explain later on in chapter 4. Level 2 process-fixes begin with building elaborate personal review systems or performance appraisals, which is most definitely not performance management! Performance appraisal is the least important activity needed for effective demonstration of performance management. Dr Deming's 14 Points for the transformation of management extends into what he notes as 'diseases' that stand in the way of effective transformation. One of these organizational diseases is the personal review system or evaluation of performance. A radical view I carry today about performance assessment is that it is misleading and strips human meaning from whatever is being measured since measures are oftentimes used to modify behaviour. What I find more useful is to establish a performance tracking system wherein each individual in the team establishes a plan of coordinated action for the year after discussions with the supervisor. The individual is now responsible to deliver on these commitments by tracking performance goals through self-assessment and knows the minimum criteria to qualify for a performance review. If the individual meets or exceeds the performance goals established even before the review period is complete, the individual flags off a request for performance review with the supervisor. On the contrary, if the individual fails to meet the established performance goals, he knows about it much before the supervisor is made aware through the process of self-assessment. The individual then requests supervisor support to accomplish the established performance goals. In such a collaborative environment, there are no losers—all win. Where there is trust, numbers do not matter and the meaning behind performance metrics is established entirely through self-interpretation. A template for such a performance self-assessment and tracking system is provided in Table 4.1, Chapter 4 while interpreting performance management process area.

Dr Deming's 14 Points for Transformation of Management: [Aguayo 1990]

- *Create Constancy of purpose toward improvement of product and service, with the aim to become competitive and to stay in business, and to provide jobs.*

- *Adopt the new philosophy. We are in a new economic age. Western management must awaken to the challenge, learn their responsibilities, and take on leadership for change.*

- *Cease reliance on mass inspection to achieve quality. Eliminate the need for inspection on a mass basis by building quality into the product in the first place.*

- *End the practice of awarding business on the basis of price tag. Instead, minimize total cost. Move toward a single supplier for any one item, on a long-term relationship of loyalty and trust.*

- *Improve constantly and forever the system of production and service, to improve quality and productivity, and thus constantly decrease cost*

- *Institute training on the job.*

- *Institute leadership. The aim of supervision should be to help people and machines and gadgets to do a better job. Supervision of management is in need of overhaul, as well as supervision of production workers.*

- *Drive out fear, so that everyone may work effectively for the company.*

- *Break down barriers between departments. People in research, design, sales, and production must work as a team, to foresee problems of production and in use that may be encountered with the product or service.*

- *Eliminate slogans, exhortations, and targets for the workforce asking for zero defects and new levels of productivity. Such exhortations only create*

> *adversarial relationships, since the bulk of the causes of low quality and low productivity belong to the system and thus lie beyond the power of the work-force.*
>
> - *Eliminate work standards (quotas) on the factory floor. Substitute leader-ship. Eliminate management by objectives. Eliminate management by num-bers, numerical goals. Substitute leadership.*
>
> - *Remove barriers that rob the hourly workers of their right to pride of work-manship. The responsibility of supervisors must be changed from mere num-bers to quality. Remove barriers that rob people in management and in engineering of their right to pride of workmanship. This means, inter alia, abolishment of the annual review or merit rating and of management by objectives.*
>
> - *Institute a vigorous program of education and self-improvement.*
>
> - *Put everybody in the company to work to accomplish the transformation. The transformation is everybody's job.*

At level 3 or the *defined level*, a common organizational framework of workforce practices and competencies, addressing business objectives with a management visibly driven by appropriate process measurements, is institutionalized. Building a robust framework to manage competencies with a strategic focus to systemati-cally grow knowledge and skills is what a level 3 process is all about. And for skill to demonstrate value, it must operate within specific contexts. When the context vanishes, so does the value of the skill. Much of this context gets established with level 2 practices of a supportive work environment conducive to nurture individual capabilities.

At the *predictable level* or level 4, advantage from having right data is taken to manage and exploit the capability of the defined framework. Nearly 70%–80% of the competency framework that was defined at level 3 is reused. Great emphasis is placed on knowledge management along with reuse of the competency frame-work, whereby minimizing variation of execution outcomes. This is possible only after establishing the fact that the framework indeed works the way it is designed to. It is only when capable people use a fairly capable process that we can have predictable performance. Workforce capability is managed quantitatively and op-portunities to exploit the competency framework are enabled by creating an empowering work environment. A skill that enables inventing skills begins to take hold with mentoring relationships and practices.

At the *optimizing level* or level 5, resilience to change is built through effective change management by ensuring continuous improvements to the established competency framework. Change management is made part and parcel of the organizational process improvement framework wherein innovative practices are tried out. A good example is: "... while at Siemens Nixdorf, Gerhard Schulmeyer instituted a process of reverse mentoring where, twenty-somethings got the chance to teach senior executives a thing or two about the future" [Hammel 2000].

While the focus of transitions from levels 1 through 3 is on organizational development, transitions beyond level 3 up to level 5 focus on practices that enable professional empowerment.

When Does the People CMM Make Sense?

People CMM has been designed to build a progressive, process-driven organizational improvement program along four process threads that span the organization, aiming at the following.

- Developing individual capability or improving individual competency
- Building workgroups and culture
- Motivating and managing performance
- Shaping the workforce

Therefore, People CMM practices make sense at any stage of organizational evolution. However, to avoid the risk of a cynical misinterpretation and going through these practices with ritualistic irrelevance, the People CMM must not be attempted for its own sake. It makes very little sense when organizations are going through troubled times with downsizing or rightsizing. Much of what I am writing in this book is at a time—the first quarter of 2002—when there has been a significant downturn in information technology (IT) and organizations are focused more on survival. But then, is the reason for such a slowdown in IT due to a lack of direction in growing the right competencies? Is there a lesson or two that can be learnt from the general lack of competency orientation which the People CMM may teach? I would be very positive about this. Besides, People CMM practices have the propensity to make sense and provide additional fillip to

Total Quality Management (TQM) [Creech 1994] programs and other process initiatives. Downturn or no downturn, TQM is something that is mandated for its own good reasons. Also, if for some reason these initiatives have not worked well for an organization, then again the People CMM may have answers to offer by providing the necessary leverage and bring relevance back to such initiatives. People CMM practices serve the purpose of providing a fulcrum to lift the load of the TQM programs provided the right power behind these initiatives can be exerted by talented and knowledgeable individuals.

Why do organizations attempt TQM at all? They do so to establish mature processes that make execution outcomes less people-dependent. If execution outcomes have to become less people-dependent and more process-dependent, then emphasis has to be placed upon the process to assume responsibility for all execution outcomes while stepping away from the easy way out of blaming people for mistakes. In a learning process, mistakes are surfaced, identified, isolated, and eliminated from the system using a powerful tool called peer reviews and management by exception. If after mistake-proofing the execution outcome through process improvements, there is a reason why the mistake has recurred, then the only assignable cause is to the very process improvement program itself—not the people who are executing the process. When process improvement ideas work well, the word is spread around in the organization so that everyone in the organization can benefit from such experiences. When they don't, the word spreads around as well so that others may not repeat the same mistake. Continuous and purposeful learning is the essence behind TQM.

The People CMM makes sense only when the entire organization is ready and willing to take responsibility for making a difference with individual learning, unit learning, and thereby overall organizational learning. It must be mentioned that if process improvement initiatives are attempted in order to game up on process owners to eliminate them from the organization, it is a sureshot formula for implementation failure! Often, assessment outcomes are stressed only to take on a constricted objective of level accomplishment or level chasing as it is called. Here again, organizations are bound to lose sight of why the process improvement initiative was initiated in the first place. Level chasing becomes an obsession sooner or later and the sponsor and his teams are advised to watch out! The People CMM will have very little relevance if the end objective of the People CMM initiative is to get to a maturity level. There is nothing like you have arrived when it comes to learning! The more you learn, the more acutely aware you become of your ignorance [Senge 1990]. Maturity level is just an abbreviation for the detailed process infrastructure that must exist to justify the soundness of implementation and institutionalization of key practices. And these practices must be created, used, and continuously improved upon by the people. So, it is important to note the strongly humanistic aspects of process improvement or change management.

Importance of People Issues

If the key premise is to build organizational capability, then there are three interacting parts to this system—people, process, and technology as a triad. A well-managed change initiative ought to consider improvements to all three of the above, taking note of the need for creating a learning environment as the necessary compeller influenced by global competition. Productivity improvement makes sense only when there is an equal emphasis placed on all three. Overemphasis of improvements to just any one of them, without suitable adjustments to the other two, will yield a lopsided change management program with poor gains and return on investment.

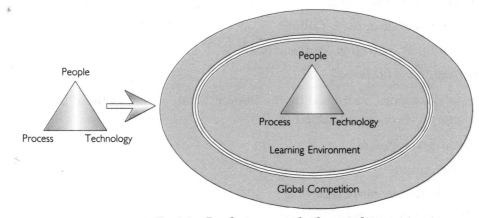

Fig. 1.1   *People–process–technology triad*

Source: Adapted from People Capability Maturity Model, Carnegie Mellon University [1995] with permission

Current Status

The current version of the People CMM is version 2.0 dated July 2001. Its principal authors are Drs Bill Curtis, William Hefley, and Sally Miller [Curtis 2002]. The current version is based on the first published version 1.0 [Curtis 1995], which was conceived as a roadmap for implementing workforce practices. Much of the philosophy governing the practices contained in version 1.0 and their effect on improving workforce capability has been reused in version 2.0. The emphasis placed on developing and improving workforce competencies with appropriate team orientation is highly pronounced in the current version 2.0. From an implementation point of view, we will see that People CMM practices have an ability to scale up in rigour and therefore provide for a continuity of purpose. The People CMM concerns itself with the domain of workforce management and development. It provides a high-level guideline to design organizational processes, which address workforce capability development. A good degree of professional and managerial judgement is required to be exercised while doing so.

Process Area Threads

The following four themes or process area threads run across the People CMM model.

1. Developing Competency
2. Building Workgroups & Culture
3. Motivating & Managing Performance
4. Shaping the workforce

Areas or disciplines addressed by the People CMM belong to these process area threads and are broadly identified as follows.

- Career development
- Compensation
- Competency development
- Culture development
- Communication and coordination
- Performance management
- Staffing
- Training
- Team building
- Work environment

Structure of the People CMM

The People CMM is organized into five maturity levels. Each maturity level is made up of a group of process areas. A process area is a collection of practices, which when established fulfills the purpose and therefore the accomplishment of goals leading to the establishment of organizational maturity. These practices are further distinguished as institutionalization practices and implementation practices. Institutionalization practices have the distinction of making the purpose behind a process area both lasting and permanent. The implementation practices enable the articulation of the activities necessary to visibly support and 'walk the talk'.

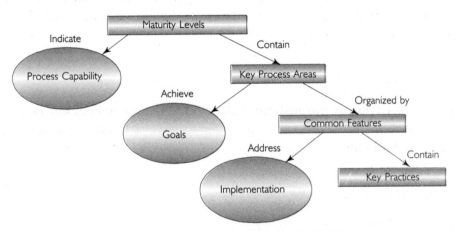

🖿 Fig. 1.2 *Structure of the People CMM*

Source: Adapted from People Capability Maturity Model, Carnegie Mellon University [1995] with permission

It is important to understand the jargon contained in the People CMM.

Maturity

Maturity indicates both the richness and consistency with which practices are applied across the organization. Since maturity is an indicator of process capability, it is a progress indicator for strategic quality planning. It offers tremendous insights into organizational ability to improve.

Process Capability

This is the range of expected results that can be achieved by following a process and the ability of a process to meet its objectives or requirements or to perform within specified limits. It is the degree of detail to which a process is enabled in an organization by supporting practices.

Key Process Area or Process Area

A cluster of related practices that, when performed collectively, satisfy a set of goals that contribute to the capability gained by achieving a maturity level. The process area is a collection of practices, which when institutionalized and implemented, accomplish the purpose and objectives behind a prescribed discipline, whereby achieving the goals.

Common Features

Common features contain the institutionalization and implementation details that an organization must be sensitive to, in order to have a lasting representation of the prescribed discipline.

Institutionalization Common Features

These are characterized into

- *Commitment to perform:* A category of institutionalization practices within a process area that describes the actions an organization must take to ensure that the activities constituting a process area are established and will endure. Commitment to perform typically involves establishing organizational policies (to set expectations for performance), executive management sponsorship, and assigned responsibilities for advising on and coordinating the implementation of workforce practices.

- *Ability to perform:* A category of institutionalization practices within a process area that describes the preconditions that must exist in the unit or organization to implement practices competently. Ability to perform typically involves resources, organizational structures, and preparation to perform the practices of the process area.

- *Measurement and analysis:* A category of institutionalization practices within a process area that describes the actions the organization must take to ensure that workforce practices are evaluated for performance and effectiveness. Measurement and analysis typically involves measuring the status of the practices performed, aggregating some measures from the unit to the organizational level, and evaluating the effectiveness of the practices performed.

- *Verifying implementation:* A category of institutionalization practices within a process area that describes the actions the organization must take to ensure that it is complying with its policies regarding workforce practices. Verifying implementation typically involves assuring that practices are being performed in compliance with policies, stated values, plans, laws, and regulations; and that executive management maintains awareness of the level of compliance.

Implementation Common Features

These are the practices and procedures implemented by the organization to satisfy the implementation goals of a process area. They collectively constitute the area of practice denoted by the title of the process area.

For any new practice, both the institutionalization and implementation have to be verified. When data deviations occur very widely from the norm, process compliance must be measured. What is equally important to ensure is the richness and consistency of application of the process.

Staged Progression

In line with continuous improvement, the People CMM takes an evolutionary growth path for organizational maturity. The staged progression of organizational maturity involves building up of capability of the governing processes in gradual steps. There are five levels of organizational maturity that define a well-defined evolutionary plateau into which an organizational process can transform. The People CMM embraces the transition management approach by advocating an evolutionary growth path for improving organizational maturity.

Five Maturity Levels

The five maturity levels of the People CMM are as follows.

1. Level 1: Initial

2. Level 2: Repeatable (Version 1.0), renamed as Managed (Version 2.0)

3. Level 3: Defined

4. Level 4: Managed (Version 1.0), renamed as Predictable (Version 2.0)

5. Level 5: Optimizing

Process Characteristics of the 5 Maturity Levels

Level I Process

Level 1 or the *initial process* is a characteristic of all low maturity organizations wherein the management processes are prone to display chaotic tendencies. Level 1 processes lack consistent workforce practices. The organization may not have adequate management talent. Skills and talents of individuals are often unutilized or underutilized. Staffing of projects with adequate skills is inadequate and therefore projects are found to be in a perennial state of firefighting. There are no clearly established performance guidelines for project teams. The compensation mechanisms and policies are visibly driven towards an overtime system. Everybody in the organization appears to be inordinately busy, but nobody knows exactly whether progress is being made on projects. Needless to say that performance measurement is either absent or considered unsafe. There is also a general apathy to improvement. Since sharing of information and knowledge is unheard of, people who are indispensable have a very high sense of job security by knowing how to exploit closely-guarded tricks of the trade! Insulation of the individual's importance is characterized by low goals and low growth. A classic level 1 process is characterized by one where everything from start to finish is by the spoken word rather than by the written letter. These organizations find documenting basic workforce practices such as job descriptions, compensation policies, and communication protocols (including escalation of matters) particularly difficult. Always centred around one individual—where the buck stops, is always very clear! A level 1 process is best characterized as being inconsistent with talent utilization and efforts to improve it.

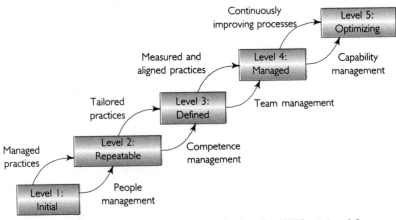

ㅁ **Fig. 1.3** *Maturity levels in the People CMM version 1.0*

Source: Adapted from People Capability Maturity Model, Carnegie Mellon University [1995] with permission

Level 2 Process

To move from an *initial* or level 1 process to level 2, basic people management practices are emphasized. Called the *repeatable process* in version 1.0 and *managed process* in version 2.0, the hallmarks of a level 2 process are to establish a foundation of workforce practices that can be improved continuously by eliminating problems that keep people from being able to perform effectively. The philosophy that governs this transformation is to address the basic and most fundamental reasons that contribute to large-scale variation in performance. Such large-scale causes of variation are known to exist because of environmental distractions, unclearly stated performance objectives, lack of relevant knowledge and skills, and poor communication and coordination of work. The underlying premise of the People CMM at level 2 is to work with aspirations and motivation of individuals to progressively reach self-actualization.

The well-documented hierarchy of needs propounded by Abraham Maslow in his Motivation Theory also suggests that an individual's physiological and safety needs must be addressed first. Activated in order, the five types of needs fulfillment eventually leads to self-actualization. Accordingly the key process areas in People CMM version 1.0 are

- Work environment

- Communication

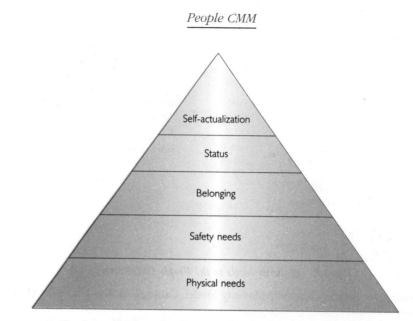

Fig. 1.4 *Abraham Maslow's motivation theory: hierarchy of needs*

Source: Adapted from SITARA People CMM Version 2.0 Model Training © 1999 with permission

- Staffing

- Training

- Performance management

- Compensation

The purpose of the practices contained in these process areas is to a large degree extrinsically influence and motivate individuals to perform. Extrinsic motivation though limiting cannot sustain performance and induce the quest for learning. These practices are employed to build a sense of commitment.

It must be emphasized that there are changes between version 1.0 and version 2.0 of the People CMM. The focus of this book is on interpreting version 2.0. Where ideas contained in version 1.0 can add value, they will be integrated in the learning. There are significant benefits in understanding both versions because the synthesis of these two versions has far-reaching effects in effective implementation. Certain practices enabling a team orientation such as team building and team-based practices are not so obviously emphasized in version 2.0. It is my belief that building effective practices around these key process areas has a significant advantage versus ignoring them altogether. If version 1.0 can help to do a better job of implementing the People CMM discipline, it would be helpful to embrace it. The focus of this book is to build a thorough understanding of both the versions and leave it to the reader to decide on the implementation approach. Accordingly, both versions will be dealt with at great length.

In version 2.0, level 2 key process areas are called

- Work environment
- Communication and coordination
- Staffing
- Training and development
- Performance management
- Compensation

Staff welfare (physical and safety needs) assumes importance and adequate measures to harmonize the work environment are taken. Training and development deals with gap analysis of individual needs and helping individuals develop a plan to minimize impact from their perceived inadequacies. A foundation for workgroup development is established through communication and coordination. Those assigned workforce management duties are trained to execute such duties and accept responsibility for ensuring that the practices are performed effectively. There is a greater consistency within and across groups, though variations of methods employed across the organization may differ. By focusing on factors that prevent people from performing their work effectively, workforce development becomes a core organizational value leading to establish a **Culture of Commitment**.

Level 3 Process

After the assignable causes that contribute to large-scale variation in performance have been addressed, the next logical step is to build a system of practices that help to manage competence. These competency-based practices are a set of tailored practices that help to identify, grow and build a competency orientation for the organization. By far, this is a steep climb from level 2.

The primary objective behind establishing a level 3 or the *defined process* is to remove inconsistencies across units by establishing tailoring guidelines, which address the specific needs of the business. An organization takes stock of the individual competencies by managing a knowledge and skills repository. By articulating the organization's competency development strategy, a plan for its future workforce requirements is established. By involving the organizational stakeholders in the development process, a sense of empowerment begins to take hold. Some of the characteristics exhibited by a level 3 process are as follows.

- Sensitivity to published surveys and their use to tailor workforce practices

- Study and analysis of core competency with an established periodicity

- Development of workforce competencies as the primary purpose behind periodic assessment of knowledge and skills

- Involvement of people in sharing responsibility for competency development

- Retraining of individuals with skills that are no longer needed

- Periodic projections of workforce needs to meet future market demands

Note: Periodic implies a frequency between engagements that is sufficient to establish context from memory as well as from records of minutes of meetings. Stipulating a weekly or a monthly or a quarterly periodicity in either the policy or procedure would soon render such engagements to a ritual, done-so-because-it-says-so! The well-meaning intention behind the activity will also be lost.

The key process areas that assist in accomplishing these objectives in version 1.0 are called

- Knowledge and skills analysis

- Workforce planning

- Competency-based practices

- Competency development

- Career development

- Participatory culture

In version 2.0, a new set of practices addressing workgroup development to build on the institutionalization of training and development at level 2 has been introduced. The process areas are called

- Competency analysis

- Workforce planning

- Competency development

- Workgroup development

- Career development

- Competency-based practices

- Participatory culture

Taking collective responsibility for organizational competency development, empowerment and participative management styles are the essential hallmarks of a level 3 process. Competency development at level 3 is about strategically growing knowledge, skills, and process abilities of individuals based on an evaluation of 'what is needed' using competency analysis. What process improvements within each workgroup competency must recognize is to ensure that improvements within their workgroups are based on recognizing the unique characteristics that describe competencies—some competencies lend themselves to innovations better than others.

Within level 3, workgroup development is the process part of team building. Practices within workgroup development influence the overall performance by optimizing the impact of growing workforce competencies. There is a great influence from organizational legacy and other cultural backdrops that dictate how effectively these practices can be institutionalized to build a **Culture of Competencies**.

Level 4 Process

At level 4, the distinction is to know the capability of the workforce in quantitative terms—'how much of what is needed is in place?' When organizations become successful with empowering individuals to take direct responsibility for enhancing organizational competency management activities, the ability to leverage experience of the organizational workforce becomes practical. Experienced individuals provide personal support and guidance to other individuals or groups. Empowered workgroups are established to enhance organizational capability management. Team building and mentoring relationships are formalized activities with well-defined quantitative objectives for managing core competencies. Therefore, there is a greater consistency in the alignment of individual-, unit-, and organization-level performance objectives to maximize potential for competency integration. Competency integration at level 4 should, however, ensure that complementary competencies distributed across workgroups are first integrated before using the improvement framework to address other integration aspects like building communities of excellence through competency communities.

The key process areas identified in version 1.0 are as follows.

- Mentoring
- Organizational competency management
- Organizational performance alignment
- Team building
- Team-based practices

In version 2.0, the process areas are called

- Mentoring
- Organizational capability management
- Quantitative performance management
- Competency-based assets
- Competency integration
- Empowered workgroups

Called the *predictable process* in version 2.0 and the *managed process* in version 1.0, process development is based on quantitative definitions for growth in workforce competencies. Standards for performance alignment across units are established with more formal team building and team-based practices that leverage value from individual mentoring. Empowerment and envisioning are so vital for team performance and quality. It must be the team's power and team's vision that compels the team and not that of their leader [Senge 1990]. The definition of the organizational workforce competencies that was established as a level 3 process is now quantitatively monitored periodically to assess their levels of growth. A combination of workforce capability and process capability assessments are used to predict process performance. Performance at different levels of the organization are analysed to determine trends and tracked against objectives. Competency integration deals with capability integration as well. Since staff

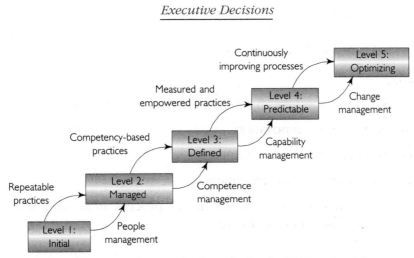

■ Fig. 1.5 *Maturity levels in the People CMM version 2.0*

Source: Adapted from People Capability Maturity Model, Carnegie Mellon University [1995] with permission

capability is known quantitatively, future trends in workforce capability and performance can be predicted for establishing a **Culture of Professionalism**.

Level 5 Process

The *optimizing level* is the highest level of process maturity in the progressive growth of organizational capability. The focus is on improving individual competencies and finding innovative ways to improve the workforce. Continuous improvement to workforce practices is possible since an environment of perpetual improvement and growth of competencies is established. All members strive to improve their own, their team's, and their unit's knowledge and skills. Motivation toward personal mastery is compelled from within individuals. Individuals don't compete with each other as much as they continuously improve upon their own performance. The inner force that compels behaviour is generated from inside individuals who constantly stimulate their memory and imagination. Achievement motivation takes on a new meaning with persistence for excellence orientation. There is a great sense of organizational bonding and a sense of involvement that serves to motivate individuals, whereby improving the overall performance of the organization.

In version 1.0, the level 5 key process areas are identified as follows.

■ Continuous workforce innovation

- Personal competency development

- Coaching

Version 2.0 identifies the level 5 key process areas as follows.

- Continuous workforce innovation

- Continuous capability improvement

- Organizational performance alignment

There are two possible ways to classify the 22 process areas. One way to think about it is along the four lines of threads.

Table 1.1　*Classification of process areas along the four lines of threads*

Levels	People CMM Threads			
	Developing competency	Building workgroups and culture	Motivating and managing performance	Shaping the workforce
5 *(Optimizing)*	Continuous capability improvement		Organizational performance alignment	Continuous workforce innovation
4 *(Predictable)*	Competency based assets Mentoring	Competency integration Empowered workgroups	Quantitative performance management	Organizational capability management
3 *(Defined)*	Competency development Competency analysis	Workgroup development Participatory culture	Competency-based practices Career development	Workforce planning
2 *(Managed)*	Training and development	Communication and coordination	Compensation Performance management Work environment	Staffing

Source: Adapted from People Capability Maturity Model, Carnegie Mellon University [1995] with permission

From an implementation point of view, there is probably a second way to classify the 22 process areas—into 'sequences'. This classification is a more natural way to look at how practices grow in capability and richness like peels of an onion surrounding the core. In the onion peel approach, we will call a foundation process area as the 'core process area' and those process areas that build on top of core process areas as the 'layered process areas'.

Basically the practices in a foundation process area 'get influenced' when the next maturity level practices in the sequence are implemented. The core process area practices also 'influence' in fundamental ways how well the practices of the layered process area can be institutionalized and performed. Based on this notion, we will see later on in this book that the implementation rigour and inherent entropy within a system dictate the richness of a process area—**'its true capability'**. And, the process area may look quite different depending upon whether

1. a process area is tending to slip back to one level below its intended capability, or

2. a process area is still operating effectively at the level it belongs when institutionalized completely, or

3. a process area has capabilities that can transform itself to a higher capability when the transition to the next level is made, where applicable.

This notion is found to be very useful during assessments when a decision has to be taken of, what I would call as a **'process harmonic'**, whether the rigour of the implementation is adequate to qualify for the rated maturity level. It is also quite intuitive and I will now describe these sequences.

Sequence I

A natural-looking progression for the training and development 'core process area' at level 2 is to transform its **foundation practices** into practices of workgroup development, competency analysis, and competency development at level 3. Further, these practices at level 3 have an ability to add the next layer of sophistication while transforming themselves into competency integration and competency-based assets. Adding more richness to these practices at level 4 would yield practices that correspond to continuous capability improvement and continuous workforce innovation at level 5.

Therefore, it is natural to expect a transition such as the following.

Training and development ▸ Workgroup development, competency development, competency analysis ▸ Competency-based assets, competency integration ▸ Continuous capability improvement, continuous workforce innovation

Sequence 2

A natural-looking progression for staffing 'core process area' at level 2 is to transform its **foundation practices** into practices of workforce planning at level 3. Further, these practices at level 3 have an ability to add the next layer of capability while transforming themselves into empowered workgroups.

Therefore, it is natural to expect a transition such as the following.

> Staffing ▸ Workforce planning ▸ Empowered workgroups

Sequence 3

A natural-looking progression for performance management 'core process area' at level 2 is to transform its **foundation practices** into practices of competency-based practices and career development at level 3. Further, these practices at level 3 have an ability to add the next layer of capability while transforming themselves into quantitative performance management and organizational capability management at level 4. Adding more richness to these practices would yield practices that correspond to organizational performance alignment.

Therefore, it is natural to expect a transition such as the following.

> Performance management ▸ Competency-based practices, career development ▸ Organizational capability management, quantitative performance management ▸ Organizational performance alignment

Sequence 4

A natural-looking progression for communication and coordination 'core process area' at level 2 is to transform its **foundation practices** into practices of participatory culture at level 3. Further, these practices at level 3 have an ability to add the next layer of capability while transforming itself into mentoring at level 4. Adding more richness to these practices would yield practices that correspond to coaching of people CMM Version 1.0.

Therefore, it is natural to expect a transition such as the following.

> Communication and coordination ▸ Participatory culture ▸ Mentoring

Work environment and compensation seem to be enabling process areas that motivate workforce to bring out their very best, more as 'extrinsic motivators'. I have seen work cultures wherein, when the workforce is naturally achievement-oriented, workers display a great sense of pride and belonging to the organization; influence due to both these process areas is only superficial if anything on the quality of work they produce and on productivity. Within the People CMM framework, these two process areas are by far the most touchy and sensitive as well. It is only when organizations are badly stuck with a level 2 syndrome that moving up to higher capability seems impossible and therefore it is only natural to point the accusing finger of blame to either poor work environment or bad compensation. Besides, the only ones asking 'why a level 2?' are the ones who seem to suffer from an identity crisis at level 1 and don't know enough about how to motivate themselves to move up in process capability.

Motivation and process capability seem to have a connection. The six types of achievement motivation begin to make sense only when the organization transforms its practices to higher capabilities.

The Six Types of Achievement Motivation

1. **Status with the experts:** gaining recognition as a leader in one's field

2. **Acquisitiveness:** desire to acquire something tangible

3. **Achievement via independence:** desire to achieve on one's own skill and merit

4. **Status with peers:** people exhibiting erroneous rituals and styles!

5. **Competitiveness:** how important is it for an individual to be a winner?

6. **Concern for excellence:** quality of a person's life is in direct proportion to their commitment to excellence regardless of their chosen field of endeavour.

Called the *optimizing process* in both versions, innovation can be attempted only when individuals are geared towards improving the overall organizational performance and competency. Alternative practices for workforce development are explored using data on the effectiveness of current workforce practices. Trials of such innovations are run as pilots, before large-scale deployment throughout the organization.

Every individual takes responsibility to improve skills and competencies of the organization. Continuous capability improvement has to do with enhancements to skills through innovative team, individual, and organizational practices. True level 5 organizations have tremendous capability to change and make change management an organizational capability. Guidance from senior and more experienced individuals to junior staff to predict and interpret trends is available as a formal activity in order to establish a **Culture of Continuous Improvement and Empowerment**.

Why the People CMM?

In the words of George Box, 'All models are wrong, but a few are useful'.

This is true of the People CMM as well. A different way to look at it is to understand that it is more of an organizational development model and not merely yet another HR (human resource) model. Taking an 'HR model' view of this framework will only limit its applicability and use within organizations. In fact, the People CMM framework is meant for the CEO, not just for the HR manager. And therefore the right stakeholder and owner for the People CMM initiative should be the CEO of the company. Chances are that best results and outcomes from the People CMM initiative are possible if and only if it is run as a 'CEO's initiative'.

Then, there is also a big question surrounding—'We have been successful all these years. This is the way we have been doing business. So why do we need to change?' Chances are you don't need to change as much as you need to understand what is it that has truly contributed to your assumption of what success means to you. Do you know enough about your core competencies that you can sustain it for now and in the future and are in a position to make money by selling on your competencies? If the answer to this question is an unquestionable 'yes', then chances are that most of what the People CMM advocates, you may have already been practising or have honed into practice. If anything, the People CMM is all about building an organizational culture of consistent performance with best practices that have been compiled from experience along with a vast body of knowledge from organizational psychology. Needless to emphasize that the People CMM is a good compilation of industry best practices for how to manage organizational change and therefore organizational transformation with a core competency orientation.

What is core competency? Core competency is a bundle of skills, technologies, and process abilities that enable a company to provide a particular benefit to customers. Within the People CMM, there is an explicit mention of commitment to perform, implying management commitment to building organizational capability. When the word commitment takes on a core competency view, it means perfecting a system of practices (the process), which renders certain customer benefits and, not just commitment to a specific process or product opportunities. Since it is difficult to compress the time taken for core competency development, it takes persistence and a great deal of effort using the 'best available resources' to get the job done. It is only when process improvement takes on such a strategic core competency view that execution outcomes become process-dependent and less people-dependent. At this stage, process improvement as a core competency can contribute to 'competitiveness'. Since competency represents a sum of learning across individual skill sets and individual organizational units, three tests for a skill to be considered a core competency are—customer value, competitor differentiation, and scalability [Hammel 1994].

There seems to be a thought that process improvement is a good investment to make in times of a downturn, such as what we are witnessing now in the last year since early 2001, where the best talent can now be *'safely deployed'* on *'add-on activities such as process improvement*! Little do organizations that think this way, realize the importance of change management. Unless change management becomes a core competency—something that is done both in good times and bad times, no matter who else does it—lasting benefits from process improvement are impossible! And, one more necessary condition—you got to deploy your best talent on change management initiatives, not the leftovers! Change management initiative ought to be the CEO's key initiative. Who else but the best resources should be working on such a key initiative? A sure way to know if you got the right person on the competency development group (CDG) or software engineering process group (SEPG) is to talk to the person's boss and tell him that you are taking his resource. If the boss yells and screams, you know you got the right person! On the contrary, if he willingly gives his resource away, you know that you got the wrong person.

Once you have the right composition for the SEPG, the next important thing to do is to characterize your current state through a structured assessment. A mini-assessment or a Class B assessment will highlight potential opportunities for improvement in your process infrastructure. While strengths will keep the organization floating, it is the weaknesses that are the liabilities, which the organization must pay particular attention to and fix using a time-bound action plan. Not every recommendation needs to be fixed immediately; some may need to be fixed first before others can be worked on. Prioritizing and fixing the process should be based on business objectives and organizational goals. And, repeat this process all over again using the IDEAL (Initiating, Diagnosing, Establishing, Acting, and Learning) approach, which is explained as follows.

The IDEAL^{SM} Model

The People CMM uses the approach of the IDEAL model to define the process of improvement. IDEAL is an abbreviation coined using the first letters for the words Initiating, Diagnosing, Establishing, Acting, Learning. It can be considered a process to improve the process improvement process itself. It is based on the Shewart-Deming cycle of Plan-Do-Check-Act or the PDCA cycle.

The stimulus for change can be proactive, that is from an opportunity to improve, or reactive, which is from danger or pain. Since exercising individual autonomy is possible only when the stimulus for change comes as a proactive response, it is useful to stay in this mode without getting into the trepidation of a fear motive becoming the reason for process change. Taking a proactive response will therefore involve the evaluation of business objectives.

Initiating

Setting the context and establishing sponsorship involves clarifying the scope of changes involved, identifying all relevant stakeholders or groups that are likely to be affected by this change, and addressing it as a collective management of the change initiative. Since most problems are management problems and not technical problems, many times it is important for the management to change first before the people in the trenches have to. In order to say we have complete sponsorship, it is important to get a 'yes!' to the change initiative from the last person in the line-up for process improvement. It is now appropriate to set up the necessary infrastructure of resources and take the necessary steps to DIAG-NOSE the business reasons demanding a change.

Diagnosing

This phase of the process improvement paradigm focuses on characterizing the current state of practice by identifying the strengths and weaknesses of the process using a formal assessment process. The assessment process is a structured review of the organizational process and product assets interpreted against the People CMM model. This cycle is repeated as and when significant improvements are perceived. The focus of this phase is to ensure that strengths become stronger and weaknesses are addressed with appropriate improvements.

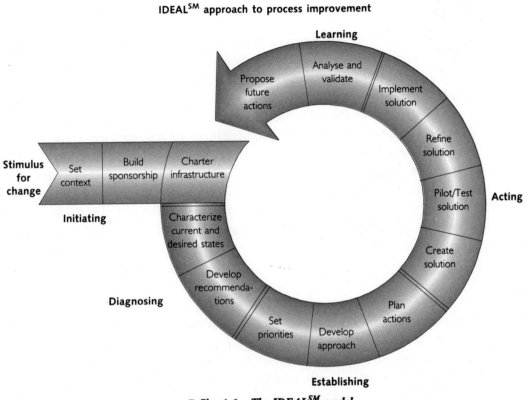

IDEAL^{SM} approach to process improvement

■ Fig. 1.6 *The IDEAL^{SM} model*

SM IDEAL is a service mark of Carnegie Mellon University.
Source: Adapted from People Capability Maturity Model, Carnegie Mellon University [1995] with permission

Development of findings and recommendations to rectify the weaknesses is based on an action plan for improving the state of practice. The findings from an assessment and recommendations form the rationale for follow-on improvement programmes. The strategy and sequence for implementing the recommendations are to be based on prioritization and documented in the process improvement action plan. Not every recommendation needs to be worked on at once; some must be addressed earlier and some later. Going for the low-hanging fruits may solve most issues.

Establishing

Setting up the right teams for process action must be based on assignment of each major recommendation to the relevant stakeholders. Team building and team-based activities are critical for effective implementation. A senior executive of the organization must formally kick off the team launch and team-building exercises. Each of the established teams must plan its own activities and become responsible for ensuring successful implementation of the process changes into the process infrastructure. Integration of the team activities is best done by a group of senior executives or the CDG—an embodiment of process champions who work to accomplish the objectives established for the process programme. Periodic reviews by the CDG, along with senior executives of the organization, are important to reinforce a positive message about the intent of the process improvement programme.

Acting

For every process recommendation worked on, it is important for the respective process owner teams (process action teams) to answer the question—'is the change getting better or is it getter bitter?' A useful mechanism to help in obtaining clarity of this information is the role played by mini-assessments or sniff tests. Every new procedure, standard, or tool that gets developed for a solution must be put through a few iterations of piloting on select projects. When pilot results prove useful, they can then be deployed over a larger organizational context to verify harmonious growth. The role played by collection of measures or metrics that directly relates to measuring the efficacy of the change is emphasized. The Goal–Question–Metric paradigm of Victor Bassili is a very useful technique to address the effectiveness of the change programme. The only way to keep the measurement and verification aspects of the change management programme to work in step and synchronously with changes induced to the process is to ensure that these activities are used to objectively evaluate the quality of new processes.

Learning or Leveraging

After an objective evaluation of the process change, it is possible to hone the practices into skill by documenting lessons learnt, revising the scope of implementation, and restructuring the CDG, if business situations have changed. Often, it might become necessary to revise the organizational approach for the next assessment. Since process maturity is a journey and not a goal, importance must be placed on repeating the cycle of improvement and sustaining the momentum from right process alignment.

Managing the People CMM Implementation Program

If importance is to be given to knowledge and skills that are required on a long term to retain human assets, it is necessary to build a system of coordinated action that helps to build commitment. It is important to note that the pattern of change that must be emphasized is on the behaviour of the system, which is the aggregate of people behaviour and interactions between systems. Since capability is more of an attribute of the organization than of a few individuals, such a systemic view is highly emphasized. Besides, organizations tend to build their own cultures based on these collective behaviour patterns. In order to be effective in building this capability, process improvement initiatives must be approached like any other time-critical project. There must be a plan with clear deadlines. The initiative must be adequately funded and staffed with the right people. Like any other project, the process improvement initiative must be governed by a plan of execution with clearly defined process owners who are accountable for the outcomes of execution.

Change management projects have the additional characteristics of carrying with them a cultural component. Trouble invariably begins when there is a head-on collision between implementing change and cultural barriers, since it is natural for people to question change from status quo. Typically compared to a frog in a hot water, organizations too don't perceive threats that appear to gradually intensify in degree and adversely impact performance. Like a frog (because it is poikilothermic) that adjusts to any gradual increase in temperature when placed in a pan of water over a flame that is gradually turned on, and eventually dies when the water reaches its boiling point, organizations too display tendencies resulting from galloping entropy. And, entropy or a natural deterioration of order and healthy organizational conditions, is a natural event that is to be expected. Complacency is bound to hasten entropy.

Change agents or advocates of a process improvement initiative must pay particular attention to this phenomenon. Old behaviour, no matter how bizarre or dysfunctional it might appear today, was a successful response at one time to the circumstance surrounding the old environment. What needs to be done is to

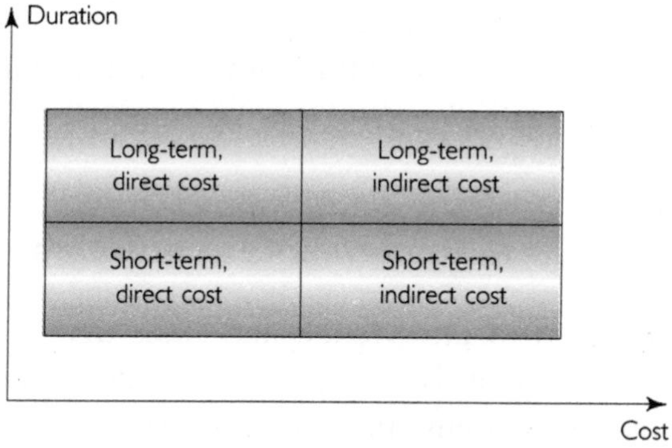

Duration

Long-term, direct cost	Long-term, indirect cost
Short-term, direct cost	Short-term, indirect cost

Cost

Fig. 1.7 *Real cost of implementation failure*

determine if current behaviour is an appropriate response in the current environment. If a two-by-two matrix is conceived as shown in Fig. 1.7, short-term implementation becomes long-term objectives and long-term indirect cost is the real cost of implementation failure. Some of the reasons for this could be the following.

- Missing leadership
- Resistance begins to increase if there too much cynicism is allowed and if indeed the change management initiative is repeated cynically
- The organization is focused only on survival.

Change agents must be role models defining the expected behaviour rather than cheerleaders who stand by the ring side. Authority gives change agents the power, but modelling the right behaviour within themselves gives them respect and credibility. To build trust, some of the characteristics this crucial role has to display are reliability, openness, acceptance, congruence, consistency, competence, character, and courage.

Inevitable resistance is to be expected because values, unwritten rules, and latent work cultures operate to either support or oppose change. This resistance to change can either be overt (in the open) or covert (hidden from view). Change agents must ensure to keep as much resistance to change as overt by actively listening to the targets of change. Targets are those for whom the change is intended and therefore have a need to either change or oppose it. They are also the people who know what is working and what is not working. There are two approaches to managing organizational transformation—the hammer approach and the transition management approach. Depending upon the context, both are recommended and have been found to be useful. The hammer approach is a 'do-it-fast' approach and is characterized by having cheap upfront cost but ongoing maintenance costs, with very little tendencies for compliance. Transition management approach is a more lasting, commitment-oriented approach with a 'do-it-right' characteristic. When there is an organizational learning disability, neither approach will work! Where the People CMM practices will not work is explained in the next section and in chapter 8 on *Limitations of the People CMM.*

Organizations where the People CMM cannot be Applied

The term 'organization' is used to mean any structured environment where a collection of people work together for the attainment of common objectives. Organizations that deal with terminal jobs for their businesses cannot and will not find the People CMM practices useful. Typical examples include cushy jobs involving clerical and other menial activities that require little or no application of new skills or knowledge. These are organizations that live by the precept: "this is the way it has been done for a number of years in the past and this is the same way it is going to be done now and in the future".

People CMM practices also have little applicability to organizations that are either complacent by virtue of being too unmanageable or have a hard time dealing with empowering individuals like government operations and government-owned businesses with deeply entrenched notions of hierarchies and seniority rather than merits of knowledge and application of skills and talent. These are institutions that offer large volumes of employment that may not be driven by criteria defined by skill or talent and usually come with thick insulations of job security. This is partly because there is no single point of ownership and the associated accountability. Work is more of an obligation, and is performed as a ritual! Organizations where the People CMM is relevant but which are unwilling to build an empowered work culture also find it difficult to deploy effective People CMM practices at the higher levels of maturity.

Characteristics of an Employer-of-Choice

'Employer-of-choice' is a very exclusive term that is shared by a finite number of organizations. These organizations are value-driven and base their recruitment and staffing decisions on a thorough evaluation of suitability of candidate profiles to the job description under consideration, based on multiple stakeholder inputs. Open positions at entry level are filled with fresh recruitments and all senior positions are normally filled by promotions from within. A successful recruitment practice that helps in arriving at the fitment decision is called 'interviews for rejection', and not 'interviews for selection'. Once a profile is selected, there is very little scope for a candidate mismatch to occur with the job description. Recruitment decisions are also based on multiple independent assessments of the candidate profile. Invariably, great emphasis is placed on ensuring candidate acceptability within more than one department or unit and a potential for continuity of service lasting up to a lifetime. The style of leadership right from the CEO down is based on empowerment in a nurturing environment that values teamwork. A general rule that is also followed is to oversupervise initially with the help of a well-structured induction programme until the person learns how to become a 'contributing member' of the organization.

When candidates start out on a new job, they are most motivated but are also most ineffective. The quality of the induction programme decides how quickly the new talent can be made to contribute to the organizational objectives. They learn the trade during both the induction programme and on the job to become motivated and effective. They also learn the tricks of the trade and become demotivated and effective. If organizations don't watch out, they soon become demotivated and ineffective. That is a clear and obvious sign to watch out for to make sure that dead wood does not develop into organizational liability. Normally, both the value and quality of a structured induction programme loses its emphasis as the organization begins to grow in size. From observation, employee induction programmes are carefully planned and executed in start-up organizations. As soon as the organization reaches its critical mass, induction programmes take a backseat. They are put on hold and done only when there are a sizeable number of fresh recruits who join the company. For this reason, it is not uncommon to see individuals attending induction programmes six to eight months after their recruitment!

An employer-of-choice has an effective process to make sure that the ability to learn and remain a contributing member of the organization is a continuous and ongoing strategic process. Investments in retraining individuals with invalid skills and on new technologies are planned with measurable goals. Job rotation and exposure to functioning of different departmental units is required and mandated for individual growth within the organization. Leadership choices are almost always based on a 360-degree evaluation wherein there is a subordinate evaluation, peer evaluation, and a supervisor evaluation.

Characteristics of Caring Employees

Caring employees take pride in their affiliation with the company they work for. Not only do they think of how they do their work, but they are also sensitive to making the day-to-day changes that are necessary to make their work more productive. A burning sense of curiosity coupled with high levels of motivation is best put to use just as a new hire joins the company. A good sense for organizational belonging, pride, and loyalty are the three important factors that are generally found missing in most organizations. If these three flames can be kindled and stoked continuously, there would be no need for a prescription-based organizational culture development programme.

Building a sense for organizational pride, a characteristic that is so very essential for employee retention and financial success, is an area that most heads of organizations or CEOs must pay particular attention to. This in itself must become one of their key result areas. The first impression of whether a company has this sense of organizational pride or not, can be judged by merely observing the signboards of the company! In some cultures, it is not uncommon to see many of these signboards either totally out of shape or lacking a character. While in other cultures, these signboards are maintained as if they are an important part of the organizational assets. Little wonder then, that such cultures and organizations demonstrate superior financial successes and results.

What Employees are Asking for?

A good way to answer this question is for the CEO or head of the organization to actually ask this question around in the organization. This question is seldom asked, nor does it get proper expression from the stakeholders of an organization. Solving the problem of attrition is impossible without periodically questioning the stakeholders on what it is that they want to have for a fulfilling professional life. After all, if eight of the significant waking hours of an individual are to be spent at work, should it not be the best part of one's life? The organization provides infrastructure and facilities thinking that these are what an employee needs. Many times, physical discomfort is not what employees want the organization to address as much as a need for a good emotional message.

While company loyalty is a positive emotion that ought to be demonstrated by every employee, the question that all levels of management should answer is—"what should be the expressed, demonstrated, and reinforced message that is consistent with the modelled behaviour?" If the message is for instance—people are our most important assets—and at the drop of a hat the organization resorts to downsizing in the name of restructuring, then there is no congruence.

What the People CMM can Offer?

It helps to build a 'learning organization' by sensitizing every nook and cranny of the organization to realize core competencies. The People CMM is a model for enhancing the workforce capability. It is conceived to organize workforce practices with a competency orientation—'what sets us apart, or what do we do that no one else does better?' Building organizational capability happens through building productivity improvement factors within workforce practices. It enhances business performance by managing intellectual assets and consolidating knowledge capital.

Why is the People CMM Particularly Relevant to Information Technology?

Application of IT to a vast array of domains is often plagued with an ever-widening supply–demand gap where the demand for qualified talent far exceeds the potential supply. This makes the People CMM particularly useful as a discipline for companies with an IT orientation. This is coupled with a galloping technology obsolescence curve that only makes matters worse. Before one realizes the true potential of the knowledge and skills that have been acquired, its applicability becomes history! By far, the phrase job satisfaction is almost unheard of in this area given this high degree of volatility and change. The naysayers of process improvement initiatives have a point to make—why add a process overhead to an already volatile and highly turbulent development scenario? The simple answer is—because we need a method to manage the madness! It therefore behoves of any serious IT company to articulate well-drawn-out strategies for talent retention through both structured and unstructured training and retraining initiatives. Knowledge and skills of the workforce ought to be kept current and fresh through a process of continuous renewal. The highly successful and widely used Software CMM (SW-CMM) addressed key issues within IT management through software engineering and management practices to establish a capable development process. People CMM practices have a propensity to enable growth in workforce competencies using a well-defined structure to grow the capability of the workforce.

In the Trenches Experience with the People CMM

IF THERE IS one model that has an ability to integrate people within an organization, it is the People CMM. It is a discipline that lets empowered individuals speak up and be heard. Process improvement in such a context has less to do with conformance and more to do with challenging status quo or established practices by engaging individuals to think of ways to do the same things better. Not only does this discipline advocate individuals to think of newer ways to build solutions but also empowers them to make the day-to-day changes necessary to keep practices fresh and current.

Organizations experiencing difficulties with change management and organizational transformation must attempt the People CMM before attempting any other model. Unlike the SW-CMM, which includes only those individuals who work with the software development process in the change initiative, or the International Organization for Standaradization (ISO) that includes only those individuals who are responsible for the establishment of a Quality Management System (QMS), The People CMM has an enormous capacity to galvanize the entire organizational workforce—starting from the janitor up to the CEO. The practices of the People CMM are about the interactions necessary for all people within the organization to work together as a team. In conjunction with TQM or SW-CMM process improvement initiatives, the People CMM provides economies of scale. Since the momentum towards a learning organization begins with TQM, it is recommended that People CMM be implemented along with other TQM programmes for sustaining a lasting representation of a learning organization. When implemented correctly with an involvement of at least 80–90% of the organizational workforce, tremendous benefits due to integration of organizational entities from across boundaries of separation are possible. In this chapter we will examine what is meant by 'when implemented correctly'.

Like any successful organizational transformation initiative or change management initiative, there has to be a well-articulated vision for "why we are doing what we are doing?" Change management that is purely evolutionary or focuses on do-it-right, can be slow and may not reach its objectives whereas, a revolutionary approach of do-it-fast may leave many people burnt out. A combination of both transition management and a hammer approach to change management is suggested for optimal and lasting results.

The fundamental principles of process change are as follows.

1. Change is a continuous process and the fundamental purpose is to 'learn-and-do-better'.

2. Major change must be initiated and supported by the top management.

3. In order to fix the process, understanding the current state of the process is fundamental.

4. Sustaining gains on improvement initiatives requires periodic reinforcement and commitment.

5. Improvement initiatives like all other time-critical initiatives require investment and compete for the best resources—which are always in short supply!

6. It requires a lot of persistence and do-it-yourself zeal to get the success formula right.

7. When it starts getting too comfortable, it is probably a good time for change.

8. Always question status quo and relentlessly pursue and explore high leverage factors.

9. The incentive for change is the change itself.

10. You need to be profitable to be good at change management.

Shared understanding and a continuous reinforcement of the above fundamental principles of change by the sponsor and his team are vital to ensure sustained commitment.

Planning the Process Improvement

The process improvement programme has to be planned, based on the scope of the assessment. An indirect way to understand the probable organizational process maturity is to look at where the highest numbers of improvements have happened in the last quarter or two. The focus of improvement is almost always visibly driven to improving the practices of process areas at the indicative maturity level. That should be the scope.

A word of caution: There is no hard and fast rule that can be used to say it takes N months to go from level X to level Y. The answer to "How long does it take to go from level X to level Y?" is "It depends!" Needless to emphasize, all assessments are 'fact-based'. Does the organization really have the necessary systems and processes in place to make sure that strengths are going to stay strengths, and is there a plan to improve upon the weaknesses in a systematic and orderly manner to transform them into strengths? Having the right systems and processes in place is only a necessary condition but not sufficient condition to operate at high process maturity. In this chapter, we will explore the sufficiency conditions, which I will relate from 'in the trenches' of what some of my best professional associations have taught me.

Sufficiency Criterion 1

Establish a strong visionary leadership council by evaluating core competencies.

The single-most important characteristic that distinguishes visionary leadership from the other styles is that when such a leadership council is used as a sounding board for ideas, with the input comes back *value added manifold*. The process of building trust is often based on frank and open communication, which is always firm. Members of this council know the intrinsic talents available in their organizations and keep an eye on the more promising individuals in the organization. Truly visionary leaders make a big difference to individual lives. They facilitate the so very crucial 'internal learning process' that eventually plays out as the single-most determining factor to be a highly capable organization.

Sufficiency Criterion 2

Establish highly talented and empowered leadership at all levels

When you have a strong visionary leadership council at the top, leadership across all levels is a natural extension within the rest of the organization. Capability of a world-class organization is actually the collective capability of this chain of leadership. They are flexible in adopting best practices, adapting to changes that are necessary, and modifying their behaviour to newer circumstances. The finesse with which they team up, organize, and reorganize is demonstrated by their ability to draw out the best performance in each other. They are also sensitive and recognize the fact that their performance operates in a broadband—ranging from poor to exceptional! There is no single value that determines their performance measure. A combination of factors determines individual performance capability and they ensure that they draw out their best performance from leveraging upon their intrinsic talents.

Sufficiency Criterion 3

Build teams of people who live by a 'can-do' attitude and are all quality champions.

In the present-day IT set-up, which requires extremely technical people who understand technology, the days of a 'traditional' quality manager are over! A technocrat who can define the boundaries for the core competencies of an organization is the best choice for today's quality manager. Having such a person within an organization and to mentor the professional teams is a definite advantage. And then it takes a whole lot of a 'can-do' attitude among people who are inspired to live out the dreams of their leaders. For people to be effective followers, they must have high self-esteem and be highly geared to accepting responsibilities. The spirit often is that the job is not done until we accomplish what we set out to accomplish! Such unstoppable teams just happen out of good chemistry and sheer good luck.

There is a strong sense of sharing of lessons learnt and they often rewrite the rules of engagement and the underlying process if they feel they no longer serve the purpose. When each individual assumes the role of a quality champion, quality does not happen by chance but gets designed into the probability of success. It is under such conditions alone, that *quality is free*. In such an orientation, not only does everybody think about *'what'* they do, but also reflect upon *'how'* they do and make the day-to-day changes that are necessary for optimal performance. It is taboo to schedule a work-product peer review, if the author of the work product feels it is not up to the mark. Extreme care is exercised while creating the intermediate work products that become inputs to phases later in the life cycle, to ensure that the hand-off is clean. The means employed are as important as the end objectives. They are naturally oriented to continuous exploration of best practices and force a change when things get too comfortable. The exhibited characteristic of such teams of individuals is that they take ideas from inception to closure by brainstorming and rapid prototyping. They normally visualize through the customer's eye by keeping a customer perspective in all of their peer reviews. Their sense of pride in their work accomplishments and their organizational affiliations to which they belong are extremely high and one can say it by looking at the manner in which they hand out their business cards!

Sufficiency Criterion 4

An organizational sponsor, supportive of proactive growth is vital.

Ideas that have business value are often actively sought out by the organization and rewarded suitably. Sponsorship is in touch with everything that is happening in the organization. Sponsors are found communicating their dreams with clear deadlines, sharing their vision for the company, coordinating action, and facilitate collective understanding. Sponsors make sure that process improvement is everybody's job—a community affair. There is clear focus on developing competencies and the will to do whatever it takes to support their growth.

Sufficiency Criterion 5

Establish gymnasiums for continuous personal competency development.

Setting up gymnasiums and learning laboratories to exercise the brains of individuals where leadership and management lessons are taught by recognized gurus and internal mentors is an organizational culture. Personal competency development is oriented towards building organizational core competencies. Personal competency development plans are laid out with a 'stick-to-your-knitting' approach. Seeing the pace with which technology changes, one is often tempted to keep moving on to newer and newer stuff. That has been the single-most important contributor for mediocrity and dilution of competencies. The only meaningful way to overcome the impact from this shifting terrain is to make sure that organizational core competencies have a long-term focus. Most individuals at all levels pursue personal learning as an obsession.

A well-articulated process improvement plan must ensure that both the necessary and sufficiency conditions are addressed to make sure that the process maturity really sticks long enough to make a positive behavioural transformation. It is my observation after spending so many years in the trenches with process improvement programmes that most initiatives seem to take an approach that is only a symptomatic treatment of the real problems that exist in the organization.

I have now come to believe that unless the process improvement programme addresses deeply entrenched belief systems and behaviour patterns, lasting or sustaining the gains of the process programme is almost impossible. In order to build such a system of coordinated action that is also resilient, it might involve dramatic changes to the way we interact with each other as human beings. We may have to change relationship styles and model the right behaviour through a shared vision.

And, since change is a 'first-principle' thing, it might require me to change first before I advocate it to the rest of the organization. The owner of the process improvement programme must understand the possible attitudes that an organization may have for the process improvement programme itself and therefore must be factored into the plan during the planning process.

- Commitment: wants it, and will make it happen. This is the nicest form for a shared vision to take.

- Enrollment: want is, but will do only whatever can be done.

- Genuine compliance: sees the benefits and therefore does what is expected and may be more if called upon to do. These are the good soldiers.

- Formal compliance: on the whole, sees a vision; does what is expected but no more.

- Grudging compliance: does not see the benefits, but also does not want to lose the job!

- Non-compliance: does not even attempt to see the benefits. "I will not do it . . . and you cannot make me do it."

- Apathy: neither for nor against vision. Retired on the job with no energy. "Why is 8 hours so long?" [Senge 1990]

Knowing the tendencies of individuals on the above attitude-scale for developing shared vision, resource allocation must be built into the process improvement plan. Picking the wrong types of individuals to champion the programme is a sureshot formula for implementation failure. And since this is such an important aspect of the planning exercise, we will explore in detail in subsequent sections.

It is also important to plan approximately five months of time to complete the People CMM assessment itself. The modus operandi of a People CMM assessment will be described in a later section.

Team Set-up, Roles, and Responsibilities

Implementing the People CMM discipline is a team effort and for best results it requires the entire organization to be enrolled into the programme. A sponsor who authorizes the change programme must be visible periodically and must regularly communicate the organizational vision. The role of a sponsor is also to fund the initiative and make sure that the business reasons that dictate and mandate the change initiative are indeed current and relevant. A sponsor is a person who has an entire organization or a group of organizations as his span of control. A team of People CMM champions should assist a sponsor to make sure that the business goals become the implementation objectives.

The role of champions in the People CMM implementation programme is to firmly believe in the reasons for change and seek sponsorship to lead the change. They are responsible for articulating the policies, owning the implementation plans, and tracking them to closure. By being sensitive to the business goals, they must be responsive and quick in managing transformation. As the change initiative progresses, there may be reasons to change the original implementation objectives to proactively respond to changing business requirements. It is the role of the champions to keep the focus on the right things. Champions usually have a division or multiple divisions for their span of control. They may or may not directly involve in implementing the change programme since a team of change agents who actually implement the change assists them.

Change agents are the torch-bearers of the implementation programme. They facilitate the change initiative by acting as catalysts. Change agents must be made up of respected individuals in the organization to whom the people in the trenches look up for solutions and inspiration. Typically, these are the project leaders and project managers who influence the shaping of individual destinies. They normally have a project or a group of projects as their span of control and make sure that the day-to-day decisions in response to the circumstances surrounding their work are in keeping with policies established by the champions. By keeping their ears to the ground and listening to what the targets or the people who actually enact the change are saying, they must be sensitive to what works and what does not work. Every new practice that is added and every change to an existing practice must carry with it a questionnaire that seeks to find out whether the change is helping the conditions get better or whether the change is making it worse.

The targets are the ones who would be able to say loud and clear whether or not the programme is working out. They are the ones who actually change and know what is working and what is not. By enrolling the entire organization within the span of control of the sponsor into the People CMM implementation programme, change agents must ensure that the commitment process is complete. This is best done by empowering targets to highlight changes that prove useful to them.

As soon as the respective champions authorize the change with the help of supporting processes guided by policies, process owners take responsibility to define and maintain the process assets. A team of process owners who actually manage effective deployment of policies, procedures, and guidelines is what determines the sustainability and the long-term success of the change management programme.

It is only when organizations have this kind of ability to perform, will the execution outcomes become process-dependent and not people-dependent. In other words, if there is an issue, it is a process issue that needs to be fixed and not an individual who is the problem.

From my own experience, the power of empowered individuals in what were called tear-down re-engineering teams helps tremendously to reduce the cycle time in which change is engineered. And the way tear-down re-engineering works is described in two cultural contexts, as follows.

Case Study I: INDIA—Team-based Practices

Based on the scope of process implementation and results of a mini-assessment or a Class B assessment (which will be described later on in this chapter and in chapter 9), recommendations are prioritized and ownership of implementing them is assigned to individuals.

Individuals who champion the solution to the themes—which are the prioritized issues and recommendations—are called the team leaders. These team leaders volunteer to find a resolution in a time-bound manner. They are also empowered to pick the resources they may need to work in a collaborative manner to come up with the solutions. Once the teams are formed after the team members give their approval to work on these tear-down re-engineering teams, the sanctity of this collaboration has to be maintained at all costs. This means that very rarely and only after a genuine case can be made out, will an individual on the tear-down re-engineering team be absolved of participation in the solution to the theme. And, solutions may take as little as a few hours to as many as a few months to arrive at. The tear-down re-engineering team cannot be dismantled until a solution is found. The attributes of a solution are that it should be an adequate and reasonable response to the circumstances surrounding the organizational context. It is impossible to come up with 'ideal' solutions because there is nothing like 'The Solution'.

Does the tear-down re-engineering team feel that they have explored all options while coming up with the solution? And, does everybody on the team feel that they have a solution, which they feel is a right response to the circumstances surrounding the theme? Is there a consensus among the team members that we can all live with the solution and stay credible when we present our solutions back to the organization? If the answers to these three questions is an unquestionable yes, then I think we have a good enough solution and the tear-down re-engineering team can be dissolved after the recommendations have been made. The theme leader will also work with the process owner to ensure that the recommendations are internalized. The role of the CDG and the executive leadership is to make sure that monthly and periodic reviews are made on the effectiveness of the practices that are internalized based on the tear-down re-engineering team recommendations. In order to keep a strategic management focus on measurement, the use of Balanced Score Card method [Kaplan 1992] with defined objectives and measurable goals was established. Besides, the team composition for themes having strategic objectives was made up of individuals representing the five perspectives of strategy, employee, customer, operations, and finance. (Also refer to *Organizational Capability Management*, Chapter 6)

Case Study 2: South Korea—Team Building

One of the best team building and problem solving exercises from a large multinational in South Korea is described here.

The head of the division is responsible for the overall success of the problem solving process. The entire division goes offsite from their regular workplace for a planned duration of time, for three days—no more, no less. Since the divisional head has an overall context of the resources available, he draws up an agenda for what it is that they are going to solve in the offsite meeting. The initial set of prioritized items are documented and teams are formed to address these issues.

From there on after the teams are established, the division meets offsite, usually on a Friday evening. There is an open house where everybody is grouped into rooms that logically assemble team members. Any additional issues that have to be discussed are identified and responsibilities are assigned to teams of individuals to find a solution. The teams live and breathe the problem in the rooms they have been assigned. Food, water, and supplies are provided into the room by people assigned this job; the team itself is not allowed to go out of the room until a solution is found. All the necessary reference materials, including Internet access, is provided for the team to hammer down the solution. At the end of each day, the moderator (who is the director of the division having overall responsibility) is given a status update on the progress made with the identification of the solution. Status updates are also quite unique. They have to be captured within a single sheet of paper! It must clearly state the objective, the planned tasks, tasks that have been accomplished, and the status of how much of the solution has been conceived as a percentage of the total.

If there are any major inputs required from sources other than those part of the division in the offsite meeting, access to such information is provided by permitting the necessary telephone calls. At no point of time will lack of inputs be cited as the reason for not coming up with a workable solution.

Other team building and team growing activities, which include outdoor games, are also part of such offsite activities. All games are common for every team with well-defined rules of when they can be played (so that teams plan their strategy and schedule them), how many people may play (to know that there are resource constraints), and what the entry and exit conditions are (to know the extent of difficulty *a priori* and know when the game is over). The objective of this team building exercise is to emphasize both interdependence and independence. Points are awarded to teams for both individual abilities (such as building a jigsaw puzzle within a stipulated time) and for team abilities (like lugging a huge log of wood for a predetermined distance). The team which acquires the most points at the end of this structured team building exercise is declared the winner. However, the valuable by-product is the indirect emphasis it places on inculcating organizational values such as stretch, speed, and simplicity, besides the team-growing and team-building benefits.

My observation from such intense solution drafting sessions is that the best ideas come when individuals are under time constraints to solve a problem and, at the same time, are forced to stay credible throughout the exercise.

Role of the Competency Development Group

The CDG is a collection of highly talented and respected group of individuals in a company who enable process improvement. The most influential leaders, who are also respected as technical and management experts, must be on this team.

The CDG is a group of individuals who make collective decisions and ensure that the process programme is on the right track. Given the dynamics of change management, a group that is cohesive and can appear credible at all times is very critical. A big mistake to make while selecting individuals for the CDG is to seek an open invitation through self-nomination! When the sponsor does this, he will end up with far too many individuals who may not have any experience in engineering change.

The danger of nominating the heads of the different units into the CDG is much the same. They may not have enough bandwidth to do a good job with change management, besides the fact that the implementation programme can get hijacked due to absolute power coming from the wrong reasons.

The right way to do this is to ask every individual in the organization to name at least five other individuals in the organization (except their boss) whom they consider as his/her mentors. Quite often, you will be surprised at the outcome—there may be a few consistent repetitions, which is an obvious choice for the CDG. Needless to add that those who are cynical to the process improvement programme are best avoided in the CDG. Unfortunately, the cynical ones also know the pitfalls. The one group of individuals who are best left out of the process programme entirely are the habitual fault finders—those who have made criticism their core competency. No organization is complete without such people in reasonable numbers—so watch out! These are the ones who sit on the fence and throw a powerful cynical influence on the targets, the ones who actually change their responses vis-à-vis the mandates of the process improvement initiative. Though Dilbert-style cynicism is good for a few laughs, it most definitely is not a solution!

The next question that comes to mind is how big should the team be? The answer to this question depends pretty much upon the calibre and willingness of the best minds available in the organization to take on additional responsibilities. Barring probably the programme manager who owns the end-to-end implementation, the CDG should not be a full-time responsibility. From my experience, if you make the CDG a full-time responsibility, this group can tend to overdo what is expected of it and also show signs of appearing to be out of touch with reality. If the CDG is a full-time responsibility, then there are two possible responses. One, nobody who likes project responsibilities more would be willing to get onto this team. Two, those who possibly enroll into the CDG are the ones who are without actual project responsibilities—the ones you should definitely avoid having on the CDG!

The recommended size for the CDG can be as few as a four-member team and as big as one with 12 members. There are advantages and disadvantages in both. Coming to closure is quick with a small cohesive team. Consensus decisions can be particularly tiring and hard to obtain with a large CDG. The disadvantage of a small CDG team is that it is subject to risks of volatility—especially in an area such as information technology where geographical mobility is something to expect.

A good way to bring in genetic diversity of thought into the CDG is to keep it a dynamic composition of at most six individuals who are rotated within the chosen dozen. They come into formation, execute their mandates, and move out voluntarily after accomplishing their tasks. It is also a good practice to sensitize individuals belonging to the CDG that their enrollment is role-based and charter-driven. The chief executive officer or the sponsor of the company must project the CDG as the organizational mentors and openly support them in their endeavours. The only known success formula for the CDG to be effective is if they are able to call their shots from the CEO's shoulders. The CEO must in fact make it a policy to promote individuals only after evaluating their contributions as members on the CDG for a reasonable duration.

What to Do and What to Avoid

Having a target process maturity at the beginning of the initiative is a definite advantage. This will enable the organization to make progressive improvements to the process areas that are in scope. The thing to avoid is level chasing. It is quite natural to look at the investments made in process improvement initiatives purely for obtaining a marketing advantage. Otherwise, there is no real return on investment given the dynamics at play.

- Unless there is a powerful enough advocate and a believer of the process programme—who is also the CEO—gains are only temporary.

- The return on investment is not fixed at all, but varies profoundly depending upon the learning orientation of the organization and its outlook to spending on acquiring intellectual capital.

- Entropy is part and parcel of the change programme; what starts out as a disciplined and well-groomed programme soon becomes chaotic without management controls and reviews.

- It requires more than just good people to run this programme effectively; they also need to be able to multitask.

- There is volatility with respect to affiliation of people to the organization due to poor loyalty factors.

Asking for a return on investment is dangerous at times, because the only incentive to change is the change itself. It is as naive and ludicrous as putting a price tag on discipline. And when put to good use, return on investment on having a disciplined workforce is nearly infinite. The right focus must be on doing the right thing for the right reason in the right manner at all times. The purpose of process improvement is to ensure that the business de-risks any adverse impact to its core competencies due to volatility stemming from perturbations from the real world—to make organizational response to business circumstances dependent on a process and not upon the execution outcome of an individual. Even the best managed companies in the world are prone to have turnover; and people leave for reasons that are best known to them. No exit interview can capture all the real reasons.

The reasons for joining a company are often to fulfil aspirations, which can be grouped to belong in the lower rungs of the Maslow's needs theory—mostly for better financial rewards or for an assumed sense of power. But, the real reasons for leaving a company are almost always emotional and belong in the higher rungs of a lack of self-actualization though such reasons often come camouflaged with the usual excuses for a better job with better rewards.

The most important reason that a person quits is because the organization does not provide enough avenues for self-expression. Financial remuneration is most definitely a tangible that is desired but it takes backseat to individual self-esteem, pride of ownership, and self-expression. It is said that pride of ownership of Apple Computers' early product, the Macintosh computer, was so great that inside the cover of early Macintosh models, moulded into the plastic, are the signatures of the design team that created it! It is almost impossible to retain an individual's interest only through a reward mechanism that does not consider other aspects of self-actualization. Therefore, the main focus of the process improvement programme should be to enable self-expression in individuals through a well-articulated mechanism of empowerment. If it is done this way, the process improvement programme itself could become the reason to arrest turnover. It is not difficult to imagine a reverse turnover wherein individuals who chose to leave an organization that is committed to high process maturity return back to the fold. And when this happens, the organizational response or the staffing process must be to accept them back into the fold and not turn them away because now you have individuals who may be willing to tattoo the organizational names on their bodies!

With respect to interpreting the practices of the People CMM, it is very important to look beyond what is expected from the model and apply it to business issues that directly impact effectiveness. For example, the communication and coordination process area can be used to better address issues of the business dealing with how confidential proprietary information is handled—data and information security and the like—rather than just focus on how inter-group coordination is achieved. In mature organizations, the corporate communication department is assigned specific responsibility to interface with entities external to organizations to communicate organizational information. Therefore, it is important to know that rather than taking a very narrow view, the communication and coordination process area may effectively address business functions and corporate issues as well.

Selecting a Lead Assessor and the Assessment Team

Lead assessors are authorized by the Software Engineering Institute to lead a People CMM assessment. These individuals have the requisite authorized training to conduct and guide the assessment process. The lead assessor brings an expert understanding of the People CMM model and the assessment method. From a sponsor's viewpoint, it is desirable to solicit the engagement of a lead assessor who is both credible and has enough implementation experience as a practitioner or as a consultant who has facilitated change management using the People CMM framework. At the time of writing this book, including the writer of this book, there are approximately 19 authorized lead assessors in the community. It therefore restricts large degrees of variation in application of the assessment method and also makes diversity due to subjective interpretations better controlled. However, it must be mentioned that since use of professional judgement on the part of a lead assessor is encouraged, there are potential opportunities during an assessment for a lead assessor to weigh different options and use personal tailoring methods. Example could include emphasis on documentary evidence versus an emphasis on actual institutionalization of the process intent. What the sponsor should know is that an assessment is a 'fact-finding' exercise. The focus of an assessment is on surfacing facts. The purpose of documentation in a People CMM assessment is to serve as a trace of execution of the process. Merely having a well-documented process with poor institutionalization of the same is as good as relegating the practice to becoming shelf-ware. My view is that such a process is worthless. I would rather see an embodiment of process institutionalization that is working well than see reams and reams of useless documentation. My opinion of an empowered work culture is that it must have a process to derive a process. If everything is specified to the last letter and the process exercises very little of the individual's innovation quotient, chances of reaching the higher levels of People CMM maturity are very remote. Process innovation is facilitated if and only if loose ends are left untied and an individual is allowed the flexibility and freedom to exercise his individual professional judgement to make the day-to-day changes that are so necessary for optimal execution. At higher process maturity, we will be able to see process innovators and process rebels (in a positive sense) rather than conformists who are process followers at best. Innovation happens only if there is encouragement provided for healthy rebellion against the process.

An appraisal of the current workforce practices is normally undertaken after deciding on a qualified lead assessor along with a trained team of about four to eight experienced professionals from the organization or the site. The mandatory training for the assessment team is as follows.

- SEI authorized introduction to the People CMM or equivalent training on the People CMM, which the People CMM lead assessor can provide

- Assessment team training on the assessment method

The assessment team composition requires a combined experience of about 25 years in business competencies of the organization, and about 10 years in management experience. Individual experience that is recommended is about 5 years of business competencies of the assessed organization, 6 years of management, and 5 years of human resource management or equivalent. The composition of the assessment team would therefore be an SEI authorized lead assessor, at least 1 member from the organization and 3–7 additional members. Some of the desirable members on the assessment team are the people who are actually responsible for workforce improvements, the members belonging in the CDG. Ineligible members are middle and senior managers, managers of interviewees, or assessment participants where there is a possibility for constrained discussions.

The most important requirement for the lead assessor and the assessment team is to stay credible at all times. The lead assessor must ensure that the team qualifies with the necessary requirements to be on the assessment team; conducts the necessary mandatory training to the degree of detail necessary for the team to function effectively; ensures that assessment principles of confidentiality and sponsor engagement are maintained at all times; and finally, after the assessment is over, submits a report to the People CMM Assessment Repository maintained at the SEI.

The typical roles of assessment team members are as follows.

- Site coordinator: arranges for site logistics, organizes on-site activities, and assists the lead assessor

- Survey facilitator: arranges logistics for questionnaire administration and monitors the survey administration

- Librarian: collects and organizes documents for assessment team review, ensures access to information, and disposes documents no longer needed by the assessment team

- Process area mini-teams: focus on assigned key process areas to ensure coverage on all key practices throughout the assessment, organize data and develop observations substantiating actual facts, develop findings, and evaluate practices and goals to develop the final rating

- Session facilitator: usually the assessment team leader who manages the interview session; keeps a control on the proceedings

- Recorders: every individual on the assessment team is a recorder. They capture notes from every data gathering session and make a list of requested documents.

People CMM assessments are consensus-driven and objectivity is ensured by focusing the assessment on identifying the facts.

Role of Mini-assessment or Gap Analysis

Much before a formal People CMM assessment is planned, it is advisable to conduct a mini-assessment or a gap analysis. The purpose of a gap analysis is for the sponsor to understand the current state of the organizational practices and understand what it takes by way of committing resources to make the next step in implementing the recommendations of the People CMM framework. A gap analysis also helps tremendously in scoping the implementation programme based on a structured understanding of both the strengths and opportunities for improvement.

The manner in which a gap analysis is conducted is by sampling representative workgroups and reviewing their practices—both documented and undocumented. A good rule to use on answering the question—"To what degree of detail should workforce practices be documented?"—is to answer the next question—"In the absence of a particular documentation, what is the likelihood of the practice becoming subject to interpretation and what are the risks?"

Obviously and intuitively, a lack of something always surfaces risks, which have to be managed adequately with appropriate risk abatement procedures. And, the next rule of thumb to use is this—without the documentation, how do we guarantee a shared vision and a shared context that can be developed? It would be ludicrous to suggest that there has to be a document supporting every practice—it is both meaningless and a tremendous drain on the ability of an individual to innovate. Besides, process execution leaves behind traces of both direct and indirect artifacts. Tangible work products such as policies, procedures, and work instructions are some examples of direct artifacts. Minutes of meetings, status reports and review records are indirect artifacts, which support as evidence of practices that may have been executed. Both tangible and intangible evidence ought to be examined by the assessment team before drawing conclusions. In a truly empowered work culture, individuals are given enough leeway in the process to innovate by permitting flexibility to tailor organizational practices.

To understand if such an empowerment exists, a sample of the organization is called forth into a discussion on the practices that are performed. If need be, process maturity questionnaires may be used in the mini-assessment to obtain an understanding of what might exist in the organization by way of both written and unwritten rules.

At the end of the gap analysis, the findings are mapped on to the practices of the People CMM framework to highlight sufficiency or insufficiency of the degree of detail of implementation. Using this mapping, suggestions and recommendations are made to the organization on how best to leverage and enhance their strengths and how to work on improvements and turn them around as strengths. If required, the organization is also prepared to prioritize these findings and establish action plans to enable remedies to the situation.

Gap analysis would have tremendous value if led by an authorized People CMM lead assessor because the expertise that a lead assessor brings to the table is expert knowledge on both the People CMM and the People CMM assessment method—a very desirable combination.

Under the three classes of People CMM assessment types, gap analysis falls under the Class C type. The other two types are Class B and Class A. Class B is a questionnaire-based assessment, which is also a self-assessment to help organizations gain an insight into their capabilities. However, the results of a Class C or Class B assessment are not used for generating maturity level ratings since both depth and coverage are not emphasized. It is a good way to obtain a 'quick look'. Class A is the standard People CMM assessment resulting in a maturity level rating, which will be described later on in this chapter.

Prioritizing the Findings

Not all recommendations need to be worked on simultaneously. Some findings have significant value for the organization and must be attempted first. When organizations embark on the People CMM initiative, there are bound to be many gaps between what the People CMM framework lays down as practices and the organizational workforce practices in use. There may be alternative practices, which are equally valuable for the organization and could be the right responses to the conditions surrounding the business. A few practices may be totally counter-intuitive, fresh, and forward-thinking. Take reverse mentoring, where fresh recruits and graduates are allowed to mentor the senior people in the organization who have either become rusty on the job or have developed dead skin that needs to be shed due to a lack of exposure to the latest developments in technology.

There is no reason to change these practices just because the alternative practice or the more counter-intuitive ones are not laid down in the People CMM framework. In fact, these practices may be more valuable than merely following a prescription of practices—the People CMM framework.

The People CMM framework, along with the findings of the gap analysis or mini-assessment, can be used as a good roadmap serving as implementation guide. A word of caution that is often ignored is that a set of findings has dependency on the organizational context. A level on the People CMM scale has a timestamp. It must not be concluded that the maturity level is 'for life'. That is the mistake most organizations commit and as a consequence they are seen to rust away within a short interval of time after they establish process capability and therefore organizational maturity. My view on this dramatic decay and wasted effort is that probably the sufficiency criteria that were identified earlier in the chapter could be missing.

People CMM Implementation Strategy

Base the implementation strategy on the findings of the mini-assessment or gap analysis. The people CMM is not a standard that has to be in place *in toto*. Considerable tailoring of the model is necessary for best applicability. The objective here is *not* to tailor the organization to fit the People CMM but to tailor the People CMM to fit the organizational needs. For an assessment, all process areas belonging up to and including the targeted level of maturity will be evaluated. Therefore, if the targeted scope of the People CMM is a level 5, then all process areas within the People CMM become relevant and need to have supporting practices to the degree of detail mandated by the model.

Each prioritized process recommendation resulting in a new practice or change to an existing practice must get an answer to 'Is the change getting better or is it getting worse?' A useful mechanism is for every change notification to carry with it a questionnaire that feels the pulse of targets that will actually live such changes. The identification of all affected groups is very important. Process improvement initiatives are similar to any other time-critical project that competes for the best available resources, undivided attention of senior management, and funding. If the CEO of the company owns the process improvement initiative, then lasting value and true idealization of process improvement objectives can be realized. If process improvement and process management become core competencies of an organization rather than supplementary activities, chances of an enduring, innovative, and purposeful programme of implementation are possible.

People CMM Assessments (Class A Assessment)

Assessment Objectives

The purpose of a People CMM assessment is to understand the site's current workforce practices through a structured study of its strengths and weaknesses. Using this understanding, the assessment helps the site to prioritize issues of considerable importance and impact. The degree of satisfaction on the People CMM process areas is also examined by mapping the observations to the practices of the People CMM. By placing emphasis on senior management sponsorship and commitment, a People CMM assessment is also used to facilitate the initiation and continuation of process improvement activities. The People CMM assessment also builds a sense of organizational ownership to the results or outcomes.

Assessment Principles

An assessment has to be approached collaboratively with active engagement of both the assessment team and the organizational stakeholders. The People CMM framework is used as a basis; the practices of the People CMM become the requirements for the assessment. All concerned stakeholders and the assessment team must enter into a confidentiality agreement which shall, at no time, make an attribution to the source of information but will be based purely on facts collected and inferences drawn using professional judgement. The focus at all times must be on follow-on action.

Assessment Participants

An executive or senior manager who publicly supports process improvement and receives the final findings briefing and the final report is called a sponsor. A sponsor interview is the very first session in a People CMM assessment. Process owners, who are the actual enablers of the process in an organization, are interviewed and allowed to review the draft and final findings. Managers or business unit heads, who are responsible for workforce practices, are also interviewed and permitted to review the draft and final findings. Non-managers or individual contributors are the enactors of the process mandates and are also called forth to represent in an interview and review both the draft and final findings.

CMM Appraisal Framework Compliance

People CMM assessment is a CAF or CMM Appraisal Framework compliant appraisal method. A CAF-compliant assessment uses multiple data points or sources of inputs to arrive at a logical conclusion on the sites' strengths and weaknesses. Some of these data points are interviews, document reviews, tools, instruments such as questionnaires, presentations, and other informal mechanisms that rely on the professional judgement of the lead assessor. These multiple data sources provide the notes necessary to make up the observations. Observations that are corroborated—seen once and heard at least twice from two different data gathering sessions—become findings. These findings are now used for making the final ratings. People CMM assessments are questionnaire-intensive. There are two types of questionnaires—individual and manager questionnaires. They have to be bought from TeraQuest Metrics, Inc. (http://www.teraquest.com) as part of the assessment process. While it is nice to have the entire organization involved in the assessment process, the typical sample size of questionnaire respondents would vary from 50% to 75% of the organization that is in scope, for both individuals and managers. Since these questionnaires are priced, the site coordinator of the sponsoring organization must determine who is best qualified to respond.

While a mini-assessment is a 'quick look in the mirror', an assessment is a more involved and detailed examination of where an organization needs to shape up to remain competitive and thrive.

Based on the source of motivation for conducting the process appraisal, it can either be termed as an evaluation or an assessment. Table 2.1 summarizes the essential differences between the two.

Think of an evaluation as a good alarm clock. What you do or how you react to the alarm does not get specified in the final report. Assessments are friendlier and their primary purpose is to collaboratively evolve a set of findings that will appraise the current state of the organization.

An authorized lead assessor, who has the qualifications and experience to lead a trained team of experienced professionals, always leads appraisals. Appraisal is based on the following.

- Review of process documentation and artifacts

Table 2.1 *Evaluations and assessments comparison*

Evaluations	Assessments
The sponsor, who is typically external to the organization, owns the results.	Being self-motivated, the organization owns the results for proactive management of process.
The sponsor determines the scope, objectives, and the needs surrounding the process examination.	The organization commits resources and makes decisions regarding process improvement based on organizational needs.
There is normally a formal interface between the evaluation team members and organizational representatives.	They are truly collaborative even when the lead assessor may be external to the organization.

- Review of tools and other process enablers

- Evaluation of responses to a structured maturity questionnaire. Maturity questionnaire is an instrument that provides visibility into where the problems lie.

- In-depth discussions with project leaders, managers, process owners, and practitioners offers a multiple perspective look at the state of practice.

- Other informal and formal cues that an assessment team can pick up from experience using professional judgement

Assessment team members must model a behaviour of credibility and authority. They must understand the principles of the assessment and the process framework thoroughly. They must be able to sift and sieve raw information and data into meaningful observations that gets transformed into pithy findings.

A good lead assessor is one who has the sense to pick the right team to do what she wants done and the self-restraint to keep from meddling while they are doing it! The challenge often is to collect relevant information from the vast body of the information available from the assessment. It is not uncommon to find experienced team members on the assessment team. It must be emphasized that the assessment team leader or the lead assessor has the final word and owns the entire assessment process. It is therefore important to emphasize that assessment team members must be good soldiers as well. They must learn to respect authority (the assessment team leader) and be willing to suspend their assumptions and engage in active listening and purposeful communication. The necessary team building and team growing activities for the assessment team have to be planned in advance by the assessment team leader. Such team training activities are typically conducted during the formal three-day assessment team training. Not emphasizing enough on such activities is a sureshot formula for building an ineffective team—which only means a loss of credibility. Assessment participants bring intimate knowledge of the current practices. They know what is working and what is not. They have a very powerful influence with process improvement and for implementing results back in their organizations. It is the synergy between the assessment team and the assessment participants that produces successful assessment results.

Team training offers a mechanism to improve skills such as recording, observing, guiding the discussion through open-ended questions, and caring enough for improving the organizational response to the assessment. Collecting organizational data at the practice level has to be emphasized in order to ensure that the observations are corroborated and has adequate coverage on the key process area. It must be mentioned again that both direct and indirect artifacts may serve the purposes of corroboration. If a practice does not have adequate corroboration, it is treated as information needed and professional judgement has to be applied while ruling practice satisfaction. The key here is to assess the impact of the judgement on goal satisfaction. The size of the organization and the scope of the People CMM framework would decide the sample size of the organization that must be used for a fair assessment. These would also provide an indication of how long the onsite assessment would last, how many people should be interviewed, and how many will respond to the maturity questionnaire. The ultimate objective for the assessment team is to ensure that it has adequate coverage on all practices of all process areas in scope to make objective decisions on goal fulfilment.

SITARA uses the template shown in Table 2.2 to report the People CMM assessment findings. Making qualitative judgements of the process is out of the scope of a People CMM assessment. However as a People CMM assessor, I have found the importance of offering the assessed entity 'value added feedback' which can assist the sponsor to initiate the follow on action plan. From my experience, most sponsors on SITARA's assessments have expressed great satisfaction when the assessment has recommended and highlighted value added judgements on the actual 'quality of practices' within the manifest process.

The primary reason for a lot of debate on the assessment results is because the assessment method clearly does not get into the merits or the quality of the process artifacts that are being assessed. During assessments, this opens up a number of questions that are difficult to interpret and justify. [Nandyal 2001] describes them to a degree that is necessary and sufficient for an intellectual understanding and an awareness of the possibilities in making interpretations. My opinion is that—the tougher the interpretation, the better is the transfer of responsibility back to the organization's process owners. In fact, while assessments are never intended to make "qualitative judgements", as a lead assessor I have made them in the interests of the organization in the final findings presentation in a section called "Points to Ponder". Observations in this section were also included in the final rating of the maturity level. Having been on both sides of the turf on different occasions—as part of the organization that was assessed and being the lead assessor, I have had some of the best insights into the possibilities of how assessments can be camouflaged! A well executed assessment must ensure that masks that camouflages the real process are unmasked [Nandyal 2001].

Table 2.2 *Assessment findings template*

Findings are of five types.
1. *Strength:* a finding consistent with a People CMM requirement in a KPA
2. *Opportunities for improvement:* a finding that does not satisfy a People CMM requirement or hurts the satisfaction of goals
3. *Points to ponder:* a finding that is needed
   - to accommodate a future domain or a future need
   - qualitative judgement from the AT
4. *Global strength:* a finding consistent with the People CMM
   - across key process areas
   - repeatedly noted
   - is of special note by the assessment team
5. *General finding:* an area for improvement repeatedly noted during the assessment or a global area of opportunity for improvement

Source: Adapted from SITARA [2000b] with permission

The final findings report is normally an assessment of the organization's adherence to the reference framework, namely the People CMM. The strengths and opportunities for improvement are used as basis to determine the maturity level of the organizational process. Each finding is based on corroborated evidence and collaborative consensus of the assessment team. When key practices of the People CMM process area fail to meet expectations, either due to an inadequate richness of the process or because the process has not withstood the test of time, it becomes necessary for the assessment team to detail such instances. The minimum duration within which a process must have been in place and have sustained is not mandated, but credible lead assessors look for a proof of process execution over a minimum of four to six months and use professional judgement when it comes to interpreting whether the process would sustain or otherwise.

After understanding the site's practices, it is possible to identify process strengths that would definitely sustain the process infrastructure, and opportunities for improvement that have to be strengthened with the help of recommendations. Identification of the highest priority issues for improvement and determination of the degree of satisfaction on the People CMM model requires expert knowledge of the model. The fundamental premise of such inferences is to ensure that transfer of process ownership back into the organization is complete and happens at the earliest. The most crucial aspect of the final findings report is to ensure that besides being credible, they help to build organizational ownership and offer a framework for a follow-on action plan through renewed commitment and sponsorship.

In order to establish objectivity, all assessments begin with a reference framework, such as the People CMM, as the process framework. By using a common framework that is well understood by everybody on the assessment team, assessment activities guide the exploration and help to ensure that interviews and discussions are conducted in an orderly and complete fashion. The scope of an assessment can also be determined using a well-documented reference framework such as the People CMM.

Strict confidentiality of the source of information is to be ensured without attribution of both People CMM and non-People CMM findings. Active involvement of senior management through a commitment process is necessary and such participation and proactive reinforcement alone helps in the buy-in from the rest of the organization. The entire assessment is to be approached with a sense of collaboration and consensus within the assessment team. The primary focus is to be placed on a follow-on action plan that uses the recommendations of the final findings.

The richness of the process is determined in the final ratings exercise that uses the final findings to abbreviate the process maturity into a single digit ranging from 1 to 5. This is the most crucial last step in an assessment that requires balance coupled with professional and management insights. Involving the management in this decision is a good professional approach. Senior management that is committed to process improvement will even choose to suggest a lower maturity rating by requesting the assessment team to focus on the impact of opportunities for improvement rather than the strengths alone. Such instances are quite rare, but are not unimaginable! The senior management in such organiza-tions believes firmly that most process problems are 'management problems' and not 'technical problems'. They also take responsibility for the current status of the process and make every effort to improve the circumstances and conditions surrounding it. Before deciding the level, the assessment team leader must ensure that the organization has also been assessed on process areas at one level above the levels she presumes the organization to be at.

The assessment report that includes the final findings, the rating, and a follow-on action plan recommended by the assessment team becomes the sponsor's confidential assessment artifact. It is now up to the sponsor to disseminate this information and make the results public. It is also the role of the sponsor to ensure that follow-on action plans are worked on and supported by qualified teams. The basic principles of action planning has to do with the following.

1. Set clear and unambiguous objectives.

2. Provide leadership by modelling desired behaviour.

3. Ensure incremental small steps are taken for each major objective.

4. Establish measures to indicate progress made vis-à-vis process objectives.

5. Obtain buy-in at all levels.

Modus Operandi of a Typical People CMM Assessment

People CMM assessments are typically a five-month exercises with the following phases.

1. Preparing phase (approximately 3 months)

2. Surveying phase (approximately 1 month in parallel with preparing phase)

3. Assessing phase (approximately 1 month)

4. Reporting phase (approximately 1 month)

Tasks in Preparing Phase

Secure Sponsor (1–2 days)

Sponsorship of the People CMM programme and ownership of results or outcomes from a People CMM assessment is by far the most crucial step in the preparing phase. Lack of a visible sponsorship and acceptance of carrying forward the change programme is in itself the biggest risk to sustaining and building a self-sufficient process improvement initiative. Sponsors must not only advocate the change, they must believe in it, and model appropriate behaviour that sends periodic reinforcing messages that are both demonstrated and expressed. The sponsor must also decide whether the desire to change is motivated by external reasons (like competition) or for the sake of making a genuine improvement to the process (to address business needs). A sponsor, who ensures that process improvement programmes become an organizational core competency with sound strategic intent, stands an excellent chance to make a lasting change to the behaviour patterns across the organization, which is what an ideal process improvement programme must demonstrate. Sponsorship is also about obtaining organizational enrolment into the process improvement programme.

Determine Scope (1–8 hours)

Based on the business objectives, the sponsor must decide upon the high priority needs that have to be addressed with adequate institutionalization and implementation practices. The People CMM framework may be used as the reference framework, since it is a good compilation of the best practices. While the immediate priorities need to be addressed, a process improvement programme must be forward-looking with respect to the scope of implementation. The scope must include a well-defined roadmap of execution with clearly articulated milestones.

Obtain Commitment (1–2 days)

Obtaining a buy-in of the relevant stakeholders of the process programme is necessary in order to build a shared context of the implementation programme. The important point is to make sure that while developing this shared context or shared vision, a sense of willing acceptance to commit to the initiative is enabled. Commitment is a pact or an agreement that has to be demonstrated by all the relevant stakeholders.

Establish Infrastructure (4–8 hours)

In a broader context, infrastructure includes tools, instruments, and training that is necessary for people on the programme to perform adequately. If the people who are performing their roles don't know what they are working on, then we don't have adequate infrastructure to carry forward the programme. So I would categorize obtaining the necessary and required training on the People CMM framework to all those who are going to be the torch-bearers for the programme as chartering the necessary resources and establishing the infrastructure.

Plan Assessment (2–3 days)

There are two types of assessments that would need to be performed. One is ongoing and periodic, which is more of a sniff test or a raincheck to see if the implementation objectives are being met. The other is more of a systematic exploration of process capability and overall organizational maturity which is the People CMM assessment. Both these types of assessments need to be planned. On the more formal People CMM assessment, the number of tasks and activities are far more than what is used on the sniff test or a raincheck. So, these tasks have to be individually planned because most of them are mandatory and required as a prerequisite to complete the People CMM assessment.

Train Team (2–5 days)

The organizational team that will be part of the final People CMM assessment must be trained on the People CMM model. Such model training is an exhaustive treatment of the subject matter and is typically a three-day course. Such training can be an authorized three-day introduction to People CMM or can be provided by an authorized People CMM lead assessor using a self-generated set of training materials.

Arrange Logistics (2–4 weeks)

It must be ensured that the chartered infrastructure is available when the implementation team needs it and required resources are also made available to meet the requirements of the assessment team during the assessment. Items on the logistics checklist include things such as access to discussion rooms, photocopy machine, high speed printer, computing resources, and so on. A logistics checklist is included as a ready reckoner in Chapter 9.

Tasks in Surveying Phase

Select Sample (2–4 days)

A sample that truly represents the organization has to be selected using random stratification, which will be described in the coming sections. This sample will be used to represent the organization in the assessment. It is a combination of individuals, managers, and process owners along with the sponsor.

Prepare Logistics (2–4 days)

In order to administer the survey, which is currently Web-based and administered online, infrastructure to help individuals respond to the survey must be provided.

Enough time must be allowed and planned for between when the survey is submitted to the individuals and when the processed survey results would be available.

Administer Survey (1–2 days)

There are two types of questionnaires—individual questionnaire and manager questionnaire. This categorization is to ensure that the wording of the question is appropriate to serve the intended audience.

For example in the work environment:

Individual Question: To what extent do you have adequate materials and equipment to perform your work?

- To a **very** little extent
- To a little extent
- To some extent
- To a great extent
- To a **very** great extent
- Does not apply
- Don't know

Manager Question: To what extent have you been made aware of methods for addressing work environment issues, such as reporting safety hazards, computer needs, and insufficient lighting?

- To a **very** little extent
- To a little extent
- To some extent
- To a great extent
- To a **very** great extent
- Does not apply
- Don't know

Both types of questionnaires have to be administered to a significant percentage of the organization as dictated by the assessment guidelines. In any organization that has a size of over 200 people, the number of individual questionnaire responses has to be 20% or more and the number of manager questionnaire responses has to be 35% or more. For an organization that has 50 persons or less, it has to be 100% of both individual and manager. A good way to select individuals to respond to the questionnaire is to use a stratified random sampling technique, wherein 20% of the individuals chosen from across the organization and is made up of 20% developers, 20% testing team, 20% design champions, 20% support team members, and so on. Not just any 20% of the organization.

Questionnaire respondents must be encouraged to write additional comments as appropriate for each of the survey questions in the space provided. The best way to administer the questionnaire, even though it is online at this time, is to build in a sense of timeliness and coordination using a common understanding. So, a proctored session where individuals assemble in one place to answer questions with active involvement of either a lead assessor or a person from the site who is best informed about the process is recommended.

Analyse Results (15–20 days)

The questionnaires are then analysed and a summary of the survey response is provided by TeraQuest Metrics, Inc., the organization which administers and evaluates the People CMM questionnaires. Analysis of the summary of questionnaire responses has to include the mean and mode calculations along with the comments that are summarized. The results of the analysis are indicators to the areas that need to be probed. Document reviews must focus on these indicators and appropriate questions may need to be scripted.

Tasks in Assessing Phase

Organize Teams (1–2 hours)

Organizing two types of teams is called for—One, the assessment team itself which actually conducts the People CMM assessment and two, the respondents of the survey who will be called forth to represent in the interviews. The primary qualifications for members who belong in the assessment team are that they must have undergone the required training on the People CMM model and the assessment team training. Whereas the criteria to select people into workforce discussions and to represent the organization in the assessment is dependent on how much they know of the workforce practices. Care must be ensured to pick a balanced number of both positively and negatively opinionated individuals. You need opinionated people for a good assessment. People with no opinions can contribute very little to an assessment!

While opinionated individuals are desirable participants on the assessment, open-mindedness is desirable for those who are going to be on the assessment team.

Brief Participants (1–2 hours)

Informing participants about their role during the assessment is very important. It is natural to expect a heightened sense of anxiety and therefore it is very important for the lead assessor to emphasize that the assessment is not an examination. It is also important for the sponsor to let the participants know that outcomes from the assessment will be used to highlight opportunities for improvement and take note of the strengths that are helpful for the organization and in no way will they be used to threaten their jobs.

Participants are expected to perform two important functions. They will respond to a structured questionnaire that addresses the People CMM practices and they will represent their site in an interview where an understanding of the workforce practices will be obtained. The first part has been discussed under *Administer Survey*.

Analyse Survey Results (1–4 hours)

Along with a frequency distribution, for every question on the survey results are provided by TeraQuest as a summary report giving the average, standard deviation and count of the sample. The scale used is a 7-point Likert scale with the following distribution.

1. To a very little extent

2. To a little extent

3. To some extent

4. To a great extent

5. To a very great extent

6. Does not apply

7. Don't know

Since time and coverage are the two enemies on an assessment, it is important to establish a criterion to assess the survey results for scripting questions. Except for the non-binary (yes/no type) and negatively-worded (meaning a low value on the 7-point scale is good) questions, one useful technique which has been found useful on assessments conducted by SITARA is the following.

- Irrespective of the average, if the standard deviation is greater than 1.0, then there is a wide variation to individual perception about the strength of the practice being addressed by the question. Obtaining better clarity on the practice during an interview is required and therefore the question that is having a wide degree of variation to individual perception is included in the scripted questions.

- If the average is 2 or below 2 (To a little extent), and the standard deviation is less than 0.5, then there is a clear understanding within the organization that the question addressing the practice is a clear weakness. So, this is included in the scripted question.

- If the average is 4 or above 4 (To a great extent), and the standard deviation is less than 0.5, then chances are that the practice addressed by the question is supported well in practice. There is a general perception that the practice is strongly supported. So, this may be excluded from direct questioning but the assessment team needs to look at indirect evidence.

Review Documents (5 days)

The purpose of documentation review is to ensure that process institutionalization is supported by practices through adequate instantiations, which are adequate and consistent with the articulated process. Documents serve as evidence or as practice implementation indicators providing a trace of execution left behind as a consequence of following organizational practices. The most important objective behind document review is to ensure that the intent behind the process is represented in practice with little or no variation arising out of interpretation.

Script Interview Questions (1 day)

Based on the consolidated report of the maturity questionnaire, an initial set of questions can be scripted based on the criterion described earlier. A good sense for practice instantiation can be obtained by documentation review. If there is consistency in both direct and indirect artifacts supporting the execution trace of a practice, then one needs to ensure that a scripted question is used to corroborate evidence from interviews. Significant discontinuities between process and practice may come up from inadequate practice instantiations. Such discontinuities are obvious candidates for scripted questions. Sufficient planning and thought must be given to how the interviews will be conducted. Depending upon the scope of the assessment (whether it is a level 2 or a level 5), there will be limited time available on hand for the assessment team to get to as much coverage as possible on the key practices of the People CMM process areas. Scripted questions have to target both process owners and groups of individuals who represent the organization.

Interview Process Owners (4–6 hours)

Process owners are generally managers, who own responsibility for key functions in the organization such as facilities, compensation, training, business strategy, quality, and technology. These are normally individual interviews as opposed to group interviews. Questions, which are asked for process owners, must ensure adequacy and continuity of purpose. Typically these interviews are 1 to 1.5 hours in duration and can be done in one single day.

Consolidate Process Owner Data in Observations (2 hours)

Data from process owner interviews must be consolidated on the same day. It is very important for the lead assessor to plan sufficient time between the close out of process owner interviews and time available until end of day to consolidate observations of the assessment team. Depending upon the scope of the assessment and prior assessment experience of individuals on the assessment team, it is more than likely that each assessment day could very well become a 15–18 hour day if the team is not closure-oriented, based on facts. It is extremely dangerous to defer consolidation to the next day.

Interview Managers (2–3 hours)

Manager interviews are mostly line managers who have direct line management responsibility. They could be business unit heads or programme managers depending upon the structure of the organization. Business unit heads have a direct responsibility to translate processes to practices within business units. To a degree, they share responsibility with process owners to keep the process current and fresh. They can be looked at as practitioners of the process.

Consolidate Interview Data from Managers into Observations (2–4 hours)

Depending upon the number of business units that are being assessed, and the number of middle managers in the organization, these could be either individual interviews or can be conducted as group interviews with appropriate participation. No more than two per group is a good way to ensure discussions of rich quality on topics that find relevance from survey analysis of manager question-naires.

Workforce Discussions (6–8 hours)

Groups of 12 to 15 individuals per group can be interviewed with questions from individual survey analysis. In order to get complete coverage on the People CMM practices, it is important to use targeted questions from the process areas that are in scope. Typically, follow-up questions are asked to obtain more clarity on the basic themes that are being discussed. Workforce discussions are normally steered by the assessment team with supporting questions rather than being interview-oriented. It is important to note that in workforce discussions certain individuals have a natural tendency to dominate the interview and a few others are reticent by nature. The assessment team and the lead assessor, in particular, must ensure that there is a good balance in discussions. If required, it will be useful to draw forth opinions of the more reticent individuals by targeting specific questions at the quieter individuals.

Consolidate Workforce Discussions into Observations (4–8 hours)

At this stage, if the assessment is under good control of the lead assessor (there is high degree of coherence and commonness of observations), the assessment observations can now be translated into findings by consolidating and corroborating facts from process owner, manager, and workforce interviews. Findings can be categorized into strengths, opportunities for improvement, and points to ponder.

Prepare Draft Findings (4 hours)

Draft findings are observations from the assessment, which are consistent, corroborated, and factual. Findings can be strengths if they are supported adequately by evidence of practice on a given People CMM process area. It is a weakness if the People CMM practice is not supported through evidence, either as stated in the People CMM or as an alternative practice. It is a points-to-ponder, if it is a professional judgement made by the assessment team by being inadequate from the organizational context. Under the category of points-to-ponder, the practice is most definitely not a strength, but a limited weakness, which may have a negative impact on the organizational ability to leverage and scale-up. Points-to-ponder may not hurt the goal and therefore may not hurt the attainment of a maturity level.

- Review with legal or sponsor (1–2 hours)

- Review with process owners (1–2 hours)

- Review with managers (1–2 hours)

- Review with workforce (1–2 hours)

All the above review sessions are done separately with the representatives of the organization participating in the assessment. Review of the draft findings with the assessment participants is absolutely critical to understand how the findings are perceived. The assessment team must take copious notes during these sessions when a first look is provided to the organization on the state of affairs in the organization. Perceptions if any in the assessment findings ought to be those of the assessment participants and not of the assessment team. Draft findings are presented in order to obtain better clarity on how the facts, which are being represented, are perceived by the stakeholders. Needless to say, if the assessment team has done a good job on the assessment, not many findings should come up for negotiation. Discussions, if any, must be to provide clarifications and not for inflicting changes to the draft findings. It is only when the assessment team approaches the entire assessment with professionalism and accuracy to representing facts, can it remain credible. The job of the lead assessor is to ensure that the assessment team will stay credible right from the word go!

Revise Findings if Necessary (as necessary)

During the draft findings presentation reviews, participants may offer clarifications and provide additional inputs. If necessary, the draft findings may need modification and the assessment team must be open for such a possibility.

Prepare Final Findings and Rate Maturity (2–4 hours)

Final findings represent the final picture of the process capability of the practices of the applicable process areas. They are used to arrive at the overall organizational maturity rating as a result. While the draft findings presentation may provide an opportunity to seek additional clarifications, a well-executed People CMM assessment will have no reasons to make major modifications to the 'factual content' in the draft findings. All the necessary word-smithing and accuracy of the facts should have been done before the review of the draft findings. It is not a good idea to modify the final findings to a degree where consensus would need to be re-established all over again. By now, the organization must have enough reasons to believe in the credibility of the findings and accept transfer of ownership of these results. Rating organizational maturity based on goal satisfaction is an optional task. If the site sponsor chooses not to go with an assessment outcome that will also declare the maturity rating, then it need* not be done. A situation such as this may arise when the sponsor expects a maturity level that is much higher than what the findings reveal. The only prudent option in such situations is for the lead assessor to insist on a 'non-rated' assessment where strengths and opportunities for improvement will be presented with no rating of the goals. Again, this situation occurs only where the lead assessor has not de-risked the assessment process from potential scope creep or has not done a thorough job of the mini-assessment to determine the possibilities of assessment outcome.

Present Final Findings (1–2 hours)

Every individual who participated in the People CMM assessment right from the opening meeting to the draft findings presentation is entitled to participate in the final findings presentation. If the sponsor feels that she would like to invite people from the organization who may not have participated in the assessment but require to know the final findings, like the chief financial officer or the chief technology officer, it would be desirable to let the assessment team leader know of such possibilities. However, having a customer or the media on the final findings presentation is a poor choice, especially if the results are not as expected. The sponsor should consult the assessment team leader before extending such invitations.

Debrief Sponsor (1 hour)

A final executive session to understand the concerns of the sponsor and to debrief the sponsor on the conduct of the assessment is a great way to complete the transfer of ownership of results back into the organization—where it ideally belongs. The importance of this session should not be diluted even though it may very well last for only a few minutes. Every minute of this final organizational debrief is worth its weight in gold.

Wrap-up the Assessment (2 hours)

This is the final step in the actual assessment process. The lead assessor facilitates the lessons learnt exercise with the assessment team as the final People CMM assessment debrief. This is the best opportunity for the team to convey "What went right and what went wrong? Next time we do the People CMM assessment, what do we do differently?" Assessment team performance review is documented.

After this debrief is complete, the assessment is torn down with the shredding of confidential information, which is made up of the People CMM assessment arti-facts maintained in the confidential trash bin during the assessment. All un-claimed and unreturned assessment artifacts make it to the confidential trash bin during the assessment period.

Tasks in Reporting Phase

Complete Final Report (1–4 days)

The final report consists of the standard forms that have to be completed as part of the kit. One of the forms which need to be completed is called the People CMM Assessment Repository Record Entry Form (PCAR). The PCAR form has to be returned to the SEI and TeraQuest.

Report Results to People CMM Assessment Repository (2–4 hours)

Submitting the PCAR form and relevant assessment artifacts, such as observation reports, draft finding presentation, and final finding presentation, along with the maturity rating to the SEI and TeraQuest concludes the process of an authorized People CMM assessment. Transfer of ownership of the results from the assessment back to the organization should be complete by now. The earlier this happens, the better are the chances for follow-on action to occur. It is the responsibility of the site coordinator to create a follow-on action plan and make it available to the SEI within 30 days of a People CMM assessment closure.

Related Chapters to Refer

📖 Chapter 9—Best Practices in People CMM Assessments

Overview of the People CMM

IT IS MY belief that knowledge of version 1.0 is helpful while implementing People CMM practices using the more recent version 2.0. Certain practices and key process areas of the People CMM version 1.0 help get the right orientation to the implementation initiative. I would also add that if this knowledge can be supplemented with the practices contained in disciplines described in other CMM models such as SW–CMM or the more recent CMM Integrated for Systems Engineering, Software Engineering, Integrated Product, and Process Development and Supplier Selection [CMMI 2002], chances are that competency development within IT initiatives will be better structured. The People CMM, in a sense, is an excellent enabler for workforce competency development while using the SITARA ODER—objective, determinants, enablers, and realignment (ODER) paradigm [Nandyal 2002]. Since competency development and nurturing practices that facilitate proactive management of competencies form the backbone of the People CMM framework, the SITARA ODER paradigm is explained in Appendix B. The SITARA ODER paradigm is a method to grow strategic intent behind workforce competency development—one of the available 'how to implement' strategies in this book.

Overview of Version 1.0

Version 1.0 of People CMM was released in September 1995 as People Capability

Maturity Model® Version 1.0 [Curtis 1995]. The model is organized as having five maturity levels. Each maturity level is made up of a collection of key process areas. A key process area, in turn, is a cluster of practices that are internally cohesive and mutually supportive to establish process capability. When the rigour of these practices is sufficient enough to satisfy a set of goals, it can be concluded that the process meets its intended objectives.

There are a total of 20 key process areas in version 1.0. Each maturity level serves as an effective foundation for building the necessary rigour and serves to improve workforce capability. In this chapter, the time tested Goal–Question– Metric (GQM) paradigm of Basili and Weiss [Basili 1984] is used to enable the necessary internal dialogue while building the supporting process infrastructure. Asking the right questions, knowing the goals of the process area, is a good way to work the People CMM framework into the organizational design. Asking a question in this new way may be worth a dozen answers. These questions can also be used to conduct an appraisal and audit of the process infrastructure after it has been established.

Questions found in this chapter require descriptive explanations and is part of the SITARA's People CMM Assessment Survey Questionnaire (PCMM ASQ) released from SITARA Process JewelBox™ [SITARA 2000] (Appendix B). PCMM ASQ is recommended to be used on a Class B People CMM assessment which will be discussed in Chapter 9 on *Best Practices in People CMM Assessments*. However, the more formal individual and manager questionnaires for People CMM assessment have to be purchased from TeraQuest Metrics, Inc. for use with a Class A assessment.

Maturity Levels and Key Process Areas in Version 1.0

Maturity level 1 is called the *initial process* or *adhoc process* and is the default level of operation. Not surprisingly, there are no key process areas that an organization is expected to perform while at this level of maturity. This does not mean that a level 1 process cannot survive and demonstrate success. A level 1 process is highly dependent upon the individuals who perform the hit-or-miss types of practices and business success is to a large degree an outcome of Dame Luck. It is generally true that the single important reason why individuals are seen leaving a level 1 organization is due to poor interpersonal relationship with their managers or supervisors [Curtis 2002]. It may be due to lack of training imparted to managers and supervisors on skills necessary to support a responsible behaviour for people management. More often than not, such preparation is assumed as part of managerial responsibilities, which are often discharged inconsistently. Two dangerous ends of the spectrum of the people management practices are very clearly visible. On one end, there are those managers who are the *laissez-faire* type, who seem to have an ability to use their goodness to get work done without stealing empowerment away from individuals. And so, the morale of the engineers who work for such managers is generally high. Risk from such a hands-off approach is that individuals soon tend to develop a 'do-what-you-want' philosophy. A certain amount of supervision based on management by exception is required. And on the other end, there are managers who are the typical Type A bosses, seen to be stepping on the toes of engineers, modifying designs without adequate rationale and virtually handing out instructions for how things ought to be done. A deep sense of insecurity could be the reason for "It is my way or take the highway!" Engineers generally feel a sense of hopelessness and are seen to be either content with what they have since they don't want to lose their jobs, or there is high degree of churn rate resulting in further deterioration of competency development.

By institutionalizing basic workforce practices and building a culture based on commitment, a certain orientation towards a disciplined execution is enabled. By addressing the reasons surrounding turnover or churn rate, with practices that will help retain talent and grow healthy relationship styles, a foundation for effective workforce practices is laid. Within the People CMM V1.0, maturity level 2 is called the *repeatable process* and is the next level at which an organization can perform.

There are six key process areas at level 2.

- Work environment
- Communication
- Compensation
- Staffing
- Training
- Performance management

At maturity level 3, called the *defined process,* a culture of professionalism is established by enabling the following KPAs.

- Knowledge and skills analysis
- Workforce planning
- Competency-based practices
- Competency development
- Career development
- Participatory culture

At maturity level 4, called the *managed process* a culture of competencies is established by enabling the following KPAs.

- Mentoring
- Organizational competency management
- Organizational performance alignment
- Team building
- Team-based practices

At maturity level 5, called the *optimizing process,* a culture of continuous improvement and empowerment is established by enabling the following KPAs.

- Continuous workforce innovation
- Personal competency development
- Coaching

Overview of Version 2.0

Version 2.0 of People CMM was released in July 2001 as People Capability Maturity Model® Version 2.0, CMU/SEI-2001-MM-01. [Curtis 2002]

The model in version 2.0 is also organized as having five maturity levels. Each maturity level is composed of process areas organized as a collection of related practices whose fulfilment enables goal satisfaction. There are a total of 22 process areas. Transitioning from version 1.0 to 2.0 is almost seamless, given the similarities behind the concepts and structure of the framework.

Institutionalization features are characterized by the follwing.

- Commitment to perform, establishes a policy with designated support

- Ability to perform, ensures the necessary preconditions for performing practices by assigning responsibilities to stakeholders who are given the preparation to support execution

- Measurement and analysis, used to assess effectiveness and improvement needs based on status measurement

- Verifying implementation, provides visibility into compliance

Implementation features describe the activities performed as

- Practices that translate the process intent into execution

With very few exceptions, the following template reveals the design of the process areas contained in the People CMM.

Commitment to Perform

- **Policy**—The organization establishes and maintains a documented policy for conducting <process area> activities. **(Level 2)**

- **Support**—An organizational role(s) is/are assigned responsibility for assisting and advising units on <process area> activities and procedures. **(Level 2)**

- **Support**—An organizational role(s) is/are assigned responsibility for coordinating <process area> activities across the organization. **(Levels 3–5)**

Ability to Perform

- **Responsibility**—Within each unit, an individual(s) is/are assigned responsibility and authority for ensuring that <process area> activities are performed. **(Level 2)**

- **Responsibility**—Within each unit, an individual(s) is/are assigned responsibility and authority for ensuring that members of the unit participate in <process area> activities, as appropriate. **(Levels 3–5)**

- **Preparation**—Individuals conducting <process area> activities receive the preparation needed to perform their responsibilities. **(Level 2)**

- **Preparation**—Those responsible for <process area> activities develop the knowledge, skills, and process abilities needed to perform their responsibilities. **(Levels 3–5)**

- **Orientation**—Individuals participating in <process area> activities receive appropriate orientation in <process area> practices. **(Levels 2–5)**

- **Support (resource)**—Adequate resources are provided for performing <process area> activities. **(Levels 2–5)**

- **Support (defined)**—The practices and procedures for performing <process area> are defined and documented. **(Level 3)**

Measurement and Analysis

- **Status**—Measurements are made and used to determine the status and performance of <process area> activities. **(Level 2)**

- **Effect**—Unit measures of <process area> activities are collected and maintained. **(Level 2)**

- **Effect**—Measures are made and used to determine the effectiveness of <process area> activities. **(Levels 3–5)**

Verifying Implementation

- **Assurance**—A responsible individual(s) verifies that <process area> activities are conducted according to the organization's documented policies, practices, and procedures; and addresses non-compliance. **(Levels 2–5)**

- **Oversight**—Executive management periodically reviews the <process area> activities, status, and results; and resolves issues. **(Levels 2–5)**

Maturity Levels and Process Areas in Version 2.0

Maturity level 1 is called the *initial process* or *ad hoc process* and is the default level of operation. While the initial level of maturity may have processes that are minimal and mostly enforced by local governmental restrictions and laws, their interpretation and administration is seldom uniform. Rigour of practices is not sufficient to qualify for an assessment.

Making the transition to a *managed process* at level 2, a foundation of management practices is established at the unit level. Managers begin to ensure that individuals are able to make personal commitments to their work. By introducing basic people management practices, units ensure repeatability of successes using the practices of the following process areas.

- Work environment

- Communication and coordination

- Compensation

- Staffing

- Training and development

- Performance management

Units can now begin to share lessons learnt and surface best practices around people management at the unit level up to the organizational level. At the *defined level* or level 3, the organization proactively identifies and develops competencies that are successful practices at the unit level as a result of performing business activities. Workforce competencies are understood and a foundation is established for coordinated action based on an understanding of workgroup competencies. At this stage of organizational development, greater sharing of lessons learnt and best practices across units is visible. A culture of professionalism, based on sharing of information with participatory management, begins to take hold of organizational practices. Taking collective responsibility for knowledge growing activities becomes everyone's overriding responsibility with individuals sensitive to identifying and growing competency assets based on tailoring of workforce practices to enrich organizational assets. Practices at the level 3 belong to the following process areas.

- Competency analysis

- Workforce planning

- Competency development

- Workgroup development

- Career development

- Competency-based practices

- Participatory culture

At this stage of organizational development, tailored practices at level 3 are quantified to accommodate practice needs that are critical to customer quality. Projects identify the constraints of operations—cost, quality, scope, and time, which are the performance parameters—and become sensitive to customers' perceptions of what is critical to quality and tailor practices to meet quantitative business objectives of both process and product quality. Qualitative and quantitative attributes for the critical-to-quality measures of both the process and product goals—characteristics without which the process or product is rendered useless—are maintained. Leverage can also be found from competency integration to improve productivity and reduction of cycle time by enabling groups working on related product lines to co-own and co-create new product architecture or designs. A typical example could be integration of systems and software development practices to meet product development objectives [CMMI 2002]. Alternatively, it could include a good degree of reuse of both knowledge assets and capabilities of subject matter experts. Customer satisfaction becomes everyone's overriding responsibility with practices belonging to the following process areas.

■ Mentoring

■ Organizational capability management

■ Quantitative performance management

■ Competency-based assets

■ Competency integration

■ Empowered workgroups

A culture that is based on empowerment of individuals can now be established to leverage value from continuous process improvement. Individuals are sensitive to personal competency development in order to function effectively in their roles within the organization. Excellence orientation coupled with a high degree of self-actualization can be seen with individual's displaying pride of ownership. The much desired fire in the belly and 'make-it-happen-no-matter-what' culture can now be perceived in most individuals who come across as highly committed individuals. Performance excellence and a high degree of individual commitment to organizational business goals become every individual's overriding responsibilities.

■ Continuous workforce innovation

■ Continuous capability improvement

■ Organizational performance alignment

Level 2 Process Areas

Work Environment

The purpose of work environment is to establish and maintain physical working conditions and to provide resources that allow individuals and workgroups to perform their tasks efficiently and without unnecessary distractions. It also involves ensuring that the work environment complies with all applicable laws and regulations.

VERSION 1.0

Goal 1   *An environment that supports the performance of business processes is established and maintained.*

Goal 2   *The resources needed by the workforce to perform their assignments are made available.*

Goal 3   *Distractions in the work environment are minimized.*

VERSION 2.0

Goal 1   *The physical environment and resources needed by the workforce to perform their assignments are made available.*

Goal 2   *Distractions in the work environment are minimized.*

Goal 3   *Work environment practices are institutionalized to ensure they are performed as managed processes.*

- How does the organization ensure safe working conditions?

- How adequate are the resources, space, and infrastructure provided to you to perform your work effectively?

- How are environmental factors and distractions affecting your performance identified and how does the organization resolve them?

- Who is responsible for assisting and advising you on work-environment-related activities?

Communication and Coordination

The purpose of communication and coordination is to establish timely communication across the organization and to ensure that the workforce has the skills to share information and coordinate its activities efficiently. Practices within this process area are used to establish a social environment that supports effective interaction and to ensure that the staff has the skills necessary to share information and coordinate its activities efficiently. Communication involves establishing effective top-down and bottom-up communication mechanisms within the organization, ensuring that all individuals have the necessary communication skills to perform their tasks, coordinate effectively, conduct meetings efficiently, and resolve problems.

VERSION 1.0

Goal 1   *A social environment that supports task performance and coordination among individuals and groups is established and maintained.*

Goal 2   *Information is shared across levels of the organization.*

Goal 3   *Individuals develop skills to share information and coordinate their activities.*

Goal 4   *Individuals are able to raise grievances and have them addressed by management.*

VERSION 2.0

Goal 1   *Information is shared across the organization.*

Goal 2   *Individuals or groups are able to raise concerns and have them addressed by management.*

Goal 3   *Individuals and workgroups coordinate their activities to accomplish committed work.*

Goal 4   *Communication and coordination practices are institutionalized to ensure they are performed as managed processes.*

- How are organizational policies, events, and practices communicated?

- What mechanisms are in place for you to maintain ongoing communication within your unit to effectively perform your role?

- How are poor interpersonal relationships handled?

- How often is your opinion sought regarding your working conditions?

Staffing

The purpose of staffing is to establish a formal process by which talent is recruited, selected, and transitioned into assignments in the organization. Recruiting involves identifying the knowledge and skill requirements for open positions, motivating all individuals to seek out qualified candidates, announcing the availability of positions to likely sources of candidates, and reviewing the effectiveness of recruiting efforts. Selection involves developing a list of qualified candidates, defining a selection strategy, identifying qualified candidates, evaluating qualified candidates thoroughly, and selecting the most qualified candidate. Transitioning involves attracting selected candidates, orienting them to the organization, and ensuring their successful transition into their new positions.

VERSION 1.0

Goal 1   *The organization actively recruits for qualified talent.*

Goal 2   *The most qualified candidate is selected for each position.*

Goal 3   *Selected candidates are transitioned into their new positions.*

Goal 4   *Members of a unit are involved in its staffing activities.*

VERSION 2.0

Goal 1   *Individuals or workgroups in each unit are involved in making commitments that balance the unit's workload with approved staffing.*

Goal 2   *Candidates are recruited for open positions.*

Goal 3   *Staffing decisions and work assignments are based on an assessment of work qualifications and other valid criteria.*

Goal 4   *Individuals are transitioned into and out of positions in an orderly way.*

Goal 5   *Staffing practices are institutionalized to ensure they are performed as managed processes.*

- How are individuals selected to work in your unit?

- How are open positions staffed, and what is the criteria used to transition individuals on their assignments within the unit?

Performance Management

The purpose of performance management is to establish objective criteria against which unit and individual performance can be measured to provide performance feedback and to enhance performance continuously. Performance management involves establishing objective criteria for unit and individual performance, discussing performance regularly and identifying ways to enhance it, providing periodic performance feedback, identifying development needs, and systematically addressing performance problems or rewarding extraordinary performance.

VERSION 1.0

Goal 1   *Job performance is measured against objective criteria and documented.*

Goal 2   *Job performance is regularly discussed to identify actions that can improve it.*

Goal 3   *Development opportunities are discussed with each individual.*

Goal 4   *Performance problems are managed.*

Goal 5   *Outstanding performance is recognized.*

VERSION 2.0

Goal 1   *Unit and individual performance objectives related to committed work are documented.*

Goal 2   *The performance of committed work is regularly discussed to identify actions that can improve it.*

Goal 3   *Performance problems are managed.*

Goal 4   *Outstanding performance is recognized or rewarded.*

Goal 5   *Performance management practices are institutionalized to ensure they are performed as managed processes.*

- How are individual performance objectives determined in your group?

- How frequently do you receive communication about your performance at work?

- How is unsatisfactory performance of individuals handled within your group?

- How is outstanding work performance recognized or rewarded?

Training and Development

The purpose of training and development is to ensure that all individuals have the skills required to perform their assignments. Training involves identifying the skills required to perform critical tasks, identifying training needs within each unit, and ensuring that needed training is received. Training activities ensure that all individuals have the skills required to perform their assignments.

VERSION 1.0

Goal 1   *Training in the critical skills required in each unit is provided.*

Goal 2   *Individuals receive timely training that is needed to perform their assignments.*

Goal 3   *Training opportunities are made available to all individuals.*

VERSION 2.0

Goal 1   *Individuals receive timely training that is needed to perform their assignments in accordance with the unit's training plan.*

Goal 2   *Individuals capable of performing their assignments pursue development opportunities that support their development objectives.*

Goal 3   *Training and development practices are institutionalized to ensure they are performed as managed processes.*

- How are training opportunities identified to support you in your work assignments?

- How do you maintain ongoing awareness of your job performance and development opportunities?

- How are you made aware of your capabilities?

Compensation

The purpose of compensation is to provide all individuals with remuneration and benefits based on their contribution and value to the organization. Compensation includes developing a documented compensation strategy, developing a plan for administering compensation, and making periodic adjustments to compensation based on performance.

VERSION 1.0

Goal 1 Compensation strategies and activities are planned, executed, and communicated.

Goal 2 Compensation is equitable relative to skill qualifications and performance.

Goal 3 Adjustments in compensation are made periodically based on defined criteria.

VERSION 2.0

Goal 1 Compensation strategies and activities are planned, executed, and communicated.

Goal 2 Compensation is equitable relative to skill, qualifications, and performance.

Goal 3 Adjustments in compensation are made based on defined criteria.

Goal 4 Compensation practices are institutionalized to ensure they are performed as managed processes.

- What is the basis on which your compensation was determined?
- Under what conditions are adjustments made to your compensation and how is equity ensured?

Level 3 Process Areas

Knowledge and Skills Analysis

The purpose of knowledge and skills analysis is to identify the knowledge and skills required to perform core business processes so that they may be developed and used as a basis for workforce practices. Knowledge and skills analysis involves identifying the business processes in which the organization must maintain competence, developing profiles of the knowledge and skills needed to perform these business functions, maintaining a knowledge and skills inventory, and identifying future knowledge and skill needs. The core competency are the knowledge and skills needed within the staff to perform an important business function of the organization. A core competency can be stated at a very abstract level, such as a need for a core competency in software engineering. Core competencies can also be decomposed to more granular capabilities, such as core competencies in designing avionics software, testing switching system software, or writing user manuals and training for reservations systems. A core competency can be decomposed into the specific knowledge and skills required to perform the business processes underlying the business function for which the competency is maintained.

VERSION 1.0

Goal 1 *The core competencies required to perform the organization's business processes are known.*

Goal 2 *Knowledge and skills profiles exist for each business process.*

Goal 3 *Core competencies are updated for anticipated future needs.*

Competency Analysis

The purpose of competency analysis is to identify the knowledge, skills, and process abilities required to perform the organization's business activities so that they may be developed and used as a basis for workforce practices.

VERSION 2.0

Goal 1 *The workforce competencies required to perform the organization's business activities are defined and updated.*

Goal 2 *The work processes used within each workforce competency are established and maintained.*

Goal 3 *The organization tracks its capability in each of its workforce competencies.*

Goal 4 *Competency analysis practices are institutionalized to ensure they are performed as defined organizational processes.*

- How does the organization determine the knowledge, skills, and abilities required for use with its current and anticipated needs?

- How are such assessments used to provide competency orientation to units?

- How frequently does your organization re-evaluate the knowledge and skills required to perform its business functions?

Workforce Planning

The purpose of workforce planning is to coordinate workforce activities with current and future business needs at both the organizational and unit levels. Workforce planning involves developing a strategic workforce plan that sets organization-wide objectives for competency development and workforce activities and developing near-term plans to guide the workforce activities of each unit.

VERSION 1.0

Goal 1   *The organization develops a strategic plan for long-term development of the competencies and workforce needed for its business operations.*

Goal 2   *Near-term workforce and competency development activities are planned to satisfy both current and strategic workforce needs.*

Goal 3   *The organization develops talent for each of its key positions.*

Goal 4   *The organization tracks performance in achieving its strategic and near-term workforce development objectives.*

VERSION 2.0

Goal 1   *Measurable objectives for capability in each of the organization's workforce competencies are defined.*

Goal 2   *The organization plans for the workforce competencies needed to perform its current and future business activities.*

Goal 3   *Units perform workforce activities to satisfy current and strategic competency needs.*

Goal 4   *Workforce planning practices are institutionalized to ensure that they are performed as defined organizational processes.*

- How are the unit's tactical and strategic competency needs established?

- How do units determine and assess the growth in workforce competencies?

- What is the frequency between such assessments and how do corrective actions ensure that unit competency objectives are fulfilled?

Competency Development

The purpose of competency development is to constantly enhance the capability of the staff to perform their assigned tasks and responsibilities. Competency development involves establishing training and other development programmes in each of the organization's core competencies.

VERSION 1.0

Goal 1 *The organization knows its current capability in each of the core competencies required to perform its business processes.*

Goal 2 *The organization develops capabilities in its core competencies.*

Goal 3 *Individuals develop their knowledge and skills in the organization's core competencies.*

VERSION 2.0

Goal 1 *The organization provides opportunities for individuals to develop their capabilities in its workforce competencies.*

Goal 2 *Individuals develop their knowledge, skills, and process abilities in the organization's workforce competencies.*

Goal 3 *The organization uses the capabilities of its workforce as resources for developing the workforce competencies of others.*

Goal 4 *Competency development practices are institutionalized to ensure they are performed as defined organizational processes.*

- How are workforce competencies defined and how are individual aspirations aligned to the organizational competency development?

- How frequently are individual competency plans reviewed and how are they assessed for effectiveness?

■ What measures are taken to ensure that growth of workforce competencies is established as an internal capability?

Competency-based Practices

The purpose of competency-based practices is to ensure that all workforce practices are based in part on developing the knowledge and skills of the staff. Competency-based practices involve recruiting against knowledge and skill needs, basing selection methods on assessing the knowledge and skills of candidates, assessing job performance against the tasks and roles assigned to the position, and basing compensation at least in part on growth in knowledge and skills.

VERSION 1.0

Goal 1   *Workforce practices are tailored to motivate individuals and groups to improve their knowledge and skills in the core competencies of the organization.*

Goal 2   *Workforce activities are adjusted to support development in the core competencies of the organization.*

Goal 3   *Compensation and reward strategies are tailored to motivate growth in the core competencies of the organization.*

VERSION 2.0

Goal 1   *Workforce practices are focused on increasing the organization's capability in its workforce competencies.*

Goal 2   *Workforce activities within units encourage and support individuals and workgroups in developing and applying the organization's workforce competencies.*

Goal 3   *Compensation strategies and recognition and reward practices are designed to encourage development and application of the organization's workforce competencies.*

Goal 4   *Competency-based practices are institutionalized to ensure they are performed as defined organizational processes.*

- What is the role of staffing on the growth of workforce competencies?

- How do you become aware of the best practices within your identified competencies?

- How has the work assignments helped you to develop knowledge and skills needed for your professional and career advancement?

- How frequently do you receive performance feedback and how does it align with the organization's competency assessment?

Career Development

The purpose of career development is to ensure that all individuals are motivated and are provided opportunities to develop new skills and workforce competencies that enhance their ability to achieve career objectives. Career development includes discussing career options with each individual, developing a personal development plan, tracking progress against it, identifying training opportunities, and making assignments that enhance career objectives.

VERSION 1.0

Goal 1   Career development activities are conducted with each individual.

Goal 2   The organization offers career opportunities that provide growth in its core competencies.

Goal 3   Individuals are motivated to pursue career goals that optimize the value of their knowledge and skills to the organization.

VERSION 2.0

Goal 1   The organization offers career opportunities that provide growth in its workforce competencies.

Goal 2   Individuals pursue career opportunities that increase the value of their knowledge, skills, and process abilities to the organization.

Goal 3   Career development practices are institutionalized to ensure they are performed as defined organizational processes.

- How are career advancement opportunities identified?

- What is the preparation you receive prior to a career transition?

- How do you go about establishing a personal competency development plan that aligns with your overall career objectives?

Participatory Culture

The purpose of a participatory culture is to ensure a flow of information within the organization, to incorporate the knowledge of individuals into decision-making processes, and to gain their support for commitments. Establishing a participatory culture lays the foundation for building high-performance teams. Participatory culture involves establishing effective communications among all levels of the organization, seeking inputs from individuals, involving individuals in making decisions and commitments, and communicating decisions to them. The purpose of a participatory culture allows the organization to exploit the full capability of the workforce for making decisions that affect the performance of business activities.

VERSION 1.0

Goal 1 *Communication activities are enhanced to improve the flow of information within the organization.*

Goal 2 *Decisions are made at the lowest appropriate level of the organization.*

Goal 3 *Individuals and groups participate in decision-making processes that involve their work or commitments.*

VERSION 2.0

Goal 1 *Information about business activities and results is communicated throughout the organization.*

Goal 2 *Decisions are delegated to an appropriate level of the organization.*

Goal 3 *Individuals and workgroups participate in structured decision-making processes.*

Goal 4 *Participatory culture practices are institutionalized to ensure they are performed as defined organizational processes.*

- How is information about business activities and performance communicated?

- How are decisions on the day-to-day business engagements made?

- How is your opinion sought and used on decisions that impact your work?

- What are the training opportunities provided to you and what are the available support mechanisms that assist you to make decisions best made by you?

Workgroup Development

The purpose of workgroup development is to organize work around competency-based process abilities.

VERSION 2.0

Goal 1   *Workgroups are established to optimize the performance of interdependent work.*

Goal 2   *Workgroups tailor-define processes and roles for use in planning and performing their work.*

Goal 3   *Workgroup staffing activities focus on the assignment, development, and future deployment of the organization's workforce competencies.*

Goal 4   *Workgroup performance is managed against documented objectives for committed work.*

Goal 5   *Workgroup development practices are institutionalized to ensure they are performed as defined organizational processes.*

- How are team charters established and used for envisioning interdependent work?

- How is the organizational standard tailored to fit your workgroup needs?

- How are ongoing assessments made to determine the progress made by your workgroup?

- How does the organization ensure growth in workforce competencies?

Level 4 Process Areas

Mentoring

The purpose of mentoring is to use the experience of the organization's staff to provide personal support and guidance to other individuals or groups. This guidance can involve developing knowledge and skills, improving performance, handling difficult situations, and making career decisions. Mentoring involves setting objectives for a mentoring programme, designing mentoring activities to achieve these objectives, selecting and training appropriate mentors, assigning mentors to individuals or groups, establishing mentoring relationships, and evaluating the effectiveness of the programme. Mentoring is the process of using experienced members of the organization to provide personal support and guidance to less experienced members of the staff. The purpose of mentoring is to transfer the lessons of greater experience in a workforce competency to improve the capability of other individuals or workgroups.

VERSION 1.0

Goal 1 *Mentoring activities are matched to defined objectives.*

Goal 2 *Mentors are selected and prepared for their responsibilities.*

Goal 3 *Mentors are made available for guidance and support to other individuals or groups.*

VERSION 2.0

Goal 1 *Mentoring programmes are established and maintained to accomplish defined objectives.*

Goal 2 *Mentors provide guidance and support to individuals or workgroups.*

Goal 3 *Mentoring practices are institutionalized to ensure they are performed as defined organizational processes.*

- How do you identify mentors who can help you with your personal development plan?

- How frequently do you get to share your development opportunities with your identified mentors?

■ How are assessments made to establish progress with respect to your personal growth objectives?

Team Building

The purpose of team building is to capitalize on opportunities to create teams that maximize the integration of diverse knowledge and skills to perform business functions. Team building involves matching potential team members to the knowledge and skill requirements of the team, training all new members in team skills, defining objectives for team performance, tailoring standard processes for use by the team, and periodically reviewing team performance. The team is a group of people that works closely to achieve shared objectives, work together on tasks that are highly interdependent, and may exercise a level of autonomy in managing their activities in pursuit of those objectives. This small number of people (often less than 10) with complementary skills is committed to a common purpose, performance goals, and work processes for which they hold themselves mutually accountable.

VERSION 1.0

Goal 1 *Teams are formed to improve the performance of interdependent tasks.*

Goal 2 *Team assignments are made to integrate complementary knowledge and skills.*

Goal 3 *Team members develop their team skills.*

Goal 4 *Team members participate in decisions regarding their work.*

Goal 5 *The organization provides standard processes for tailoring and use by teams in performing their work.*

■ How is collaborative work facilitated in your organization?

■ How does the organization ensure that individuals leverage complementary skills?

■ How is project-specific tailoring of workforce practices facilitated?

■ How are you made aware of internal resources that may help you with your competency development?

■ How are team-based objectives established for competency development?

Team-based Practices

The purpose of team-based practices is to tailor the organization's workforce practices to support the development, motivation, and functioning of teams. Team-based practices involves ensuring that the work environment supports team functions, setting performance criteria and reviewing team performance, involving team members in performing workforce activities, and reflecting team criteria in individual compensation decisions.

> **VERSION 1.0**
>
> ***Goal 1*** *The organization adjusts its workforce practices and activities to motivate and support the development of team-based competencies within the organization.*
>
> ***Goal 2*** *Workforce activities are tailored to support the needs of different types of teams within the organization.*
>
> ***Goal 3*** *Team performance criteria are defined and measured.*
>
> ***Goal 4*** *Compensation and reward systems are tailored to motivate improved team performance.*

- How are teams formed and how is ongoing communication among team members maintained?

- How is team performance assessed and how is teamwork recognized and rewarded?

- How does the organization support and promote team-based activities?

Organizational Competency Management

The purpose of organizational competency management is to increase the capability of the organization in its core competencies and to determine the effectiveness of its competency development activities in achieving specific competency growth goals. Organizational competency management involves setting measurable goals for growth in the organization's core competencies, defining and collecting data relevant to them, analysing the impact of competency development activities on achieving these goals, and using the results to guide the application and improvement of competency development activities.

VERSION 1.0

Goal 1 *Measurable goals for capability in each of the organization's core competencies are defined.*

Goal 2 *Progress towards achieving capability goals in the organization's core competencies is quantified and managed.*

Goal 3 *The knowledge and skills-building capability of the organization's competency development activities is known quantitatively for each of its core competencies.*

- How are individual competency profiles established?
- How are individual competencies assessed to ensure alignment with overall organizational goals for competency development?
- How are competency assets identified and used?
- How are workforce competencies requiring complementary skills integrated?

Organizational Capability Management

The purpose of organizational capability management is to quantify and manage the capability of the workforce and of the critical competency-based processes they perform.

VERSION 2.0

Goal 1 *Progress in developing the capability of critical workforce competencies is managed quantitatively.*

Goal 2 *The impact of workforce practices and activities on progress in developing the capability of critical workforce competencies is evaluated and managed quantitatively.*

Goal 3 *The capabilities of competency-based processes in critical workforce competencies are established and managed quantitatively.*

Goal 4 *The impact of workforce practices and activities on the capabilities of competency-based processes in critical workforce competencies is evaluated and managed quantitatively.*

Goal 5 *Organizational capability management practices are institutionalized to ensure they are performed as defined organizational processes.*

- How are target capability profiles established for the identified workforce competencies?

- How are the results of quantitative analyses concerning the organization's capability in its workforce competencies used?

- How does the organization establish quantitative goals for capability development in its critical competency-based processes?

Organizational Performance Alignment

The purpose of organizational performance alignment is to enhance alignment of performance results at the individual, team, unit, and organizational levels with the appropriate goals and to quantitatively assess the effectiveness of workforce practices on achieving alignment. Organizational performance alignment involves setting measurable goals for aligning performance at the individual, team, unit, and organizational levels; defining the data and analyses; collecting the data; analysing trends against objectives; acting on exceptional findings; analysing the impact of workforce practices on performance alignment; and reporting results.

VERSION 1.0

Goal 1   *Measurable goals for aligning individual, team, unit, and organizational performance are defined.*

Goal 2   *Progress towards achieving performance alignment goals is quantified and managed.*

Goal 3   *The capability of workforce activities to align individual, team, unit, and organizational performance is known quantitatively.*

VERSION 2.0

Goal 1   *The alignment of performance among individuals, workgroups, units, and the organization is continuously improved.*

Goal 2   *The impact of workforce practices and activities on aligning individual, workgroup, unit, and organizational performance is continuously improved.*

Goal 3   *Organizational performance alignment practices are institutionalized to ensure they are performed as defined organizational processes.*

- How are performance goals established and aligned for individuals across units?

- How is cross-group sharing of lessons learnt and best practices enabled?

- What is the feedback mechanism that helps in timely corrective and preventive actions?

- What are the performance measures used to understand organizational workforce competencies?

- In interdependent and collaborative work, how are competencies leveraged to offer the best competency alignment?

Competency Integration

The purpose of competency integration is to improve the efficiency and agility of interdependent work by integrating the process abilities of different workforce competencies.

VERSION 2.0

Goal 1   *The competency-based processes employed by different workforce competencies are integrated to improve the efficiency of interdependent work.*

Goal 2   *Integrated competency-based processes are used in performing work that involves dependencies among several workforce competencies.*

Goal 3   *Workforce practices are designed to support multidisciplinary work.*

Goal 4   *Competency integration practices are institutionalized to ensure they are performed as defined organizational processes.*

- How does the organization leverage value from multidisciplinary work?

- What are the project management activities and organizational infrastructure supporting collaborative work?

- How is a common shared vision for competency development and integration of complementary team competencies established?

- How does the organizational process repository enable integration of competencies?

Empowered Workgroups

The purpose of empowered workgroups is to invest workgroups with the responsibility and authority for determining how to conduct their business activities most effectively.

> **VERSION 2.0**
>
> **Goal 1** *Empowered workgroups are delegated responsibility and authority over their work processes.*
>
> **Goal 2** *The organization's workforce practices and activities encourage and support the development and performance of empowered workgroups.*
>
> **Goal 3** *Empowered workgroups perform selected workforce practices internally.*
>
> **Goal 4** *Empowered workgroups practices are institutionalized to ensure they are performed as defined organizational processes.*

- How are teams assisted and supported with decision-making that is best made by them?

- How are practices tailored to support project-based activities?

- How are individuals and teams supported by knowledgeable experts within the organization?

Competency-based Assets

The purpose of competency-based assets is to capture the knowledge, experience, and artifacts developed in performing competency-based processes for use in enhancing capability and performance.

> **VERSION 2.0**
>
> **Goal 1** *The knowledge, experience, and artifacts resulting from performing competency-based processes are developed into competency-based assets.*
>
> **Goal 2** *Competency-based assets are deployed and used.*
>
> **Goal 3** *Workforce practices and activities encourage and support the development and use of competency-based assets.*

Goal 4 *Competency-based assets activities are institutionalized to ensure they are performed as defined organizational processes.*

- Where are the lessons learnt and best practices captured and how are they used on projects?

- How are competency assets identified and kept current with the changing organizational capability profile?

- How often is the asset library assessed and how is the assessment result used?

Quantitative Performance Management

The purpose of quantitative performance management is to predict and manage the capability of competency-based processes for achieving measurable performance objectives.

VERSION 2.0

Goal 1 *Measurable performance objectives are established for competency-based processes that most contribute to achieving performance objectives.*

Goal 2 *The performance of competency-based processes is managed quantitatively.*

Goal 3 *Quantitative performance management practices are institutionalized to ensure they are performed as defined organizational processes.*

- How is feedback provided on project performance with respect to the identified critical-to-quality measures?

- How are process capability baselines established?

- How is sub-process variation stabilized and how are corrective actions rendered?

- How is the impact due to special and common causes of process variation determined and minimized?

Level 5 Process Areas

The purpose of personal competency development is to provide a foundation for professional self-development. Personal competency development consists of a voluntary programme for continuously improving individual work processes. This programme involves developing goals and plans for personal work activities, establishing and using defined personal processes, measuring and analysing the effectiveness of these personal processes, and implementing improvements to them.

VERSION 1.0

Goal 1   *Individuals know their capability in each of the competencies involved in their work.*

Goal 2   *Individuals continuously improve their knowledge and skills in the competencies involved in their work.*

Goal 3   *Participation in improving personal competencies is organization-wide.*

- How are training opportunities ensured to enable individual's competency development objectives?

- How are personal competency development plans established?

- What are supporting infrastructural mechanisms available to individuals that help to capture individual learning?

- How are organizational development activities aligned to foster individual learning opportunities?

Continuous Capability Improvement

The purpose of continuous capability improvement is to provide a foundation for individuals and workgroups to continuously improve their capability for performing competency-based processes.

VERSION 2.0

Goal 1   *The organization establishes and maintains mechanisms for supporting continuous improvement of its competency-based processes.*

Goal 2   *Individuals continuously improve the capability of their personal work processes.*

Goal 3   *Workgroups continuously improve the capability of their workgroup's operating processes.*

Goal 4   *The capabilities of competency-based processes are continuously improved.*

Goal 5   *Continuous capability improvement practices are institutionalized to ensure they are performed as defined organizational processes.*

- How are causes of defects identified and minimized?

- How do you suggest improvements in your work processes?

- How have the self-improvement programmes you have undertaken in the recent past helped you improve your performance?

Coaching

The purpose of coaching is to provide expert assistance to enhance the performance of individuals or teams. Coaches engage in close relationships with individuals or teams to guide development of skills that improve performance. Coaching involves selecting appropriate coaches, analysing data on personal or team performance, providing guidance on methods for improving performance, and evaluating progress toward goals for improving performance. Coaching is the provision of expert assistance to enhance the performance of individuals or teams.

VERSION 1.0

Goal 1   *Coaches are selected for their expertise and prepared for their responsibilities.*

Goal 2   *Coaches work with individuals to improve their personal competency and performance.*

Goal 3   *Coaches work with teams to improve their team-based competencies and performance.*

- How is coaching made available to you in order to improve your performance?

- How are coaches selected in your organization?

- What is the mechanism used to collaborate with your coach for setting quantitative goals for improvements in performance?

Continuous Workforce Innovation

The purpose of continuous workforce innovation is to identify and evaluate improved workforce practices and technologies, and implement the most promising ones throughout the organization. Continuous workforce innovation involves establishing a mechanism for proposing improvements in workforce activities, identifying needs for new practices, surveying and evaluating innovative practices and technologies, conducting exploratory trials of new practices and technologies, and implementing the most beneficial ones across the organization. The purpose of continuous workforce innovation is to identify and evaluate improved or innovative workforce practices and technologies, and implement the most promising ones throughout the organization.

VERSION 1.0

Goal 1   *Innovative workforce practices and technologies are evaluated to determine their effect on improving core competencies and performance.*

Goal 2   *The organization's workforce practices and activities are improved continuously.*

Goal 3   *Participation in improving the organization's workforce practices and activities is organization-wide.*

VERSION 2.0

Goal 1   *The organization establishes and maintains mechanisms for supporting continuous improvement of its workforce practices and technologies.*

Goal 2   *Innovative or improved workforce practices and technologies are identified and evaluated.*

> **Goal 3** *Innovative or improved workforce practices and technologies are deployed using orderly procedures.*
>
> **Goal 4** *Continuous workforce innovation practices are institutionalized to ensure they are performed as defined organizational processes.*

- How are incremental and innovative improvements to the competency assets rendered?

- How frequently does your organization evaluate innovative workforce practices and technologies?

- How are innovative workforce practices and technologies that prove beneficial in a trial implementation adopted in an orderly way across your organization?

Summary of the Key Differences between Version 1.0 and 2.0

At level 2, protection from burnout was addressed by the process. The process is used to define practices to enable balancing individual workloads. Within version 1.0, team focus came in a little too late at level 4. Team building has now moved down from level 4 to level 3 in workgroup development process area.

Cross-functional work is now better supported at level 3 with regrouping of practices into process areas, which are mutually exclusive between maturity levels and internally cohesive. With the introduction of three new process areas—competency-based assets, empowered workgroups, and competency integration—the right environment for 'predictability' is established along with mentoring. Quantitative performance management and organizational capability management at level 4 establish the much needed quantitative reference for a predictable process.

The focus of the book henceforth would be on interpreting key process areas contained in both versions of the People CMM. We will reuse concepts from People CMM version 1.0 where such practices don't seem to be obvious in version 2.0. What I will not do, however, is to state verbatim either the practices or sub-practices from the People CMM model because such information is already available off the SEI website as freely downloadable model descriptions. Table 3.1 summarizes and provides for a comparative view between versions 1.0 and 2.0.

Table 3.1 *Grouping of process areas in the two versions of the People CMM*

Level	Version 1.0 Key Process Areas	Version 2.0 Process Areas
2	Work environment	Work environment
	Compensation	Compensation
	Staffing	Staffing
	Training	Training and development
	Performance management	Performance management
	Communication	Communication and coordination
3	Workforce planning	Workforce planning
	Career development	Career development
	Knowledge and skills analysis	Workgroup development
	Competency-based practices	Competency development
	Competency development	Participatory culture
	Participatory culture	Competency analysis
		Competency-based practices
4	Mentoring	Mentoring
	Organizational performance alignment	Organizational capability management
	Organizational capability management	Quantitative performance management
	Team-based practices	Competency-based assets
	Team building	Competency integration
		Empowered workgroups
5	Coaching	Continuous capability improvement
	Continuous workforce innovation	Continuous workforce innovation
	Personal competency development	Organizational performance alignment

Source: Adapted from People Capability Maturity Model, Carnegie Mellon University [1995, CMU/SEI-2001-MM-01] with permission.

The overall organizational process maturity definitely has an influence on how well an individual process area is performed. Therefore, the notion of continuous process improvement in principle applies actually to how well a given process area is performed. Mere fulfilment of the practices, as stated in the People CMM, has a tendency for process fossilization to set in rather early, whereby offering a low leverage solution to process implementation. And, the tendency to roll back to old ways is often the case. The critical issue with change management is that sooner or later we will know that we made a mistake; but how quickly is this feedback available? One of the characteristics of a high maturity process is that such feedback is almost real-time and permits for timely management decisions by effective mistake-proofing. What is useful in this context for enabling a high leverage solution is to make sure that the capability of each of these process areas is individually improved continuously as progressions are rendered to the overall organizational maturity. The dynamics of implementing process improvement using the People CMM framework is often disjoint, discontinuous, and abrupt. In other words, organizational behaviour—which is nothing but a synergistic sum of individual behaviours—cannot evolve slowly in measured steps. It has to be dynamic, restless, and has to change in leaps and bounds in order for such change to be modelled as a successful response to the rapid dynamics of the surrounding organizational context. For example, rapidly changing technology dictating what core competencies are necessary, dynamic affiliation of people dictating staffing and retention mechanisms, geographical and global opportunities dictating how career development has to be addressed, and so on.

My belief also stems from the fact that even in high maturity organizations we tend to see more of the process followers and implementers and less of the process innovators and rebels (in a positive sense). The fizz-factor as I would like to call the effervescence due to enthusiasm is missing because of change agents becoming mere process conformists. In order to address this fizz-factor, my recommendation is to look at process improvement in a slightly different manner—as a continuous innovation rather than continuous improvement. In other words, as we improve the overall organizational response as the maturity increases, we must be able to perform the practices at the lower levels of the quote-unquote People CMM maturity framework in a different manner. It is in this notion of being able to perform the same practices differently as the organization transcends maturity level, where lasting change and sustaining gains on change management are possible. This sense of proactive restlessness is what dictates how long a process improvement programme lasts. There is big difference and an explicit distinction between what we do to merely fulfil the requirements of a model and how well we do it in order to make sure that these practices are there to stay. To make the fizz-factor explicit, and to understand and interpret the key process areas, the approach taken in the remainder of the book is to look at how the process area looks from one level below and from the level at which it belongs when it is institutionalized and how it would look if the next level is also enabled, where applicable.

In other words the template that is followed throughout the interpretation of the process areas is to provide the reader with a view of the following.

- How does a process area look from one level below?

- How does a process area look at the level it belongs when institutionalized?

- How does a process area transform itself when the transition to the next level is made, where applicable?

It is in this last view that high leverage potential due to enabling a process area can be unearthed. By infusing enough fizz and verve into the process improvement programme sustaining the gains is possible. Needless to add, these factors are not exhaustively covered due to limitations imposed on the size of the book! While discussing one of the possible People CMM implementation approaches, we have understood that practices belonging to the lower-level process areas can potentially transform into practices at the higher-level process areas using the sequences mentioned in chapter 1. Depending upon the overall organizational maturity, there is a natural tendency for process areas at any level to exhibit a subdominant trait, either due to positive influences from enabling higher maturity process areas or shades of gray from lower maturity process areas showing up in the implementation. In other words, it is natural to expect process areas to exhibit their own individual capability levels due to influences from overall organizational maturity.

Sequence 1

Training and development ▶ *Workgroup development, competency development, competency analysis* ▶ *Competency-based assets, competency integration* ▶ *Continuous capability improvement, continuous workforce innovation*

Sequence 2

Staffing ▶ *Workforce planning* ▶ *Empowered workgroups*

Sequence 3

Performance management ▶ *Competency-based practices, career development* ▶ *Organizational capability management, quantitative performance management* ▶ *Organizational performance alignment*

Sequence 4

Communication and coordination ▶ *Participatory culture* ▶ *Mentoring*

Sequence 5

Work environment, compensation

Source: Adapted from SITARA Process JewelBox™, SITARA Technical Report [2000] with permission

We will now interpret the process areas based on the above sequences. To get the best perspectives and the most from the interpretations, it is recommended that all related process areas within a sequence are read in one continuous flow.

Interpreting the Level 2 Process Areas

LEVEL 2 PROCESS CHARACTERISTICS

THE FOCUS AT level 2 is on establishing a basic foundation of practices within units that can be continuously improved. The focus of improvement is on minimizing the impact of environmental distractions, setting and clarifying performance objectives, building knowledge and skill-based infrastructure, and improving communication and coordination of all constituent entities within the organization. This foundation of workforce practices is established to evoke a response that is directed towards improving conditions that would otherwise limit unit performance. The institutionalization goal of all of the level 2 process areas is at the unit level.

The primary objectives at Level 2 are as follows.

- Establish workforce practices at the unit level

- Eliminate problems that keep people from being able to perform their work responsibilities

- Establish a foundation of workforce practices that can be improved continuously

■ Address the most frequent problems that keep people from performing effectively, which include

  • Environmental distractions

  • Unclear performance objectives

  • Lack of relevant knowledge and skill

  • Poor communication

■ Establish a sense of responsibility and discipline in performing basic workforce practices

Staffing

How does the staffing process area look from one level below?

Staffing decisions are *ad hoc* and arbitrary. Recruitment of people into positions is impulsive and driven by urgent needs. 'We need 50 Java programmers by next weekend'—is the type of single line requirement, which is handed over to the recruitment staff. And then, the recruitment staff move earth and heaven to find these resources. Use of headhunters or placement agencies is often extensively relied upon. Evaluation of the headhunter or placement agencies is seldom done with respect to, making sure that these agencies really know and understand how to interpret such single line requirements. Everybody from the recruitment staff down to the headhunters get busy using a search macro for the word 'Java' in their respective resume databases!

Headhunters and recruitment agencies are often totally ignorant about the expertise they are trying to provide. Standard headhunter practice is to shoot blind e-mails to individuals in the industry—"We came across your resume on the Web which fits an immediate requirement of our client urgently. Here are the requirements.... If you feel you don't fit these requirements, please give us the reference of somebody you know who does!"

It goes without saying that those who seek the help of recruitment agencies or headhunters are in desperate need for a change. How would a person, who is desperate for a job, ever perform with a sense of loyalty to the organization, which the position commands?

In an offshore development activity, typically the onsite coordinator calls the shots. The onsite coordinator responsible for the project will need 50 Java programmers by the next weekend. The recruitment staff collaborates with placement agencies that succeed in lining up the requisite number of heads. Those assigned staffing responsibility do a mediocre job on meeting such recruitment targets.

In manager interview sessions of a typical level 1 organization, a noteworthy characteristic would be that most interviews conducted to recruit individuals are after office hours or over weekends with no clear guidelines or preparation that may be necessary for getting the right resources. From an assessment point of view, it is useful to interview the receptionist of a company and find out how many times the receptionist had to keep the interviewee waiting and the reason for that. The reason for keeping interviewees waiting could very well be because there was not enough staff available to conduct the interview! In many level 1 organizations, those who get to interview candidates for a job are those who are unoccupied at the moment. It is not surprising then, that a level 1 reeks of mediocrity. Many managers are found turf guarding! Even for recruitment at senior levels, the only basis used is to make sure that the person who is being brought on board is not smarter than the peer level that she/he would eventually constitute. And, most definitely it will be somebody who is not better than the person she/he is going to report to. It is not surprising then to note that in such a work environment, which is visibly driven by scarcity mentality and lack of personal competency development initiatives particularly at the upper echelons, it is very rare to find a person who is better qualified than the supervisor being recruited. Even if such recruitments do happen, individuals who come on board voluntarily exit gracefully since more often than not, they are set up for failure.

When individuals want to leave, they just decide to abscond or don't show up. The organization has learnt to ignore their presence with no formal mechanisms in place such as exit interviews to track the reasons behind why there is a no show in its employed staff. In work cultures that provide cost advantages and resort to the use of a buffer team called the bench, project assignments to such resources is often poorly managed.

There are many other ways to characterize a level 1 staffing process. Questions such as "How many hours of a day do you typically spend on recruitment decisions—either on entry or exit interviews?" or "What is the selection/rejection rate that you use to base your recruitment plan?" directed at those making staffing decisions provides for tremendous insights into whether the capability of the staffing process area is at a level 1 or higher.

While making staffing and recruitment decisions on people being sourced externally to the organization, a level 1 organizational maturity context is not objective but is dependent upon industry grapevine. While referral checks may be performed, there is no objectivity to ensure accuracy of information about the person. When the staffing process area practices are not institutionalized, work load is not balanced since resource estimates are more of 'guesstimates'. As a consequence, there is no ownership to work commitments. It is very likely that since talent and skills are mostly underused and often abused in such a set-up, individuals find the workplace not challenging enough and perceive career stagnation. Since *ad hoc* staffing methods are employed with weak evaluation of fitment of candidates to the needs, there is a possibility for bad hires to retard team-based activities and thereby have a negative influence on team productivity.

How does staffing look, at the level it belongs when institutionalized?

It is very important to note that this process area is not called 'recruitment'. Most level 2 initiatives involving this process area look at it primarily as fix in recruitment, which is a low leverage process solution.

In order to ensure that qualified individuals best execute work that is committed to them, a formal process of seeking talent, recruiting, and transitioning individuals into their assignments is practised. Since having the right talent and skills is a great influencer and enabler of organizational performance, much importance is attached to the staffing practices to serve as foundation practices. A level 2 process infrastructure establishes a policy that describes the ground rules for performing staffing activities. The policy clearly states and has answers for the following critical questions. "What are the criteria for selecting individuals into the organization vis-à-vis the different job positions? What are the staffing procedures that are necessary to be performed and followed while making recruitment decisions?"

In a level 2 process, bench management or buffer team management is particularly well conceived. Individuals on the bench are put through specific training programmes in certain specialized and emerging areas of the organization's core competency. As the competency terrain shifts, retraining activities of staff on the rolls is coordinated between the resource management or staffing department and the training and development.

DEFINITION: CORE COMPETENCY

- *Short definition—accumulated knowledge*

- *The combination of technology and production skills of an organization that creates its products and services and provides its competitive advantage in the marketplace [Prahlad 1990]*

- *The specific organizational abilities that*

  - *Deploy knowledge, skills, and talents of individuals, using*

  - *Operating processes (methods, tools, and procedures) of the organization*

  for consistency in execution and the realization of tangible and intangible benefits [SITARA 2000]

The above definition of core competency encompasses more and includes the use and maintenance of the development process as well—an important competency asset.

At level 2, the staffing process is a lot more structured. Those assigned staffing responsibility are seen to proactively engage in purposeful interviewing. They use a well-defined criterion to select individuals to appear for personal interviews. Job requirements are written down as a list of both the nice-to-haves and mandatory requirements. They use a thorough screening process for resume evaluation. A shortlist of candidates is maintained based on an evaluation of individual experience, fitment, and use of a structured interview format to probe whether the candidate meets the job requirements. The emphasis of staffing at level 2 is on ensuring that individuals with right capabilities (knowledge, skills, and talents) are recruited.

Job descriptions for every critical position in the organization are maintained, analysed for applicability, and revised, both periodically and on an event-driven basis.

Note When the word 'periodic' is used, it means that it should be as frequent as to allow easy recall of the previous context. Stipulating a weekly or a monthly periodicity in either the policy or procedure could be stifling and would very soon render such engagements to a ritual—done because the policy says so!

Potential sources of talent such as universities, training institutes, and other learning centres are researched and placements are made through direct on-campus recruitment. Career fairs, open houses, and other mechanisms such as site visits for potential candidates are used as mechanisms to make every effort to source the right talent for the job. Reliance on notifying internal job openings through announcements and employee referrals is more predominant. Those assigned staffing functions execute staffing activities with care and attention to ensure both suitability of individual to the job profile and the overall organizational value system.

Succession plans are established to promote individual growth, and thereby unit growth and organizational growth through a well-defined programme of implementation. Questions such as "How does one get promoted to the next level of job responsibilities?" have objective (as opposed to being subjective) criteria. The objective criteria could clearly spell out the minimum levels of accomplishment or attainment that an individual must exhibit before he or she can move up the value chain. For example, to become a project leader, an individual must have executed at least two or three development projects involving the domain applying the full process life cycle. To become a project manager, a project leader must have expert knowledge of all the different support functions of a project such as testing, quality assurance, configuration management, and release management as a practitioner. To become a programme manager, a project manager must have gone through (in addition to the above) process management, relationship management, and team building and team growing activities. And so on . . .

How does staffing, transform itself when the transition to the next level is made?

Staffing projects with the right mix of individuals using objective criteria and staff management is an organizational competency. The organization is prepared to execute both high-risk and low-risk projects with expertise to manage both risk takers and avoiders. Managing the interactions between a high maturity organization with a low maturity process is in effect an outcome of strong staffing practices. By enabling a high capability staffing process area, the question of "how does a high maturity organization deal with other low maturity organizations (customers, projects, and other execution activities)", gets adequately answered through leverage resulting from growing workforce competencies.

When level 2 processes get enabled, organizations become sensitive to burnout and risks due to individual obsolescence. Organizations make it a rule to rotate resources out of projects at a logical conclusion and put them through a process of self-renewal. When staffing is performed to a high degree of process capability, the organization establishes certain ground rules for promoting individual learning and manages risks of its intellectual assets becoming obsolete. A policy that states the percentage of time in a calendar year that an individual needs to go through a self-renewal process is established. And a procedure that describes the objectives that an individual needs to accomplish during the forced hibernation is also made explicit. Objectives could be for self-learning, or for internalizing things that were learnt from project execution, or for establishing a collective shared vision around newer competencies developed by the individual, or it could be for orchestrating a formal training programme for knowledge sharing. Preventing burnouts by rotating individuals through a bench is a human resource function that is planned and reviewed with all concerned stakeholders.

Individuals who go through the self-renewal programme establish defined objectives of how they would contribute to personal competency development, their unit competency development, and may be even to the overall organizational competency development. Organization is also structured in such a way as to foster such thinking. Software resource centres or software engineering research labs are established to function as conduits to promote internal organizational learning on workforce competencies required for demonstrating strategic advantage.

When succession plans are established for individuals, everybody in the organization accepts and respects such decisions and facilitate individual transformation, rather than preventing the person from accomplishing the desired objectives. A high staffing process capability becomes visible when everybody in the organization promotes the growth of their co-workers rather than becoming an obstacle and hindrance. The human resource function becomes a proactive facilitator for such overall organizational development through active engagement in the staffing activities that orient towards competency development. When an individual is known to be on a collision course with such healthy organizational development, the human resource function steps in and takes corrective action as necessary and appropriate. The organization develops a mechanism to engage in purposeful dialogue through a process of periodic staff debriefs facilitated by the human resource functions.

Depending upon the level at which the recruitment has to happen, multiple levels of people in the organizational responsibility structure interview candidates to determine fitment, which culminates with the CEO personally meeting the individual. Such a multidimensional assessment is used to evaluate acceptability of the interviewee for positive attitude, self-motivation, and ability to work as a member of a team. There is no other quick-fix available for building organizational bonding except that every concerned organizational stakeholder (CEO down) takes staffing activities seriously and meets the new recruit. This is best done through periodic induction programmes that are initiated by the CEO.

Sequence 2

Staffing ▶ *Workforce planning* ▶ *Empowered workgroups*

Related Process Areas

Level 3: Workforce planning

Level 4: Empowered workgroups

Communication and Coordination

How does the communication and coordination process area look from one level below?

The communication of policies and management decisions is often indirect. You know what the boss is thinking through his secretary! Employee suggestions are seldom requested and when obtained there is very little follow-up. There is no time for discussion or dialogue. Decisions are made for everyone else to follow. At times, the organization exhibits a false sense of having communicated the message by expecting behaviour change based on individuals who are set up to demonstrate the expected behaviour. Since there is very little documentation supporting organizational policies and procedures, the only way to know anything is to ask around. And if you don't get an answer, make your assumptions because nobody knows it anyway. This is especially true of policies (e.g., travel policy, use of official e-mail, what constitutes company confidential information, and intellectual property) and their interpretation. There is very little guidance by way of a handbook describing the employee code of conduct.

Coordination of project activities using periodic team meetings with the objective of developing shared vision and understanding the project commitments is seldom established. Project meetings, when conducted, seldom have any agenda or known set of objectives that have to be accomplished. There is often an inordinate wastage of time on frivolous discussions when such meetings do take place. Project team meetings have no role plays—a moderator controls the discussions, a recorder keeps track of the action items and the progress made, and decisions are therefore one step forward and two steps backward.

Workgroups don't cluster in a single work area. They may be separated and dispersed so widely within the organization that team building and team activities are very loose in content and structure. Often, people from unrelated functions such as sales and marketing and accounts sit alongside the development folks, that unrelated information and information that is best respected and categorized as need to know gets diffused and becomes grapevine or sheer gossip. In other words, this process area in the garb of level 1 organizational maturity can be renamed as 'Gossip and Grapevine!'

Communication and coordination operating at a level 1 capability when viewed in relationship to other process areas, like performance management or staffing decisions or opportunities for training and development and so on, has a negative impact on their respective individual process capabilities as well. For example, promotion opportunities are provided but with no rationale governing them. And, individuals who get promoted are improperly recognized due to poor communication of the message. Many times, organizational anarchy prevails because nobody knows who is responsible for what. It is a failure of the communication aspects of this process area. Many times, the origin of such anarchy of communication is due to the senior management. Role clarification and changes to organizational structure, which have to be communicated to everybody in the organization by the senior management, seldom happen.

Employee suggestions and feedback are seldom requested and, if requested, they literally go into a black hole! No decisions are taken on such feedback instruments nor do the employees offering them feel good about making recommendations. A cynical environment of "nothing happens to our suggestions" prevails. "We know we filled out something that we were told to fill in". Or "provided the feedback to our management and we don't know what they did with it nor do we understand why they asked for our feedback!"

Frequent breakdowns in coordination efforts based on miscommunication and unclear understanding of individual objectives results in unclear work prioritization. This leads to indifference, apathy, and dissatisfaction due to interpersonal conflicts, unproductive meetings, and overall organizational dysfunction. In a level 1 set-up, you say what the boss likes to hear! The bearers of bad news are often considered anti-establishment and therefore looked upon differently. There is yet another cynical form this takes—typecasting. People are seen to be walking around with huge imaginary brass plates with the positions they hold branded on them. "He is only a Quality person!" or "She is only good at C language". The word 'only' is a very scary form of communication in such organizations! Type-casting also takes on a rather unpleasant variation with extreme generalizations, such as "He is not a dependable person at all" or "She is not good for anything". Communication is mostly indirect and often unpleasant. If X has a problem with Y, X is seen to be discussing his interpersonal problems with Z, rather than confronting the issue directly with Y. What is even limiting for highly motivated individuals is the job titles and job descriptions. They obscure the full range of contributions that individuals are able to make.

To a large degree, establishing formal communication and coordination mechanisms within the project, unit, or division and within the organizational context helps to streamline and improve the effectiveness of the rest of the process areas.

How does communication and coordination look, at the level it belongs when institutionalized?

To establish authenticity and control of information, organizations that establish a level 2 communication and coordination process capability need to know the rules. This, 'need-to-know' rule is enabled by grouping individuals belonging to a workgroup cluster in a single work area so that they may discuss, share, and keep the dialogue of exchanging information centred around the issue that is being debated or discussed.

Information that is communicated best by an individual within his span of control gets empowered to be made by this individual. Those having project responsibilities are encouraged to voice their concerns openly and freely in a manner that encourages overt communication. Employees not only make recommendations for changes or suggestions for improvements but are also empowered to take responsibility to engineer a solution through an active collaboration of other organizational functions.

Well-defined responsibility structures are established at the project, unit, or division level and at the organizational level for communication and coordination activities to be effective. Driven by the CEO or head of the organization, an environment based on trust and esteem for individual dignity becomes established by giving the right to comment the degree of freedom that it deserves to improve the conditions surrounding the day-to-day execution of work. Communication of message assumes three forms—reinforced, expressed, and demonstrated—whereby a sense for authenticity of intentions gains hold leading to improving trust and confidence. Information that is necessary for individuals to be effective with their job responsibilities is made available and deployed over the company infrastructure (typically over an Intranet). Changes to process infrastructure are communicated after they are reviewed internally.

Periodic organizational interface meetings or town hall meetings driven by the CEO or the head of the organization are conducted. In large organizations, these could be telecast internally with a landing desk to take calls from employees distributed geographically. And in the cases where the organizational size is not big, the entire organization converges in one place to obtain a common understanding of the organizational context. The CEO ensures that she/he communicates the necessary changes to everybody in the organization with "before you hear anything else said about this topic, hear it from the horse's mouth" attitude.

This level of transparency and openness creates a conducive work environment wherein individuals share information and keep any resistance overt (as opposed to keeping it covert and secretive). Communication is mostly direct and professional. If X has a problem with Y, X is seen to be confronting the issue directly with Y at a professional level. It is also natural to see that when communication is professional, the issue that is being discussed is not in anyway linked to the person. There is often a tendency to spar at the problem with mutual respect until there is a resolution and the involved individuals depart as friends. The feeling one gets in a mature organization is that "differences of opinion are not generally wrong or bad; but, what would I see if I look through the other person's perspective". On most technical matters, "if I share all that I know about the problem and the other person shares all that he knows about the same problem, chances are that my ability to logically process this information is about the same given similar knowledge, skills, and process abilities". In such elevated forms of interpersonal communication, everyone stands to gain, there are no losers! It may be useful to digress a bit here and relate this to Sumo wrestling—there is grace at the end of a match with the winner and his opponent leaving the ring respectfully with no fanfare associated with the winner.

The most important message that must be communicated and reinforced periodically is about the organizational value, culture, and belief systems. This is particularly useful when new recruits join midway and have no other mechanism to understand them. For those who are with the organization, periodic reinforcement of this message serves to enhance recollection of the shared vision. In mature organizations, relevant stakeholders conduct periodic organizational debriefs during such town hall meetings on security policies and on general organizational expectations from employees.

How does communication and coordination transform itself when the transition to the next level is made?

As the organization transcends maturity level 2 and takes the next steps, which enable empowerment to take hold, communication and coordination assumes a new meaning—that of developing a 'Shared Vision'. Openness and interpersonal interactions become not only tolerant but also very genuine. A true sense of caring and purpose in what is being done begins to take effect with a management philosophy stemming from 'collective leadership' and management by exception—where management reviews happen only if the empowered level seeks such a clarification. Management style supports empowerment and lets empowerment stay at the level it was delegated to, long enough without snatching it back at the first opportunity!

A higher process capability communication and coordination process area becomes visible when people feel and exhibit an open sense of loyalty to their employer and to the group they belong. Employee suggestions for change or about circumstances are automatic and forthcoming—as if it was their birthright. One does not need to goad people into speaking up. It would be instructive to observe the employee suggestion form to figure out if this process area is enabled to perform at a higher process capability or not. One of the ways to know it is if the employee suggestion form also has a section for the individual to express his or her opinion on the possible solutions. For every recommendation or suggestion for change, there must be a justifying implementation offering the rationale.

The CEO or the head of the organization demonstrates a behaviour of absolute transparency and this behaviour is mandated to be demonstrated from top to bottom and from left to right. Decisions are taken at the level they are best made and if there is any reason why an issue is escalated, the question that gets asked is, "Did you discuss this with your manager?" If the answer is yes, then the concerned manager is brought in along with the person who escalated the matter and the next question that gets posed to both the individuals is, "What was the decision that was taken and why was it not acceptable?" On the contrary, if the answer to the first question is no, then the solution would be "First discuss this issue with the concerned manager and get back to me if and only if you both cannot resolve it.

If this culture of respect for authority and a communication stance of congruence are made explicit in the organizational hierarchy, then a lot of unnecessary waste of time and effort in the games people play can be avoided. One of the important prerequisites for communication to sustain is that there must be an equally well-recognized organizational ability to listen. With effective organizational listening mechanisms in place, pushing control down to the right level where the decision is best made, is enabled helping build a participatory culture based on empowerment.

In any human interaction, the three things that come into play are the self, the context, and the others. Virginia Satir [Satir 1991] identifies the following communication stances.

The Blaming Stance

The individual feels he is OK but the context and the others are always not OK, which means the only reason why his world is topsy-turvy is because of the others and the context is not OK. Such individuals invariably have an accusing finger of blame pointing to the context or other individuals.

The Placating Stance

The individual feels a deep sense of worthlessness. He feels he is always wrong and the context or the others are right. In other words, the self is not important, but keeping the others and the context happy is the single-most important purpose in the individual's life.

The Super-reasonable Stance

The only thing that matters is the context. Neither are the feelings of the self nor of the others, is important. It is "what do the facts reveal?" The sense of super-reasonableness comes out best in people working in the IT sector!

The Irrelevant Stance

Neither is the self nor the context nor the others important. Everything is hunky-dory and nothing matters to such individuals.

The Congruent Stance

This is the most desirable stance, where an individual balances between self, others, and the context and keeps a sense of emotional equilibrium.

Communication and coordination process area can also be looked at from the seminal work of Larry Constantine on *Organizational Paradigms* [Constantine 1993], where the categorization of organizations is into the following four types—open, closed, synchronous, and random.

Sequence 4

Communication and coordination ▸ *Participatory culture* ▸ *Mentoring*

Related Process Areas

Level 3: Participatory culture

Level 4: Mentoring

Performance Management

How does the performance management process area look from one level below?

Individuals are inadequately prepared to meet the challenges of the job they are supposed to perform. Poor performance is further compounded by the fact that clearly stated performance objectives are seldom established for recruited individuals. When candidates start out on a new job they are most motivated but also the most ineffective. By learning the trade, they become motivated and effective. They also learn the tricks of the trade and become demotivated but are still effective. If organizations don't watch out, they soon become demotivated and ineffective. It is very common to observe individuals who are just putting in time and whiling it away planning for what matters over the weekend! This cycle of neglect due to undersupervision or unstated performance objectives to be more precise may be a reason why even a potential star performer ends up becoming a mediocre or an average performer. The other factor affecting individual performance is the gross neglect of good programme management leading to 'overgoaded-always-under-pressure' situations. Under such circumstances, it is natural to expect individuals cutting out what they consider as 'extraneous activities'. When extraneous activities are cut down to the bare bones and all weekends are spent as well on project activities, there is nothing more that can be done to enhance performance. This leads to burnout, disillusionment, and employee turnover.

Performance management at this level of capability is seldom institutionalized as an organizational practice. It is more of an annual ritual performed with no guidance. Performance appraisal forms may be used, but rather inconsistently. There is no genuine intent on the part of the supervisor to make sure that the feedback being provided to the person being appraised is in line with the objectives set forth for the individual at the beginning of the exercise. Within the context of IT, where individual mobility is high, timely performance appraisals seldom happen because performance management at a capability level 1 is still not institutionalized to the necessary degree of detail.

In other situations, performance appraisals are perceived as a threat. They are viewed with much apprehension since such appraisals are considered mechanisms for unsettling an individual from his job function. In a more cynical work environment, performance on the job is never permitted to exceed set thresholds since the organization begins to fear that either the individuals who are now competent and demonstrate more than average performance would leave the job function or would begin to demand better compensation. So, the supervisors always maintain a tight control and stamps out any possibility of an individual demonstrating superior performance. In fact, there are work cultures that underplay the significance of training and development to such an extent that it is almost cynical. "Why should we provide better training opportunities to individuals and then have to deal with a high probability of losing them to our competition? So, we will not invest in training individuals." That is the reasoning.

Performance evaluation is not done because it is not possible due to confusing directions with subjective evaluations based on unclear objectives. Organizations also run into the evaluation fever head-on, where a considerable number of days are spent in a performance review ritual. In most organizations, which have barely figured out the reasons for a performance review, such reviews are geared towards compensation revisions and salary increments; not so much for competency development. Unfortunately, performance reviews or appraisals are the least important of activities to be conducted to demonstrate performance management.

How does performance management look, at the level it belongs when institutionalized?

Performance management is usually an annual exercise conducted to ascertain an individual's contribution over the year. Performance appraisals are used as mechanisms to determine the individual's contribution to the project, unit, and the organization and are used as bases for making decisions on promotions, compensation administration, and for making individual career decisions.

At the beginning of each appraisal period (may be quarterly, half-yearly, or yearly) individuals are asked to proactively bring forth their potential contributions planned for the duration. These are called variously as key result areas or objectives or key focus areas. The appraiser and the person being appraised both agree, through a process of consensus, the perceived value contribution that these objectives or key result areas may have for advancing the individual's career objectives and achieving the unit goals and overall organizational business objectives. Depending upon the appraisal period, different types of measuring instruments may be used.

Performance appraisal forms are used to systematize and make consistent the process of obtaining an individual's ideas on his/her contribution in the last one year on the assignments executed by him. Factors that either hindered performance or enabled outstanding accomplishments are normally requested. In order to make sure that the organization can offer the individual an avenue for furthering his/her career interests, individuals are encouraged to bring forth their career interests into an open discussion with their respective supervisor. Individuals are also asked to rate their own overall individual performance on a predetermined scale.

The supervisor now rates the individual appraisal and contribution and discusses potential reasons for disagreement until both the appraiser and appraisee are in concurrence. Development needs and training programmes are identified to ensure that any individual inadequacy is addressed.

These appraisal forms are then evaluated by the supervisor and, in a one-on-one debrief, issues and concerns on individual performance are fed back to the individual. On matters requiring either an escalation or external resolution, the concerned individuals are brought into the context for discussions. Performance requiring timely recognition is identified and suitably rewarded. Rewards need not always be linked to monetary gains. Rewards could be a letter of appreciation or recognition of outstanding performance, which could operate at the more meaningful emotional plane. After all, a salary or compensation package is designed to be equitable with the contribution package of an individual. When individuals go above and beyond their regular job requirements, such exemplary performance can always be compensated in a manner that has little impact on the economics.

The big question that needs to be asked is why should a performance appraisal system have a defined periodicity. Especially if we are dealing with a large organization, can this ritual not become an overwhelming and a daunting task?

How does performance management transform itself when the transition to the next level is made?

Individuals come across in discussions as if they are in control of their destinies with career development taking on an orientation towards personal competency development. If an individual feels inadequate to perform on the job, he either self nominates into a structured training programme sponsored by the organization or seeks out such advancement personally. The role of individual competency development is to such a high degree that individuals actively seek opportunities to better their performance through constant honing of skills and knowledge and application of these to their job functions. Individuals are also sensitive to the contributions they make and take personal measures towards effectively improving their performance on the job. The supervisor's role is to facilitate superior individual performance—more as a mentor and a coach. Assuming that the right choices were made at the time of recruitment, lack of adequate demonstration of performance by an individual is viewed as a failing on the part of the supervisor! Therefore, the supervisor ensures that adequate resources, infrastructure, and provisions are made to evoke the best performance of individuals. Project teams take on a competency orientation with every individual in the team working towards common organizational objectives by bringing the best performance out of every team member.

Performance evaluation is periodic and ongoing rather than done once annually. The individual responsible for demonstrating his or her performance calls the shots. A diary of events leading to superior performance and inferior performance is maintained and the individual alerts his supervisor when she/he feels that she/he is ready for a performance review. Any perceived inadequacies such as lack of training or resources are brought to the supervisor's attention immediately and every effort is made to remedy the situation. The normal response of a supervisor for such perceived inadequacies would be: "Give me one reason to prove that by remedying this situation, you will be more productive, or you will be better able to deliver quality work products or improve customer satisfaction and I will do everything under my control to assist you."

Table 4.1 *Performance self-assessment and tracking system*

Actions/ Personal Goals	Measurement mechanism	Worst case	Planned level	Best case
1. Project Commitments				
2. Organizational Development				
3. Key Initiatives				
4. Personal Competency Development				
Self Assessment Period:				
Personal Commitment:				
Supervisor Approval:				

Source: Adapted from SITARA Process JewelBox™ © 2002 with permission.

Management offers a conducive and responsible work environment that facilitates individuals to express their viewpoints and ideas by encouraging them to write white papers and technical reports and to publish their ideas in technical forums. We will discuss more of this in the work environment process area. The critical question to know if performance management is operating at a high enough capability is to ask—"Can you outline the high and low points in the last two quarters with respect to the organizational performance and your contributions to it?"

> ### Sequence 3
>
> ***Performance management*** ▸ *Competency-based practices, career development* ▸ *Organizational capability management, quantitative performance management* ▸ *Organizational performance alignment*
>
> ### Related Process Areas
>
> *Level 3: Competency-based practices, career development*
>
> *Level 4: Organizational capability management, quantitative performance management*
>
> *Level 5: Organizational performance alignment*

Work Environment

How does the work environment process area look from one level below?

There is absolute disregard for personal productivity factors. When appropriate work environment standards and procedures are not institutionalized, overtime is a rule rather than an exception. Organizational infrastructure is not conditioned enough to support individual work commitments. One of the most important distractions in a level 1 environment is time wasted on frivolous activities and unproductive meetings. An example of a frivolous activity is to provide status updates after every meeting to justify the minutes of the meeting! A level 1 scenario is best described as one where the minutes are maintained and the hours are lost! Environmental conditions are often inadequate to support and motivate individual performance. Distractions and continuous interruptions to work are perceived as the strongest demotivators by the workforce during interviews. There is very little scope of team building, because the individuals belonging to a product development team are seldom aggregated in a common area. They may be distributed all over the place and there is very little scope of negotiating and understanding individual commitments.

Examples of a typical level 1 work environment include situations, where multiple contractors who have no common understanding of the organizational process work alongside the organizational programme managers to deliver on commitments! In a situation such as this, it is almost impossible to know who is working on what part of the problem. Each individual is free to define the technical architecture without an overriding organizational process or architecture. As a result, tools used are not common across the project. Assumptions made are purely individualistic and the place where the final product is tested invariably is on the field! There is great imbalance of workload on the team; some are overworked while others play Solitaire. Workforce defines its own work rules including the hours they worked. One of the most important deficiencies in a level 1 work environment such as this is an absence of a structured process or an articulated method to develop software and related artifacts. An absence of the very crucial management tracking and oversight process to ascertain closure of committed work. It begins with this absence and gets compounded with several personal styles and preferences, which lead to expensive waste of both individual time and productivity.

Periodic health check-ups and fitness tests during the initial recruitment are not enforced strictly. In such work environments mandatory pre-recruitment medical check-ups are conducted more because of governmental laws. Organizations underscore the significance of such mandatory health check-ups before accepting the joining report.

Sexual and environmental harassments seem to have very few escalation mechanisms. There are no clear-cut policies as to what information and pictures office spaces can display and what cannot be displayed. Examples of what this might mean are—cubicles display lewd pictures; individuals receive low performance rating for not partying with the boss; there is poor regard for personal preferences and value systems with culturally sensitive issues such as consumption of alcohol and the like.

Yet another example of an inadequately supported work environment could be a situation where individual work spaces are nothing more than a row of pigeon holes subjected to a lot of interruptions affecting the quality of professional work. Tom DeMarco and Tim Lister [DeMarco 1985] demonstrate with the help of data that people who work in noisy, interruption-prone space are less effective and more error-prone.

The next context is one of the weirdest forms that I have witnessed. This was in Bangkok in Thailand, a country where critical decisions are taken after checking with Mother Nature—stellar combinations in the sky! There is a time based on astrological significance for installing equipment and taking crucial decisions. I also noticed a strange workforce practice in a services company—the significance of business dominance is based on head count! So, there were times during my rendezvous in this location when I noticed school kids occupy chairs in an office just to show head count!

A more recent observation was where I found large beehives hanging off rooftops. The above examples are things that happen day in and day out in certain organizational contexts, which have no systems in place for administering effective work environment practices.

How does work environment look at the level it belongs when institutionalized?

An organization addresses issues concerning inadequate resources and frequent interruptions to work (degrading performance) on a priority basis by identifying such work conditions through surveys. The facilities management is responsible for the overall upkeep of the physical environment and ensuring resource requirements to individuals who accomplish committed work in a timely and collaborative manner. There is a well-defined process for individuals to raise requisitions and the facilities management will ensure adequate support to procure additional infrastructure periodically. Work environment is effective only when a combination of multiple requirements, including safety and health of workforce together with physical needs of individuals, are met. Periodic fire drills and spraying of work space with disinfectants are conducted to maintain healthy working conditions. Clearly-stated policies are communicated to individuals about the minimal expectations from individuals during and as long as they are in employment. Organizational policy on substance abuse and consumption of alcohol on the job and the repercussions are clearly stated in code of conduct manuals. Within the same context, individuals and managers are sensitized to the do's and don'ts of the use of official infrastructure in the conduct of business and for personal matters.

Individuals are subjected to a pre-joining medical health check-up. Only if they are found to be medically fit, will they be permitted to join the rolls of the organization. Thereafter, the organization sponsors and mandates periodic health check-up camps where either medical professionals come to the work spot to conduct these check-ups or the employees are told to go to pre-qualified diagnostic labs and hospitals to get through to a thorough screening and test for both contagious and non-contagious diseases. Appropriate corrective actions are mandated by the organization.

Sexual harassment is addressed within the area of the work environment. It includes addressing issues of both environmental harassment such as creation of a hostile and offensive workplace and quid pro quo harassment wherein sexual activity is a precondition for employment and growth. How sexual harassment problems are surfaced and resolved would be an appropriate question to draw insights into organizational sensitivity to this issue. The organization establishes very clear policies on what constitutes harassment. For instance, there is a very clear organizational statement on what can be displayed in a cubicle and what cannot be. Photographs that have a religious or a lewd connotation are definitely not permitted. Often, improving the overall work environment has shown a remarkable influence on employee satisfaction by affecting the morale and thereby improving productivity.

How does work environment transform itself when the transition to the next level is made?

The organization takes upon itself the role of being a responsible corporate citizen by advancing the state of practice for a healthy work environment. Individuals are sensitized to safety rules and standard emergency evacuation procedures. Organizations truly believe in a healthy mind in a healthy body. They provide for resources to keep their workforces trim and fit along with ensuring a creative work environment with enough recreational infrastructure. In an area such as IT, which is primarily a desk job where the involvement of physical activities is very minimal, there is often an impact on health arising out of sedentary lifestyles. Organizations charter infrastructure and trained professionals into gymnasiums and health centres which provide facilities such as swimming pools and games involving physical activities. In large organizational infrastructures, resident doctors, physical therapists, and doctors on call are available with supporting medical infrastructure.

Ergonomically appropriate tools are chosen to ensure that occupational stress is reduced to a bare minimum. For example, individuals are provided awareness on cumulative trauma disorders (CTDs), which affect soft tissues and nerves in the long term with repetitive use of same muscle group such as carpal tunnel syndrome and tenosynovitis or 'tennis elbow'.

On more serious issues concerning protection of confidential and proprietary information, organizations conduct regular and periodic orientation programmes and audits to ensure protection of intellectual property. Systems and processes with appropriate infrastructural support ensure protection to confidential and proprietary information. Individuals exhibit and demonstrate a great degree of concern and personal commitment to protect what is in the true interest of the organizations they work for, which is the protection of intellectual property to prevent loss to valuable corporate assets—core competency. It is only when the work environment supports such a healthy view towards core competency orientation, can the jump to the next maturity level at level 3 be rendered seamless.

Sequence 5

Work Environment, compensation

Related Process Areas

Level 2: Compensation

Training and Development

How does the training and development process area look from one level below?

Training and development is left entirely up to the individual with no sense of involvement from the organization. More often than not, the training and development policy is 'we hire the best, and fire the rest!' Training programmes are *ad hoc* in their administration, often impulsive and provided without forecasting organizational needs. Internal competencies are grown more because of project needs rather than a need that is based on an assessment of required skills. There is no guidance available from either the project supervisor or the unit manager for individuals on identifying training needs based on individual career objectives and team requirements. Individuals are left to feel that they are on their own. If there is a training function within the organization, it is more than likely that it is staffed with coordinators who have no competence or qualifications to actually determine the merits of training programmes sourced from external training sources. The only job of the training coordinator within the training department appears to be to publish an annual training calendar without actually determining the organizational needs. It is very likely to see the training function missing a representation in the management committee or management council, which is normally established to review organizational performance on a periodic basis. The attitude of individuals in such an organization would be that 'the organization does not prepare me for my future, I might as well learn whatever I want by myself'.

Training and developmental opportunities are not programmed into individual yearly calendars. The only individuals who get to attend training programmes are those who are not productively engaged on project activities and the only way to attend a training programme is to become unproductive. This starts a vicious circle.

Training opportunities are not aligned with overall career objectives or organizational goals. Mandatory training programmes such as process training and induction training are often mistimed, happening only when there are enough individuals on board. It is not uncommon that induction training is provided to individuals after a considerable lapse of time! Needless to add, individuals would have learnt not only the trade by themselves but also the tricks of the trade, which is what works to the detriment of the organization. Highly dependent upon the decision-maker or the supervisor, there is no rationale for a waiver on mandatory training programmes. Ignorance of advancements in tools and technology coupled with a general resistance to learn characterizes a low capability training and development change initiative.

How does training and development look at the level it belongs when institutionalized?

Derek Bok's statement—'If you think education is expensive, try ignorance'—sums up well the importance of training and development. Training and development addresses both aspects of short-term or tactical needs of the project and the long-term, strategic needs of the organization. Individuals are made aware of the organizational competencies and potential strategic directions in order to help them pursue training opportunities. Individual training needs are identified based on such informed decisions and aggregated at the unit level for timely administration of training and developmental activities. Periodic discussions on individual developmental needs are also used as bases for timely administration of competency development.

Adequate funding is provided and a proactive training and administration staff helps to grow the individual learning orientation by actively sourcing training resources. A well-structured training and development administration team includes a balanced proportion of team leaders, project managers, and divisional heads. Decision-making around individual training needs within such a team is balanced and timely. Mentoring or some other rudimentary form of counselling is also resorted to, in order to ensure that individuals feel safe and secure while being put through a developmental programme.

In mature development environments with strong competency orientation, individuals are perceived to be engaged on 'productive and billable activities' such as project activities only for about 10 calendar months in a year. The other two months are allocated for personal competency development and personal renewal. Such a mechanism ensures that burnout is minimized and individuals are provided with an opportunity to foster a learning orientation. Role-based training is also provided in the critical project skills that require specialized learning.

Those assigned training responsibilities within the organization are provided the necessary orientation and preparation necessary to be effective as instructors. Train-the-trainer programmes are normally provided to internalize capability and dissemination of information obtained from external sources.

Competency enhancements and individual demonstration of acquired knowledge as results of training programmes are objectively evaluated by the supervisor through an effective performance management and review system. Well-defined criteria that establish an individual's proficiency in the subject matter are used as bases for making waiver decisions on required training. A well-executed training and development programme ensures that a training database of individuals, who have received specific training programmes is maintained giving a picture of the knowledge and skills acquired by individuals.

A summative evaluation such as the use of the Kirkpatrick Model to measure effectiveness of the training programme to accomplish its stated goals is normally in place.

Donald Kirkpatrick's Model is a hierarchical model for evaluating training based on learning and results. These levels can be applied to technology-based training as well as to more traditional forms of delivery. [Kirkpatrick 1998]

Level One: Reactions–What did the learners think of the training?

Level Two: Learning–What did learners learn during the learning experience?

Level Three: Behavior–What learning and skills did learners apply on the job?

Level Four: Results–What changes in results and productivity have been observed on the job? [Rothwell 1994; Brown 1992]

How does training and development transform itself when the transition to the next level is made?

Leaders in the organization demonstrate a passion for organizational transformation with training and development. Corporate socialization events, such as staff meetings, highlight to a good degree the extent of leadership involvement in the learning process. A recent Harvard Business Review interview by Diane L. Coutu [Coutu 2002] sums up 'the anxiety of learning' to be of two types—'learning anxiety' and 'survival anxiety'. Whereas learning anxiety is an organizational disability coming from the individual's fear of change that often threatens individual identity and self-esteem, 'survival anxiety' is what truly contributes to learning due to the fundamental trait of coercive persuasion. Learning anxiety comes from the most difficult sentence to make public—'I don't know enough'! Often, organizational goals established for learning are non-negotiable and cascades down from the highest level of authority. Leaders in the organization establish a psychologically safe environment for others by becoming true learners themselves.

A question that will reveal a high process capability is to get reasonable answers to "What are the organizational goals for competency development and what has the company learnt about its successes and failures over the years?"

I have personally experienced that a high degree of individual commitment to learning comes with the creation of 'brain-trusts'. Since it is difficult to change the whole system, a brain-trust usually works as a group of individuals who decide to have well-meaning intentions for each other by openly sharing ideas and topics of common interest and just lift-off the ground.

Within a highly capable training and development process area, a training database of individuals having critical skills and knowledge is maintained along with a defined expiration policy! Knowledge and skills are rendered obsolete if the specific skill has not been in use by an individual for an extended period of time. Such decisions are based on evaluating results from administering proficiency examinations or mandating individuals to go through periodic certifications awarded by standard certification bodies.

Sequence 1

Training and Development ▸ *Workgroup development, competency development, competency analysis* ▸ *Competency-based assets, competency integration* ▸ *Continuous capability improvement, continuous workforce innovation*

Related Process Areas

Level 3: Workgroup development, competency development, competency analysis

Level 4: Competency-based assets, competency integration

Level 5: Continuous capability improvement, continuous workforce innovation

---

Compensation

How does the compensation process area look from one level below?

Compensation decisions and administration are *ad hoc*. The compensation package is not quite in sync with an individual's contribution package. And compensation decisions are not based on ensuring equity or parity within the system but are largely dependent upon what one can negotiate. In some cultures, where asking the age of a person at the time of recruitment is not taboo, compensation is based on age! Indirectly, this is also linked to the entry-level position an individual gets to keep. Revisions to compensation and reward administration are made without establishing appropriate correlations to performance and value contribution. They are dependent largely on a parity structure that is dictated by the job position more as a socialistic system. Compensation reviews, if any, happen without considering business performance and external benchmarks such as compensation surveys. While evaluating the individual and manager responses to the survey questionnaire, three categories of individuals belonging in the overpaid, underpaid, and equitable clearly stand out. While motivational aspects of pay–performance link establishes a general rule that individuals who feel overpaid seem to show better commitment and greater job responsibility, it is not quite true! The only possible guarantee from those who definitely know that they are overpaid is that they are most likely to stick around in the organization longer than normal. But they are sure to leave the moment their compensation gets into the next state of becoming equitable to their contribution. Or, much worse, if it tilts into the possible state of becoming underpaid because of a performance review!

A culture that is based on irregularities in compensation administration tends to build a different type of mentoring mechanism called cronyism! Bosses and supervisors often play the game of favourites. And these are generally the ones who are rewarded disproportionately. More often than not, compensation and rewards are discussed openly and comparisons are made. With no guiding strategy for the administration of compensation, individuals are not clear if disparities do exist. And since there is no rationale offered by the organization, the single-most important reason for individuals exiting the organization is due to a feeling of frustration over inequities and lack of fairness.

At the time of recruitment, compensation decisions are also not based on criteria that recognize the individual's perceived value—educational qualifications, prior work experience, and the job profile that is being matched. With a poorly managed staffing process, practices within compensation seem to aggravate matters. If staffing is unplanned and reactive to the demands of 'urgent' requirements, then it shows on the compensation process area where 'hot talent' is in-sourced at any cost. Large sign-on bonuses and attractive incentives, besides an abnormal pay package, tend to upset internal parity. It is more than likely that such a perception-driven recruitment decision that the hot talent is the right talent may soon turn out to be based on wrong assumptions, which further overwhelms and upsets the balance in the system.

It is more than likely that the reward mechanism actually promotes wrong behaviour! For example, if the organization rewards a project manager for exceptional ability to turnaround a project that is failing, then more and more managers will soon make pretences that the project is actually failing and ensure a successful ending only to get the reward! By doing so, the organization indirectly communicates that if one needs to get recognized, he needs to first mess up the project and then turn it around. Project managers in such a system are seen to visibly appear busy, fire-fighting an impossible project only to make pretences of eventually turning it around! A loose compensation system is generally visible in a lousy development environment, which is inadequately supported by systems, processes, and oversight mechanisms.

How does compensation look at the level it belongs when institutionalized?

Coordinated at the organizational level, compensation addresses the equity theory where a balance between inputs and outcomes based on perception of individual value is established. When recruitments are made, compensation decisions are based on the perceived value contribution of the individual by making an assessment of the individual's qualification, job experience, and perceived potential. Compensation decisions based on staffing exercises in mature organizations are based on consolidation of feedback from multiple perspectives. If there is a fitment issue, it is discussed with the concerned individual and appropriately communicated to all relevant stakeholders and recorded in personnel records. Access to personnel records having sensitive information such as compensation is restricted.

A compensation strategy based on well-defined criteria recognizes individual contributions and makes necessary adjustments, as necessary. The compensation system is designed scientifically to ensure that top performers are rewarded and recognized while a percentage of the low performers are given adequate opportunities to improve and demonstrate capabilities before offering them an exit option. The basis for the administration of compensation and changes to it are periodically communicated by knowledgeable process owners to all individuals in the organization. In order to make the compensation system equitable, it is normally linked to a peer group though individual rewards are provided for demonstrated performance. Pay for performance is based on motivational aspects of pay–performance link.

Compensation from the point of view of the organization is understood as a cost to the company. Within such a system there is a well-defined allocation of the reward mechanism, which forms part of the organizational investment in the individual's future by providing training and developmental opportunities. Such strategies are communicated to the individual to ensure that a match is established between individual career objectives and overall business objectives. The cost-to-company factors both strategic and tactical training needs of an individual while making compensation decisions.

Compensation surveys are used as external benchmarks to ensure that while keeping compensation equitable, parity is ensured both internally and externally. And when necessary, corrections are made to adjust inequities.

How does compensation transform itself when the transition to the next level is made?

Employees are compensated for the skill portfolios they possess, which indirectly helps build flexibility and team orientation. Compensation systems, such as incentives and bonuses, are designed to build and grow team orientation and are not so much for demonstrating individual excellence based on the function an individual performs. Profit sharing, bonus, and incentive schemes, which promote individuals to highlight best practices that help to improve process–product interface points. Compensation and rewards at this level are to provide both individual self-actualization and monetary gains. Numerous opportunities are provided for individuals to display their innovativeness through employee suggestion programmes or process improvement initiatives to improve work culture and for building organizational core competency. Such efforts are rewarded amply.

Moving away from individual incentives, the organization structures the reward mechanism around team orientation and community of practices. Emphasis of compensation practices is placed on improving the efficiencies within workgroups and motivating team-based attitudes and behaviour to build communities of excellence.

Sequence 5

*Work environment, **compensation***

Related Process Areas

Level 2: Work environment

Interpreting the Level 3 Process Areas

LEVEL 3 PROCESS CHARACTERISTICS

THE FOCUS AT level 3 is to exploit the synergy of practices across units and help the organization gain strategic competitive advantage by developing competencies that can be combined. A level 2 process provides a good foundation to make sure that a fundamental ability to accomplish business activities exists. What level 3 establishes is a strategy for the organization to realize that it has this ability and to recognize it as a workforce competency. This strategy includes refocusing training and development practices on developing workforce competencies and providing graduated career opportunities to address the defined workforce competencies. This transformation has an impact on the conduct of the basic workforce practices of performance management, compensation, and related practices in the work environment that support development of workforce competencies. It is useful to understand the symbolic significance of having a strategic framework and plan. Individuals feel more secure when they understand the existence and intent behind a strategic framework. Better yet, if such a strategic competency development framework, usually about 10 pages long goes through an SEPG or CDG review with the front-line leadership signing its agreement to it.

The focus of practices up to and including the level 3 is towards ensuring organizational development. The institutionalization goal of all of the level 3 process areas has to be interpreted at the organizational level.

The primary objectives at level 3 are as follows.

- Remove any inconsistency in how workforce practices are performed across units

- Adapt workforce practices to the specific nature of business this is done as follows—

  - By analysing skills required by the workforce and business functions it performs

  - By identifying core competencies required to perform the business

  - By adapting workforce practices to develop the specific knowledge, skills, and process abilities

  - By identifying best practices in workforce activities or those of other organizations and tailoring them as the basis for adapting enhanced workforce practices

- Gain strategic competitive advantage from core competencies

- Adapt workforce practices to the specific nature of business

- Define core competencies after analysing skills required

- Adapt and tailor workforce practices to meet organizational objectives

- Develop core competencies and plan/support career development strategies

- Let a common organizational culture exist that emphasizes growth of the organization's capability in its core competencies and sharing of responsibility by the entire workforce

Definition: Workforce Competency

Workforce competency represents a distinct integration of the knowledge, skills, and process abilities required to perform business activities that constitute organizational core competency.

Definition: Competency Community

Members of the workforce who share knowledge, skills, and process abilities of a particular workforce competency constitute a competency community.

Knowledge and Skills Analysis (Version 1.0)

Refer to Competency Analysis.

Competency Analysis

How does the competency analysis process area look from one level below?

In their rudimentary form, knowledge and skills of individuals may at best be collected without any form of analysis as to their currency and applicability. A resume bank having individual profiles is maintained along with a training database providing information about the specific training programmes attended by individuals. However, there may be no criteria to ensure that such descriptions are not outdated. And the integration of the resume bank to the skill-set database of acquired training is not complete. Individual profiles are as current as what the individual makes it out to be without any direction and guidance from the organization to ensure that individuals update their training records. Since the process of analysing the skills-set database is *ad hoc*, skills acquired by self-learning and through self-sponsored training programmes are seldom brought to the attention of the organization and therefore remain unnoticed. The true capabilities of individuals are not known and, as a consequence, workforce capability cannot be assessed.

How does competency analysis look at the level it belongs when institutionalized?

A description of workforce competencies within a competency dictionary is maintained at the organizational level. A process asset library comprising process artifacts and process descriptions that are in use at the organization is established and maintained. Each of the workforce competencies has a definition that includes the minimal criteria for the knowledge, skills, talent, and process abilities that an individual must possess. Individuals are assessed on their proficiency with the help of certification and proficiency examinations. Available resource profiles for existing competencies are maintained, based on aggregation of individual proficiencies by a competency development centre. The competency development centre is also responsible for coordinating realization of individual training needs with the training department to ensure a planned growth of competencies within business units. An example of resource profiles could be a tally of the number of individuals who are beginners, novices, practitioners, masters, and experts. An analysis of organizational workforce capability against these dimensions is periodically made to determine the depth of organizational competencies.

SITARA 10W5D Competency Hierarchy Model and SITARA Domain-Competency Sandwich Model [SITARA 2001] are two innovations from the SITARA Process JewelBox™ that enable analysis of organizational competencies. They are described in what follows.

SITARA 10W5D Competency Hierarchy Model

The 10W5D is a structured competency hierarchy model that identifies organizational competencies to have a span of at least 10 wide competencies (10W). Each competency is further organized into 5 level deep capabilities (5D). For example, program management, software engineering, reliability engineering, and so on could be the 10 wide or broad categories of competencies. Within each of these competencies, the organization needs to identify a minimum of 5 different capabilities to demonstrate that the competency is truly enabled. Within program management, for example, the potential candidates for 5D are the following.

- Product specification
- Design management
- Product line management
- Programming languages
- Communication strategies

The above example indicates that it is only when the organizational competency description for programme management demonstrates adequate capability within the identified 5D, can true potential from having program management as a competency be realized. In fact, this is a fan-out process, wherein each one of the 5Ds themselves can further be broken up into mini-competencies. For example, Honda's competency with small engines is used to develop a product line of lawn movers, motorcycles, and so on.

I would like to leave the reader with a thought. While developing competencies is important, what is more important is to recognize and build efficiencies within the acquired competencies by becoming sensitive to the domains of operation. This leads to the following.

SITARA Domain-Competency Sandwich Model

The 10W5D is based on yet another SITARA innovation—Domain-Competency Sandwich (Fig. 5.1).

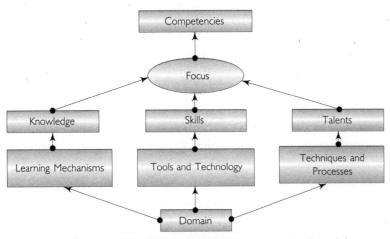

■ **Fig. 5.1** *SITARA Domain-competency sandwich model*

Source: Adapted from SITARA Process JewelBox™ © 2002 with permission

The reasoning of the model is as follows. Competency development has a bearing upon the domains of expertise that the organization intends to build. And when a focused combination of knowledge, skills, and talent is applied to the domains of specialization, competencies tend to grow. The enabler for acquiring knowledge is a learning mechanism that is supported by the organization. Learning mechanisms could include formal training programmes, conferences, symposia, and so on. Skills are rendered meaningful, if and only if they are supported by adequate tools and technology, which the organization has to acquire. Individuals have a certain natural ability, which is called talent that gets perfected by repeated practice through effective techniques and processes. One of the most important factors that help improve productivity is gaining familiarity with the types of problems encountered and solutions developed, based on practice and more practice. SITARA 10W5D can now be applied after a deterministic and inferential evaluation of the specific knowledge, skills, and talent is made.

The analysis of competencies is based on periodic assessments of both tactical and strategic needs of the business, mostly dictated by customer opportunities. There is a good integration of activities between the delivery side of the business and strategic operations, which does business forecasting and projections. Changes to competencies, are based on competency development plans after a thorough impact analysis to workforce functions by all affected constituencies of the business.

How does competency analysis transform itself when the transition to the next level is made?

Units are sensitive to growing workforce capabilities through the use of process profiling techniques. A process profile is a pictorial representation of the capabilities of the different process areas that constitute organizational competency. Use of quantitative feedback on process execution is normally resorted to during analysis to ensure that the causes of variation are understood. Leverage and return on investment is made possible by integrating the capabilities of the different competencies such as software and systems engineering. A well-defined and thoroughly tested reuse repository is part and parcel of the process asset library. Having such a knowledge repository of best practices resulting from workforce experiences along with work products that are easy to access and use is the foundation upon which workforce capabilities begin to get capitalized. Variation of execution outcomes from competency-based activities is integrated into the process improvement framework.

Sequence 1

Training and development ▸ *Workgroup development, competency development,* **competency analysis** ▸ *Competency-based assets, competency integration* ▸ *Continuous capability improvement, continuous workforce innovation*

Related Process Areas

Level 2: Training and development

Level 3: Workgroup development, competency development

Level 4: Competency-based assets, competency integration

Level 5: Continuous capability improvement, continuous workforce innovation

Workforce Planning

How does the workforce planning process area look from one level below?

Business units make staffing decisions based on *ad hoc* and mostly perceived strategies for competency growth. There is a lack of coordination of activities between the strategists doing customer opportunity forecasting and business delivery functions. As a result, workforce is often retooled on technologies based merely on a gut reaction of potential opportunities without thorough validation. There is generally a lot of direct cost sunk into unrealizable competency development activities.

There is no sense of managerial accountability to use existing idle staff that is already recruited—because 'it was someone else's decision to hire them!' Since business units resort to uncoordinated hiring, there is a gross overstaffing situation in one business unit and gross understaffing in another. Staffing activities are not linked to strategic growth of competencies within business units. Since competency integration is not understood, units seem to maintain separate silos of similar competencies. There is a greater risk of underutilization and suboptimal deployment of talent on projects. Unit level workforce requirements and plans are not coordinated by a group such as the resource management team. Critical positions in projects do not have well-established succession plans. The organization tends to develop and grow all types of competencies without exploring partnerships, alliances, subcontracting, and supplier management to its advantage. As a result, business efficiency is often sacrificed.

How does workforce planning look at the level it belongs when institutionalized?

Based on the competency architecture, both tactical and strategic workforce requirements at the unit and organizational levels are planned. A resource management team, comprising individuals who are trained in coordinating and deploying the right talent for the unit needs, ensures timely induction and release of resources back to the common resource pool. This plan is now made the basis for establishing the staffing requirements. Hiring is linked to a business strategy, which also dictates the underlying principles for growing workforce competencies.

Critical positions in the organization have well-defined succession plans established for individuals and these plans align with career objectives. Existing workforce capabilities along with a mapping of individual experience profiles are documented per competency category. The competency dictionary defining workforce competencies is updated for the new skill categories which are identified in the competency development plan. Competency development plans are maintained by individual business units providing a growth plan and a direction for harnessing workforce capability. The competency development plan drives recruitment plans and staffing decisions. There is greater consistency between unit-level accomplishments and organizational competency goals. The competency development centre assists business units in establishing a plan for growing workforce competency levels on both its tactical and strategic needs. Workforce planning activities are based on adjusting resource levels for business units as a result of periodic competency analysis, and tracking business unit performance against established targets. The organization proactively manages partnerships, alliances, subcontracting, and supplier management relationships to improve its business efficiency and leverage workforce augmentation.

How does workforce planning transform itself when the transition to the next level is made?

Managers and supervisors are sensitive to the profitability of business and ask the right questions before making staffing decisions—Why do we need to recruit so many project leaders?' or 'Where is the need for 10 programmers when we can rotate staff from the resource pool?' Through careful planning and timely induction of needed resources from an organizational pool of resources, work assignments are normally made to ensure that overtime is an exception rather than a rule.

Sequence 2

Staffing ▶ ***Workforce planning*** ▶ *Empowered workgroups*

Related Process Areas

Level 2: Staffing

Level 4: Empowered workgroups

Competency Development

How does the competency development process area look from one level below?

Individuals are not given a direction to grow and generally perceive a lack of opportunities. Individuals set low goals for themselves or, at times, goals that are out of sight. This no-gain feeling is generally due to unstructured development of individuals, which is mostly through what the supervisor feels is important for the individual. In most cultures, where lifetime employment is assured, individuals who leave their destinies to a paternalistic boss or supervisor, are common. There is also a tendency in such work cultures for individuals tending to do the same thing over and over again all their professional life without needing to learn new things or change the way they work. The positive thing about such a highly repetitive job is that 'practice and more practice ensures very narrow limits of variation in outcomes' and therefore has a bearing on product quality. The flip side is that individuals are rendered useless, should the domain change or should technology force a change. A high degree of obsolescence is the risk.

How does competency development look at the level it belongs when institutionalized?

While the units focus on improving workforce capabilities through training and development, the organization focuses on competency development. By creating an awareness of workforce competencies through a published competency dictionary and information about available development opportunities, individuals embark on self-nominating themselves into proficiency development programmes. These competency development programmes are sourced from both internal and external sources. Such development initiatives address individual needs fulfilling skills, knowledge, and process abilities. Graduated learning opportunities are provided for individuals who are at different proficiency levels—beginner, intermediate, and advanced stages of learning. Setting goals which may be out-of-reach (also called stretched goals) helps ignite the human spirit and permits the individual to take charge of his/her competency development activities.

The organization supports growth of competencies by actively supporting and funding the creation of competency communities. Such communities, in turn, apply the necessary peer pressure to help individuals take personal initiative to ensure competency development. A useful by-product of competency communities is the identification of internal mentors and coaches who facilitate and help catalyse the learning process by vocalizing individual learning experiences. Mentors share lessons learnt by them from first-hand experiences and offer learning aids to hasten the process of competency development. Creation of a community of practice is also fostered to enable learning in formal settings through sharing of war stories. There is a great degree of emphasis placed on developing individual capability.

Competency communities publish their development activities and integrate their learning into the overall organizational competency framework by providing information on the latest advances in their competencies, best practices, competency profiles, and lessons learnt through newsletters. An individual's performance objectives are linked to growing organizational workforce competencies. Key results are measured and tracked against specific accomplishments to competency development.

How does competency development transform itself when the transition to the next level is made?

A well-defined competency development or outlook template is used to objectively assess each of the workforce competencies, which are identified based on competency analysis, using for instance the SITARA 10W5D Competency Hierarchy Model. These competencies are translated into individual plans for knowledge, skills, and talent development. The organization provides a well-defined guideline to ensure that individuals are sensitive to the fact that both underutilization and overuse of a skill is a liability. Table 5.1 illustrates one of the formats for a competency outlook template.

Table 5.1 *Competency Outlook Template*[*]

- Name of the competency
- Pre-requisite supporting competencies
- Competency roadblocks
- Competency facilitators
  - Reasons for undemonstrated or underutilized ability
  - Reasons for competency to be recognized as having demonstrated ability
  - Impact of overused competency
  - Causes for the identified competency roadblocks
  - Specific learning disabilities
  - Specific learning mechanisms in place at the unit level
  - Specific individual learning mechanisms in place

Source: Adapted from SITARA Process JewelBox™ © 2002 with permission

Individuals are seen to contribute to intellectual activities like paper publication, writing technical white papers, and filing patent applications. Where applicable, they participate on standards committees such as the The Institute of Electrical & Electronics Engineers, Inc. (IEEE) and define both technology and process standards. Individuals take keen interest in becoming members of professional bodies and technical societies. The organization actively supports and sponsors individual affiliations to professional bodies. To understand the extent of self-limitation imposed by the work environment if any, an assessment question could be—'What are the avenues available for individuals in the organization to express their capabilities?' My belief stems from a long-held fact that unless individuals are geared to contribute to professional journals and technical forums, they are not likely to grow beyond their present competence levels. Intellectual curiosity is what kindles the flames of competency development. Organizational learning has to do with individual learning at all levels in the organization, beginning right at the top. A feeling that 'no one does it better than us' begins to take root.

Sequence 1

Training and development ▶ *Workgroup development,* **competency development**, *competency analysis* ▶ *Competency-based assets, competency integration* ▶ *Continuous capability improvement, continuous workforce innovation*

Related Process Areas

Level 3: Workgroup development, competency development, competency analysis

Level 4: Competency-based assets, competency integration

Level 5: Continuous capability improvement, continuous workforce innovation

Career Development

How does the career development process area look from one level below?

Individuals slip into the traps of the Peter and Paul principles. The Peter principle rules when individuals tend to get promoted to their 'level of incompetence' and since they cannot move out, they get stuck. Promotion systems do not concentrate upon the individual's demonstrated potential. When individuals tend to reach a level of incompetence, there is no supporting mechanism within the organization to gently move them back to a position in which they can function effectively. The organization does not prepare individuals adequately for their new assignment when they are promoted.

The Paul principle is the gradual obsolescence of individuals as they lose touch with the competencies they once possessed. Individuals are seen to have retired on the job with no initiative to learn and take advantage of technological break-throughs and changes within the competency communities. By becoming too conservative, they resist innovation and change and suffer from amnesia.

Both these situations are indicative of a haphazard growth and are clearly associated with organizations that view 'organization men' to hold the reins of the company or hold the fortress; competency and demonstrated capability are secondary. Career patterns tend to encourage superficiality as some individuals move rapidly up the value chain. Career opportunities at the next level are invariably tied with better compensation or reward structure and those who are perceived as 'organization men' are seen to occupy such positions without regard to their abilities to deliver. Cronyism and playing personal favourites are often overtly encouraged.

How does career development look at the level it belongs when institutionalized?

Individuals have different needs at different points in their professional life. Career development addresses such needs through a combination of traditional career ladders where a person's span of control and authority increases in direct proportion to where he lives on the organizational chart. Dual ladders enable individuals to take a more technical focus with increasing influence within the competency community or the community of practices. The fuel that fires such competency communities are the extensive interpersonal networking and openness to new ideas. Snaked ladders are also available for individuals who want to increase the breadth of influence where they are visible more as competency community builders. Irrespective of the ladder of individual choice, a defined policy governing promotions and criteria based on the individual's demonstrated potential is defined and used to make such decisions. A pen-picture established by the individual during a performance management review is used as the basis to decide mid-course corrections. Career development opportunities are made available to all those who take the individual initiative to demonstrate their worth. Use of 360 degree evaluations to obtain all-round perspectives of what the peers, subordinates, and supervisor think about the individual is used to base promotional decisions.

Each competency community maintains a well-defined documented procedure describing the criteria for promotions and career advancement. Performance management reviews and periodic self-assessments with good supervisor oversight are used to ensure timely professional advancement and corrective actions using counselling meetings. Well orchestrated career development practices address the two important needs of individuals—enabling competency development activities by establishing personal development plans and offering a rich career opportunity by enabling competency-based promotions.

Individuals with shadow responsibilities work alongside their immediate supervisors to facilitate their smooth transition into their potential next assignment. Outstanding performers are put on a fast track of growth and provided with specific training opportunities available exclusively for top achievers in leadership and management disciplines.

How does career development transform itself when the transition to the next level is made?

Individuals are sensitive to self-introspection while setting up personal goals and use deeper questions such as 'What do I want to do in my career that I haven't yet done?' Mentors and coaches who are assigned the job of grooming individual careers ask the important question—'What is the toughest problem facing your career?' and enable individuals to take appropriate remedial steps to minimize impact to personal development plans. Mentors and coaches keep an eye on the more geared and promising individuals in the organization and assist them with learning opportunities that enable realizing their true potential.

Sequence 3

Performance management ▸ *Competency-based practices,* **career development** ▸ *Organizational capability management, quantitative performance management* ▸ *Organizational performance alignment*

Related Process Areas

Level 3: Competency-based practices, career development

Level 4: Organizational capability management, quantitative performance management

Level 5: Organizational performance alignment

Competency-based Practices

How does the competency-based practices process area look from one level below?

Workforce practices of identifying and growing competencies are mostly outdated and employees soon limit their potential. Individuals generally perceive a slow development path. The choice of business model also plays a significant role in the merits of the competency-based practices. In a pure body-shopping mode of operation, there is very little scope to nurture competency-based practices. In a consulting type of business model, individuals have to always perform at the cutting edge. The level of competency-based practices therefore varies within the same organization depending upon the focus established for different business units. Adjustments to compensation are mostly position-centric and not based on an individual's demonstrated competencies. There is therefore very little incentive for individuals to proactively grow organizational workforce competencies.

Even within a competency community, there is very wide variation in individual competencies and as a result practices are not consistent. The degree of variation is huge in execution outcomes even among teams working on similar competencies. Teams are generally not aware of their competency profiles and their activities are not governed by performance goals mandated by the work or competency requirements.

How does competency-based practices look at the level it belongs when institutionalized?

Competency profiles established for individuals belonging to different competency communities, together with workforce practices of recruitment, performance management, promotions, compensation, and so on are used to develop competency-based workforce practices. Assignments of individuals to projects are based on professed and demonstrated competencies. Periodic review and revisions to workforce practices is enabled by integrating the competency development activities into the process improvement framework. Performance feedback to individuals is also based on competency objectives established by units for individuals. Unit objectives for competency development are translated into staffing practices that improve and grow competencies by sourcing the right talents, developing them and motivating them. Compensation and reward structures are evolved to address competency-based adjustments. Competency-based practices could be multidisciplinary or can be specific to a single discipline. If it is multidisciplinary, then adequate practices that support integration of competencies are visible.

For example, when an organization is transitioning from the SW-CMM to the CMM Integrated—Systems Engineering/Software Engineering, it establishes a target capability profile for the process areas in the CMMI framework [CMMI 2002]. Each business unit will map this target capability profile to its internal competencies and ensure creation of practices that support accomplishment of the capability levels on the organizational process areas, which belong to a competency category. For example, organizational process areas could be segregated into process management, project management, support, and engineering competency categories. If the organizational goal is an optimizing capability level or level 5 for the verification practices, which belong in the engineering competency category, then units have to ensure adequacy of practices which support attainment of such a capability level for verification. Some of these workforce practices can include the following.

- Establish quantitative objectives for process performance based on the critical-to-quality parameters driven by customer needs and business objectives

- Stabilize the performance of the sub-process, which lends itself to effective process control to achieve the process performance objectives

- Identify and correct root causes of defects and other causes of process variation through a continuous process improvement programme.

Business units establish a supporting training plan to ensure that individuals understand the full significance behind the target profile and learn new practices, if any, that will help them accomplish objectives. The units might adopt a phase-wise deployment wherein the first half of the year a certain capability will be targeted at the unit level and after this profile is accomplished, the next target profile is staged as illustrated (Fig. 5.2). Articulating such strategies at the unit level is enabled by assessing 'what is needed', developing plans that describe 'a timeline for fulfilling the needs', and by directed action plans which and 'provide implementation details'.

How does competency-based practices transform itself when the transition to the next level is made?

This is usually multidisciplinary when the transition to level 4 is made. Therefore, not every competency required for the business is home-grown. A combina-

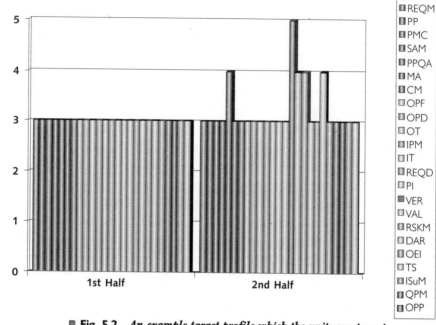

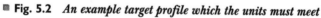
Fig. 5.2 *An example target profile which the units must meet*

REQM—Requirements Management
PP—Project Planning
PMC—Project Monitoring and Control
SAM—Supplier Agreement Management
PPQA—Process and Product Quality Assurance
MA—Measurement and Analysis
CM—Configuration Management
OPF—Organizational Process Focus
OPD—Organizational Process Definition
OT—Organizational Training
IPM—Integrated Project Management

IT—Integrated Teaming
REQD—Requirements Development
PI—Product Integration
VER—Verification
VAL—Validation
RSKM—Risk Management
DAR—Decision Analysis and Resolution
OEI—Organizational Environment for Integration
ISuM—Integrated Supplier Management
QPM—Quantitative Project Management
OPP—Organizational Process Performance

tion of a strong supplier agreement management process together with competencies that are business imperatives within the strategic framework and intent of the organization is used to deliver upon commitments. Competency-based practices within such a high leverage system include ability to evaluate supplier processes and supplier work-products. With a highly capable competency-based practices process area, the technical prerequisites that enable competency integration at the next level get established.

Sequence 3

Performance management ▸ ***Competency-based practices***, *career development* ▸ *Organizational capability management, quantitative performance management* ▸ *Organizational performance alignment.*

Related Process Areas

Level 3: Competency-based practices, career development

Level 4: Organizational capability management, quantitative performance management

Level 5: Organizational performance alignment

Workgroup Development

How does the workgroup development process area look from one level below?

In the Forming–Storming–Norming–Performing–Synergy cycle of team behaviour, teams are caught struggling between the forming and storming stages. The teams are at best a loose coalition of individuals with limited knowledge of the objectives that they are supposed to accomplish. Within a workgroup, there is a poor organization of roles and responsibilities. Across workgroups, intergroup conflicts arise out of dependencies that are ill-conceived. There is a great dependency on the project leader or the team leader for decision-making. Conflict resolution and escalation process are seldom visible, since each individual in the team behaves and functions as an independent autonomous entity. This is a typical situation when the team composition is made up of external consultants who are not drawn from a single organization. Staffing of resources and work assignments to individuals do not have a basis. Teams are found to have steep learning curves, since skill profiles of individuals vary widely and generally do not complement each other.

Teams are disbanded without archival of work products into a configuration management system and of lessons learnt into a knowledge repository. Since roles and responsibilities are not properly defined, commitments are made to customers without team consensus and, as a consequence, confusion reigns supreme. When things go wrong, there is very little information available for

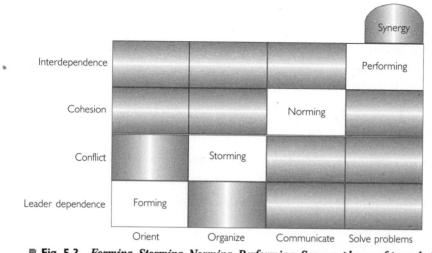

■ **Fig. 5.3** *Forming–Storming–Norming–Performing–Synergy phases of team building*
Source: Scholtes 1998.

postmortem and mid-course corrections. Composition of workgroups is often dynamic and therefore very little scope is available for ensuring accountability.

How does workgroup development look at the level it belongs when institutionalized?

Being the process part of empowerment, a well-defined programme is established to increase empowerment and facilitate envisioning areas of responsibilities through team charters. Individual roles and responsibilities on the project are clearly established. Operational process descriptions giving detailed work instructions are made available for workgroups to independently function without unnecessary management oversight. Teams begin to move out of the storming phase and use periodic team sync-and-stabilize mechanisms to move into norming and performing phases of team development. The work environment supports effective workgroup development by ensuring intra-group proximity to maximize alignment of interdependent work. Accountability for project outcomes is clearly specified and teams are made up of individuals with complementary skills. A shared vision of the objectives is enabled by frequent project interaction meetings.

Work breakdown structures that are drawn up during problem decomposition identify process dependencies that ensure maximum intra-group cohesion and minimum intergroup coupling. Workgroups make use of tailored processes, which permit better structuring of work elements after a team evaluation of project constraints (i.e., time, scope, quality, and cost). Formal project closure activities along with the creation of retrospective reports help to enable knowledge management. Reassignment of individuals to other projects is after formal project closure and archival of competency assets such as work products, process assets, and product artifacts. The foundation of practices for performing competency-based assets through asset capture is laid within workgroup development. Workgroups establish operating procedures based on project characteristics by tailoring the organizational standard process. Experiences with the use of tailored practices and project assets are captured before workgroups are disbanded. Individuals belonging to a competency community (also called the home organization) contribute and internalize emerging best practices and lessons learnt from work execution within their workgroups (also called project organization) into knowledge repositories maintained by their respective home organizations.

How does workgroup development transform itself when the transition to the next level is made?

Teams have well-defined champions for critical project phases such as design, process development, and validation. Synergy and team harmony is ensured by those assuming leadership roles by personally demonstrating the behaviour they advocate for teams. Normally a list of banned words is also maintained to ensure that their use is prohibited in the best interests of workgroup development during brainstorming. Individuals integrate lessons learnt into the project at every phase of project execution through a process of causal analysis and resolution meetings. Team decisions are normally driven by effective decision analysis processes with full team participation. Multiple types of decision-making techniques for both technical and management decisions are advocated. Independent decisions are encouraged by the team for task-level decisions requiring minimal project leader involvement. Consensus decisions are used for resolving intragroup issues that require multiple internal stakeholder commitments. Coordinated decisions are used as mechanisms to ensure good inter-group visibility for decisions requiring external stakeholder commitments. Escalation of issues up to the senior management is a well-defined process and is resorted to after team reflection. Organizational policies support a host of decision-making techniques to maximize the use of empowerment and permit decisions to be taken at the most appropriate lowest level of authority.

Some examples of decision types include the following. *[CMMI 2002]*

- Command: *The leader examines the issue and makes a decision alone.*

- Consultative: *The leader receives and examines inputs on the issue from relevant stakeholders and makes the decision.*

- Collaborative: *Issues are raised by any relevant stakeholder (including the leader), the issues are discussed, and the solutions are voted upon. Rules are needed to determine whether this vote is binding on the leader.*

- Consensus: *Issues are raised by any relevant stakeholder, including the leader, and are discussed until all members of the integrated team can live with and support the decision.*

- Structured: *Major issues may be decided using formal evaluations. The steps in formal evaluations may be carried out in a collaborative way.*

Sequence 1

Training and development ▸ **Workgroup development**, *competency development, competency analysis* ▸ *Competency-based assets, competency integration* ▸ *Continuous capability improvement, continuous workforce innovation*

Related Process Areas

Level 2: Training and development

Level 3: Competency development, competency analysis

Level 4: Competency-based assets, competency integration

Level 5: Continuous capability improvement, continuous workforce innovation

---

Participatory Culture

How does the participatory culture process area look from one level below?

Information on business performance is normally not provided. Most individuals are in the dark as to the strategic intent and the purpose of the business. The contributions individuals make and their significance to the overall accomplishment of organizational objectives is seldom understood. Information on potential opportunities and job assignments is provided randomly in informal conversations with the big boss.

There is often a high level of bureaucracy and procedural gridlocks that is best described with the help of an analogy. How many people are required to change a fused bulb? If you answered 6, then you are right in such a system! One to identify that there is a problem with the bulb, second to establish the fact that the bulb has a blown fuse, third to determine if it should be replaced or can be repaired, fourth to pronounce the bulb dead, fifth to authorize the purchase of a new bulb, and sixth to actually replace the bulb...and probably a seventh—the process assurance person who will oversee the execution of all these activities!

A list of exceptionally performing individuals, which obviously is a very short list, is maintained and these individuals are grabbed by managers seen to indulge in turf-guarding wars. Decisions to move individuals in and out of projects are based on projects getting critical all the time with a strong senior management involvement at all times—since empowerment is a far-fetched idea.

Information that is required for effective team functioning and coordination of team activities such as resource availability, travel schedule, and individual calendars is not made available. Team and organizational meetings are scheduled without obtaining necessary consensus. Project issues are analysed until it is too late—a typical pattern of paralysis by analysis is visible to a large degree. Limited use of knowledge management, reuse of project experience, and integration of the process improvement framework to leverage workforce competencies renders meaningless the overall benefits that could accrue. Therefore, individuals demonstrate a sense of withdrawal and are not in touch with day-to-day realities. Possible attitudes demonstrated for shared vision are as follows.

- Grudging compliance: Does not see the benefits, but also does not want to lose the job!

- Non-compliance: Does not even attempt to see the benefits. "I will not do it ... and you cannot make me do it."

- Apathy: Neither for nor against vision. Retired on the job with no energy. "Why are eight hours so long?"

How does participatory culture look at the level it belongs when institutionalized?

Being the foundation for decision-making, a system that supports automation of data collection and processes for consensus building, nominal group techniques, wide-band Delphi, multi-voting, conflict resolution, brainstorming, and the like are defined. Roles such as decision-maker, participant, input provider, and group coordinator are assigned in formal decision analysis meetings. Three types of decision-making processes—independent, coordinated, and consensus decisions—are normally supported and used in practice.

Information about organizational events and tracking of requisitions made by individuals for project execution is automated to a high degree. Visibility of individual engagements is provided through a central resource planning and tracking tool. Business goals cascade down from the CEO to the last individual in the organization using either a Balanced Scorecard Method or through a commitment building process. Possible attitude of individuals to shared vision could range in the following.

- Commitment: Wants it, and will make it happen. This is the nicest form for a shared vision to take.

- Enrollment: Wants is, but will do only whatever can be done.

- Genuine compliance: Sees the benefits and therefore does what is expected and may be more if called upon to do. These are the good soldiers.

- Formal compliance: On the whole, sees a vision; does what is expected but no more.

Participation of individuals in co-designing strategies involving recruitment, selection, decision-making, and redressing issues concerning them, is highly visible with a majority of them participating on teams besides their own project. Brainstorming, round-table reviews, and speakout forums are used to bringing large numbers of stakeholder perspectives into context before a framework of action is established. In short, a participatory style of management creates the ownership necessary for ensuring that responsible decisions are made by individuals. A foundation for empowered workgroup practices is established when an effective method for improving the workplace uses people participation in activities that are not part of their day-to-day work functions.

How does participatory culture transform itself when the transition to the next level is made?

Individuals are sensitized to their overriding responsibilities to the organization and the fundamental value system. The senior management periodically reinforces organizational beliefs and value system and policies supporting protection of intellectual property. Adequate resources and funding are provided to enforce information security and individuals willingly participate in protection of competency assets. A prioritized list of organizational goals and the key initiatives are used and translated into unit-level objectives for every individual to ensure his/her fulfilment. With a highly capable participatory culture in place, the much-needed sociological factors that enable competency integration at the next level get established. A council such as the Software Engineering Council authorizes and supports individuals to take risks and the initiative to exceed their briefs and authority and start new initiatives within the framework of action. In fact, this was how the People CMM initiative got brewing at Intelligroup Asia in the Fall of 1999. A process improvement proposal to set up 'Super Action and Tear Down Reengineering' for sensitizing the organization to both humanistic and profitability issues led to a fully funded CEO initiative. Intelligroup went on to become the first commercial People CMM Level 2 in the world [Intelligroup 2000].

Sequence 4

Communication and coordination ▸ ***Participatory culture*** ▸ *Mentoring*

Related Process Areas

Level 2: Communication and coordination

Level 4: Mentoring

Interpreting the Level 4 Process Areas

LEVEL 4 PROCESS CHARACTERISTICS

REAL LEVERAGE FROM process improvement becomes visible only when organizations make the crucial transition from level 3 to level 4. There is a very strong tendency for organizations to resist change after attaining level 3, since beyond the defined process maturity, there have to be strong compelling forces that relentlessly question status quo. Oftentimes, the SEPG or CDG comprises individuals drawn from the organizational workforce with part-time responsibility. Since such individuals also have project responsibilities that invariably override time spent on organizational key initiatives, there is a great tendency for an organizational process to stagnate and fossilize.

Therefore, the focus at level 4 is to make sure that workforce competency communities master their competency-based processes. Integration of competencies involving multidisciplinary activities can safely be attempted after the basic workforce competencies are mastered. An example of a well-compiled multidisciplinary model offering an environment for product development is the Capability Maturity Model Integration (CMMI) model. Quantitative understanding of process capabilities is facilitated through use of six-sigma techniques for process calibration or application of the higher maturity process areas of the CMMI model itself. Maturity of the organizational process ought to be understood using either the SW-CMM or the CMMI since such an understanding is implicit within the definition of workforce competencies. Process performance data ought to be collected and reasons for special causes of process variation analysed using root-cause analysis techniques and verification and validation practices. Reuse of competency-based assets through a well-maintained reuse repository is normal practice in a level 4 process infrastructure to minimize variation.

Focus of practices from the level 4 up to a level 5 is toward ensuring professional empowerment. The institutionalization goal of all level 4 process areas is at the unit level. If every unit has an ability to demonstrate either a tailored version of the organizational process definitions or makes use of these definitions as is, then there is a greater degree of confidence that ensures these practices are supported within the organization.

The primary objectives at Level 4 are as follows.

- To use the experience of the organization's workforce to provide personal support and guidance to other individuals or groups—

  - A program of mentoring and activities designed around mentoring relationships is established for effective team building and team-based practices.

  - Criteria for selecting individuals or groups to be mentored and those assigned mentoring responsibilities is established.

  - Mentors meet periodically and occasionally evaluate whether they are achieving their objectives.

  - Organizational growth in each of the core competencies is quantitatively measured.

  - Performance results at the individual, unit, and organizational level to appropriate quantitative goals are assessed.

  - Workgroups are empowered to make the necessary changes to their work processes that best address their needs while fulfilling business objectives and stated values of the organization.

  To capitalize on managing its core competencies as a strategic advantage—

  Quantitative foundation for evaluating trends in the capability of the organization's workforce, is established.

  Development of teams that complement knowledge and skills is ensured.

- Team-building activities are performed to improve their effectiveness.

- Workforce practices support team development and performance

- Mentoring is used at both the individual and team levels.

- Growth of the organization's capability in its core competencies is monitored to retain knowledge and help in organizational growth.

Competency Integration

How does the competency integration process area look from one level below?

Practices are not sufficient to support collaborative work due to poor inter-group and intra-group communication. Individuals work on the different competencies and domains in a disjointed fashion. Competencies are grown in vertical silos or as stove-pipes inhibiting alignment of competencies. Workgroups are found to reinvent solutions that have already been conceived since access to a common competency repository of assets is not supported. Since there is a very poor appreciation for partnering relationships competition among competency communities is visible even among two business units belonging to the same organization; often even bidding for the same project as competitors! Work execution requiring collaboration among multiple disciplines or within multiple competency communities is not supported by a common organizational strategic framework. Since individuals are not trained on supporting leadership mechanisms and leadership styles business units work to cross-purposes whereby conflicting with the overall organizational growth objectives. Many times, under the pretext of building agile work units, organizations tend to make the mistake of wilfully abetting internal competition.

How does competency integration look at the level it belongs when institutionalized?

In multidisciplinary types of work, by consciously making efforts to improve interdependence, interactions between the systems development process, software development process, and the product development process are interwoven. Organization offers the necessary guidelines and supporting processes to help create an environment for integration along with performance expectations for both individual and team excellence. And the project management practices define team commitments, work plans, and project information for managing the project and supporting risk management.

The project organization is based on individuals drawn up from the different competency communities who have the responsibility for the successful execution of the project besides growing competencies within their competency community. Possibilities for conflict arising out of such multidisciplinary work are avoided by articulating common improvement strategies and facilitating the much-needed internal dialogue within the boundaries of the defined organizational standard development process and the competency development framework. Different mechanisms that help collaborative work are deployed as standard practices and includes use of communication tools such as chat, e-mail, web-casting, net-hail, and net-meeting and a host of other culturally acceptable sync-and-stabilize forums such as offsite meetings, and so on. Common development and maintenance tools are used along with a common process language to facilitate decision-making.

Practices resulting from establishing a participatory culture provide for the formation and sustenance of integrated teams. Alternative practices supporting empowerment, such as establishing team charters, defining operating procedures based on roles and responsibilities, and assigning team members appropriate to meet the competency demands of the project are actively pursued by workgroups to keep minimal coupling between competency communities and offer maximum cohesion within competency communities. Additional competencies, as needed, are often supplemented through effective supplier agreement management and proactive identification of the sources of competencies external to the organization. A common shared vision of competency activities is established by aligning the unit's and the organization's shared visions.

How does competency integration transform itself when the transition to the next level is made?

The organizational structure directly supports a high degree of growth for the workforce competencies as shown in Fig. 6.1. One such mechanism is a competency-based structure called the home organization or functional organization to which individuals normally belong. They are drafted to work on project development opportunities called team organization and return to the home organization after completion of work responsibilities. Such a matrix structure is more ideally suitable in an R&D type of an environment. [SITARA SE/JUNE 2001]

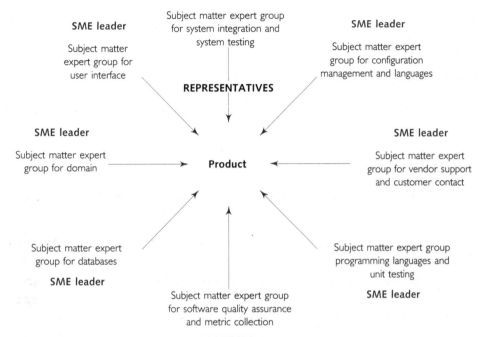

SME leader

Subject matter expert group
for system integration and
system testing

SME leader

Subject matter
expert group for
user interface

SME leader

Subject matter expert
group for configuration
management and languages

REPRESENTATIVES

SME leader

Subject matter expert
group for domain

Product

SME leader

Subject matter expert
group for vendor support
and customer contact

Subject matter expert
group for databases

SME leader

Subject matter expert group
for software quality assurance
and metric collection

SME leader

Subject matter expert group
programming languages and
unit testing

SME leader

SME leader

Fig. 6.1 *Example of home organization–project organization structure*

Source: Adapted from SITARA Process JewelBox™ © 2002 with permission [SITARA Technical Reports: SITARA SE/JUNE2001]

Note: SME–Subject Matter Expert

Sequence 1

Training and development ▸ *Workgroup development, competency development, competency analysis* ▸ *Competency-based assets,* **competency integration** ▸ *Continuous capability improvement, continuous workforce innovation*

Related Process Areas

Level 2: Training and development

Level 3: Workgroup development, competency development

Level 4: Competency-based assets

Level 5: Continuous capability improvement, continuous workforce innovation

Team Building (Version 1.0)

■ Refer: Workgroup development at level 3 and empowered workgroups

Team-based Practices (Version 1.0)

■ Refer: Competency-based practices at level 3 and empowered workgroups

Empowered Workgroups

How does the empowered workgroups process area look from one level below?

At level 1, the manager is seen to be ineffective at managing his resources and is more at a whims-and-fancies level. At level 2, the manager spends most of his time managing his resources. At level 3, the manager is seen managing the process. Decisions are often impulsive at these three levels with scant regard for performance ownership. Learning and orientation towards learning is mostly extrinsically motivated for better compensation and rewards resulting from efficiencies of operation.

How does empowered workgroups look at the level it belongs when institutionalized?

A high trust environment is the hallmark of an empowered workforce. Individuals are seen to request management support while making decisions only with a view to seek clarification. The management by exception renders the role of a manager to enable people who work for him/her to make appropriate decisions. If after the manager provides the necessary clarification and information necessary for decision-making to the individual, the individual decides to make another choice then the management system is mature enough to realize that the individual did so after exercising professional judgement. Everyone in the organization actively supports the choice of the decision type and the resulting outcomes, made by the individual.

Compensation as an extrinsic motivator is only to reinforce the intrinsic motivators of proficiency development and for gaining recognition as a leader in one's field, or with a concern for excellence. Money as an extrinsic motivator is limiting and cannot sustain performance. It is best described with an analogy. You cannot keep throwing chunks of meat at a crocodile hoping that one day it will become a vegetarian! In like manner, behaviour that is rewarded gets repeated and compensation and reward mechanisms are designed to promote empowerment and envisioning, which are so vital for team performance and quality. It must therefore be their power and their vision that compels them and not that of their leader. [Senge 1990]

Speak up and speak out programmes are common to encourage overt discussion on issues concerning all aspects of the strategic competency development framework. Team-based quality circles are more often visible within competency communities. Individuals are seen to use the process improvement framework effectively by tailoring workforce practices to better suit the demands of the project. Teams learn how to produce extraordinary results by demonstrating their power of reasoning by setting positive team goals while encouraging individual debate.

How does empowered workgroups transform itself when the transition to the next level is made?

A system of coordinated action that best utilizes organizational expertise is visible with a high degree of influence from organizational mentors and coaches. People will do things for money, more for a good leader but the most for a belief. And belief is one of the greatest motivator anywhere in the world. Mentoring and coaching are designed to help in factors that build a high trust environment that promotes belief in oneself and one's abilities. Mentoring and coaching are recognized as alternative management styles that rely on skills that create skills in others. Competencies that are necessary for an individual's personal development programme towards building a high-trust environment are identified. They could include reliability, openness, acceptance, congruence, consistency, competence, character, courage, and so on.

The use of partners in learning process is highly encouraged within empowered workgroups of a competency community.

Sequence 2

Staffing ▸ *Workforce planning* ▸ ***Empowered workgroups***

Related Process Areas

Level 2: Staffing

Level 3: Workforce planning

Quantitative Performance Management

How does the quantitative performance management process area look from one level below?

The process infrastructure with a level 2 system enables individuals to set personal objectives and mostly the focus is on the individual with very limited feedback. At level 3, workgroup objectives are established for project data such as cycle time, schedule and cost performance, defects, and competency development and feedback on execution usually is at the end of completion of the process. Such a feedback mechanism results in an afterthought.

Performance requirements are not quantitatively defined but are mostly qualitative since neither the customer nor the project teams make any effort to understand the critical-to-quality parameters. Therefore, results are not predictable and changes consume a good part of the development lifecycle. Feedback if any is often too late.

How does quantitative performance management look at the level it belongs when institutionalized?

Feedback on project performance with respect to the critical-to-quality measures and effectiveness of teamwork is real-time and in-process. Such timely feedback enables mid-course corrections to be effected and helps to control the effect of variation on process outcomes.

Workgroups apply quantitative and statistical techniques to manage process performance and product quality. Quality and process-performance objectives for the project are based on project characteristics after applying the necessary tailoring options and from those established by the organization. The project's defined process therefore comprises, in part, process elements and sub-processes whose process performance can be predicted. At a minimum, the process variation experienced by sub-processes, which are critical to achieving the project's quality and process-performance objectives, is understood. Corrective action is taken when special causes of process variation are identified using causal analysis techniques.

Process performance is characterized by both process measures (e.g. cycle time, and defect removal efficiency) and product measures (e.g. defect density and validation reports). The use of six-sigma techniques for process calibration based on statistical representation of process data in control charts, bar graphs, Pareto analysis, and so on is visible. There is strong connection of the quantitative aspects of the development process to performance indicators of the team. Metrics are used to steer the process of discovering and uncovering facts and trends in a process, rather than to characterize and quantify people with a view to modify their behaviour.

How does quantitative performance management transform itself when the transition to the next level is made?

One of the obvious manifestations of a high capability quantitative performance management process area is a highly capable verification and validation process. Mistakes and problems are surfaced effectively only to ensure that there is a process solution that prevents them from happening again. The practices make use of very effective causal analysis techniques to identify the root causes of problems and the process programme ensures that these causes are insulated from occurring in future process outcomes. Techniques such as the five-whys are used to ensure that linear simplification of single cause–effect relationship does not lead to misleading analysis. The five-why technique is to ask 'why did this happen' and go after answering this iteratively five times by 'what else could be the reason', all the while ensuring that no individual is assigned blame.

Sequence 3

Performance management ▸ *Competency-based practices, career development* ▸ *Organizational capability management,* **quantitative performance management** ▸ *Organizational performance alignment*

Related Process Areas

Level 2: Performance management

Level 3: Competency-based practices, career development

Level 4: Organizational capability management

Level 5: Organizational performance alignment

Organizational Capability Management

How does the organizational capability management process area look from one level below?

The capability of work processes is normally understood only as a gut feel. The project estimates for schedule, cost, and effort is based more on a 'we-can-do-it' philosophy rather than on an objective analysis of capability data. Therefore burnout, disillusionment, and an individual sense of being overworked is visible. Process capability baselines using statistical techniques are not established for the critical work processes such as design review effectiveness, verification, and validation. As a consequence, causes of variation in process execution are not known. There is a wide range of performance results stemming from varying competency profiles of the workforce. Post-mortems for instance are conducted more as a ritual mandated by the defined process and not with a view to maximize learning from mistakes made and identifying the best practices that were the success factors. There is also a poor link between project execution and archiving of project retrospectives, which enable capturing capability information based on outcomes from use of organizational competencies. The skill-set database capturing organizational competencies based on project execution is seldom updated and impact to it is not understood.

Since capability determination has a dependency upon a strong metrics programme, the lack of a solid rationale for metrics collection works to the detriment of capability management. Individuals perceive that data collection is oriented towards behaviour modification rather than steering actions to discover facts. Metrics based on historical data without capturing the context behind the data (i.e. what was the expertise of the individuals who produced and provided the numbers, what tools did they use, etc.) is as bad as having wrong or no data. There is yet another type of dysfunctional use of metrics, to change or modify individual behaviour to fit the so-called organizational benchmark. Two of the most famous software metrics, which have a tendency to modify individual behaviour, are forcing a comparison of defect count and productivity data to organizational benchmarks. There is very little guidance available from metrics champions to enable an understanding of "what do the numbers or the trend actually reveal? Is it about the calibre of those who were responsible to produce them (past tense!) or of those who *will* use these historical measures to produce better numbers?"

Competency communities seem to make ineffective use of process assets and synergy that could result from integrating competencies since practices take a short-term view of project execution. Therefore, not as many innovative solutions are documented either, for future use within the organization.

How does organizational capability management look at the level it belongs when institutionalized?

Organizational workforce capability is known in quantitative terms based on analysis of the skill-set database for both specific and critical skills. Project estimates become more realistic and accurate since such estimates are based on capability data. Training plans are modified appropriately to ensure that the overall organizational objectives for capability development in both the tactical and strategic needs are met. Individuals are put through a training process and their performance on the acquired competencies is managed. Practices such as best practices review make good use of the newly acquired workforce competencies in designated focus areas of the workforce by internalizing them within the process improvement framework.

Data from repeated iterations of the process and tailoring of process based on critical-to-quality characteristics is used as input to determine process efficiency and process capability baselines. Process capability baselines are typically aggregated for tailored processes which have similar critical-to-quality needs (i.e. cost, time, quality, and scope) and along with the project context (i.e. what was the expertise of the individuals who produced the numbers, what tools did they use, how long was the development cycle, what was the maturity of the customer's process, etc.).

Software capability baselines, which are based on a strong metrics programme, are used more to steer organizational learning to discover and uncover facts about the process that they did not quite know of. It is used more like a balance sheet, which is good as on date and less as a comparative tool. Management clearly understands that having a mature software process is not the only contributor to the numbers and therefore accounts for the 'engineering genius' that is behind producing the numbers. The software process is only as good (or as bad) as the people who use it. Having a process is a necessary but not sufficient condition to operate at high process capability.

How does organizational capability management transform itself when the transition to the next level is made?

Good use is made of integrating and aligning workforce competencies to reduce cycle time. The use of Balanced Score Card techniques [Kaplan 1992] as an approach to strategic management with a focus on measurement is visible. The balanced scorecard translates vision and strategy into a tool that effectively communicates strategic intent and motivates and tracks performance against the established goals/objectives.

A vision describes the ultimate goal and strategy is a shared understanding about how the goal is to be reached. The balanced scorecard is then used to translate vision into a clear set of objectives. These objectives are further translated into a system of performance measurements that effectively communicate a powerful, forward-looking, strategic focus to the entire organization.

The balanced scorecard uses four distinct perspectives to measure performance. The *strategic perspective* directs attention to the organization's people and infrastructure. The development of a true learning organization supports success in the next balanced scorecard perspective, the *operational perspective*. The operational perspective focuses attention on the performance of the key internal processes that drive the business. These internal processes need to be seen through the customer's eye—*customer perspective*. It is only then that process improvements will have a lasting sponsorship and financial success. *Financial perspective* measures the ultimate results that the business provides to its shareholders. Together, these four perspectives provide a balanced view of the present and future performance of the business.

I have piloted the balanced scorecard using what was called the tear-down re-engineering teams with one more perspective with useful results to report—*employee perspective* [Intelligroup 2000]. One of the most useful results is the high degree of employee commitment to the capability development programme; Intelligroup Asia transitioned from level 3 to level 5 on the SW-CMM in a mere 12 months. This perspective is needed to insulate and isolate erosion to the 'knowledge base'. Competency identification and development is possible only with the creation of appropriate mechanisms to identify, retain, and grow knowledge, skills, and talent. It has also been observed that building a sense of internal ownership through the employee perspective is the only lasting way to increase dividends and return on investment. Besides, it requires a patient study and organizational contribution (through employee perspective) to get the right balance. SITARA's current attempts with the balanced scorecard method suggests establishing the following three main criteria as prerequisites.

I. Internal Hand-offs

Every measure selected for a balanced scorecard should be part of a chain of cause and effect relationships that represent the strategy.

2. Enablers and Performance Drivers

Measures common to most companies within an industry are known as 'lag indicators'. Examples for a lag indicator include improved market share or customer retention. The drivers of performance ('lead indicators') tend to be unique because they reflect what is different about the strategy. A good balanced scorecard should have a mix of both lead and lag indicators.

3. Linked to Financials

With the proliferation of change programmes underway in most organizations today, it is easy to become preoccupied with a goal such as quality, customer satisfaction, or innovation. While these goals are frequently strategic, they also must translate into measures that are ultimately linked to financial indicators.

Based on the strategic intent, organizational objectives are defined for both the enterprise (horizontal business units) and the unit levels (vertical business units). For example, as a human resource strategy, training and development initiatives can be identified to have an impact on the five different perspectives within the organization. Therefore, objectives are established and goals are defined for each of these five perspectives at both an enterprise and business unit level. The function of human resource development (HRD) is now to serve as an enabler and facilitator for realizing the objectives behind the strategic intent. Identifying, as many of the HRD enablers as possible (and practical) is important for each of the strategic intents.

- Alignment of individual goals
- Training and development
- Compensation and bonuses
- Periodic performance appraisal
- Career counselling
- Job rotation assignments and profile enrichment
- Periodic clarification of organizational objectives and goals
- Employee suggestion systems
- Performance appraisal through an objective process

Any strategic HR objective will have to fan out into all the five areas as in the following illustrative example.

Objective	Superior performance through training
Finance	Increase human resource capital, reduce human resource cost
Operations	Workforce competency development, skills diversification, capability build-up, organizational learning and innovation
Customer	Enhanced performance, improved skills, better solutions, customer confidence
Employee	Career development, skills enhancement, improved morale, self esteem, keeping current with technology
Strategic	Training and development initiatives

Sequence 3

Performance management ▶ *Competency-based practices, career development* ▶ **Organizational capability management**, *quantitative performance management* ▶ *Organizational performance alignment*

Related Process Areas

Level 2: Performance management

Level 3: Competency-based practices, career development

Level 4: Quantitative performance management

Level 5: Organizational performance alignment

Competency-based Assets

How does the competency-based assets process area look from one level below?

Duplication of effort and reinventing of solutions happen all the time since organizational learning is not a collective exercise. Capitalization of workforce capabilities is seldom demonstrated since practices such as best practice reviews, post-mortems, and project retrospectives are not planned into the project engagements. Leverage of individual experience and work products is limited stemming from a 'not-invented-here' syndrome.

Workgroups that have suffered from bad experiences with having reused previous work products which have not been debugged seem to hold the organizational belief system opposing reuse. Even when there is a reuse mechanism in place, integrity of the reusable assets is very doubtful since there is very minimal supporting documentation describing how to use them.

How does competency-based assets look at the level it belongs when institutionalized?

Having a strong competency-based assets programme to capture knowledge and experience to perform processes that further enhances competency-based practices and performance is a self-feeding process. Process assets are available for use by the projects in developing, maintaining, and implementing their defined software process. Knowledge management and a strong focus on reuse is therefore a strong foundation in organizations that begin the level 3 transition.

A well-established process asset library is documented and maintained. The software process assets typically include the following.

- Competency dictionary describing workforce competencies
- The organization's standard software process (including the software process architecture and software process elements)
- Descriptions of software life cycles approved for use
- Guidelines and criteria for tailoring the organization's standard software process
- The organization's software process database
- Library of software process-related documentation

How does competency-based assets transform itself when the transition to the next level is made?

Workgroups actively archive best practices and lessons learnt resulting from the use of organizational process along with tailoring options to match critical-to-quality requirements of the project. Both successful and not-so-successful designs are archived along with best practices and worst practices based on post-mortem reports into repositories known as the white book and red book, respectively.

Before creating any new design or work product, the reuse repository is actively researched to ensure that a similar solution is not being built all over again. A separate group of individuals maintain the knowledgebase and reuse libraries and are assigned responsibility to coach and mentor projects with the use of assets from the reuse library. A team of professionals, whose only responsibility is to create deployable ready-to-use components, is also visible. Such a team called the SWAT Team (skilled with advanced technologies), corporate research and development team, or the software engineering council is also empowered to survey and research both process and technological changes in the organizational domains of expertise and ensure that they sensitize the organization with the most current technological advances.

Sequence 1

Training and development ▸ *Workgroup development, competency development, competency analysis* ▸ *Competency-based assets, competency integration* ▸ *Continuous capability improvement, continuous workforce innovation*

Related Process Areas

Level 2: *Training and development*

Level 3: *Workgroup development, competency development, competency analysis*

Level 4: *Competency integration*

Level 5: *Continuous capability improvement, continuous workforce innovation*

Mentoring

How does the mentoring process area look from one level below?

Sharing of lessons learnt and the process of helping individuals realize their true potential is informal. Individuals normally know where to get help on specific competencies and request such assistance when they are stuck driven by a need. Since reusable assets are normally not archived in a central repository, there is very little leverage of organizational capabilities. Mentoring could be masquerading under the guise of cronyism with morale problems getting surfaced from time to time. Individuals are seen to be pushed into positions of authority that they are not capable of handling.

Individuals perceive a disproportionate face time with their supervisors. Those who have a way of making the supervisor feel important get the greatest attention. Late bloomers generally have a raw deal since supervisors and personnel managers tend to overlook their career potential.

Mentoring does not have an objective and invariably is supervisor-centric since the only purpose such a relationship serves is career advancement.

How does mentoring look at the level it belongs when institutionalized?

Mentoring is a formal process that is structured to enable learning. A checklist is used to measure progress and learning on established targets and goals. Growing out of a healthy participatory culture that establishes knowledge sharing, mentors aid in the development of workforce capability and assist with the creation and use of competency-based assets. A programme of performance excellence is in place. Typically, empowered and experienced professionals are enlisted to provide guidance to project managers to improve business performance to achieve organizational excellence.

The organization identifies individuals with higher potential and grooms them for key positions that require high trust and delivery capability through a process of mentoring. Mentoring is used to build highly directed teams, focused on growing the identified workforce competencies. Mentoring relationships are facilitated by using an organizational framework and structure of competency communities. Individuals naturally flock to competency communities to gain affiliation with subject matter experts. Process of selection of mentors and formalizing the mentor–protégé relationships is based on the perceived value addition from such relationships.

Mentors are provided guidance on the objectives and the process of conducting mentoring activities for the duration of learning. Personal competency development plans are drawn up for individuals and such plans are monitored and tacked periodically. Once the grooming is complete, the protégé is given the necessary push to take the initiative to succeed in the new assignment. Thereafter, it is up to the protégé to decide the next course of action on the mentoring relationship. Most solid mentoring relationships, which are established with a purpose of growing and nurturing talent in individuals, live a lifetime. So, it is more than likely that individuals may have mentors external to the organization, with whom they maintain excellent rapport and from whom they are willing to learn. However, institutionalizing a mentoring programme within an organization requires the creation of competency development centres with communities of excellence or competency communities to which individuals perceive an internal stake as well in their personal competency development and learning process.

Needless to emphasize, mentors are highly knowledgeable individuals within their competencies, have a natural ability to teach, and are excellent communicators. Such individuals are of the leadership material and the whole organization is bound to gain by nurturing and growing such individuals. Mentors are selected for their desire and ability to teach besides having a natural thirst for knowledge. They are recognized by the organization and rewarded suitably. These are individuals who are looked upon as role models and are easy to spot. Speaking of role models, it might be useful to maintain two lists of role models—one list containing the positive role models (those that the individual draws inspiration from and aspires to become) and the other list of negative role models (whom the individual despises and does not want to become).

How does mentoring transform itself when the transition to the next level is made?

Mentoring takes on an advanced form, that of 'coaching' where coaches are seen to set stretched performance targets and carefully monitor team accomplishments. In its highly refined state, reverse mentoring is often resorted to wherein coaches themselves become good learners—it's always a two-way process.

Coaches have well-defined tasks to perform.

- Understand the needs of their protégés.

  - Establish the learner's top five strengths and top five needs.

  - Establish the causes of these to develop a common understanding.

  - Engage the learner in dialogue and reflection to define the need.

- Assist the protégé to take personal ownership by defining a structured plan of learning.

  - Help the learner accept the needs.

  - Get a person with whom the learner has rapport to positively reinforce the need.

  - Sell the learner a balanced strategy to work on the needs.

  - Set a specific time-frame of no more than a month to try these items repeatedly.

■ Support the process of learning by making resources available for individuals to demonstrate excellence

- Development costs both time and money.

- The learner needs continuous feedback, emotional support, and reinforcement. More effective learners reduce insights to rules of thumb.

■ Celebrate successes with protégés at every opportunity

- Find ways for the learner to demonstrate the learning. And, celebrate success.

Coaches provide just the necessary inputs to the workgroups, who exercise their ingenuity to come up with solutions of the breakthrough type. These could be in the areas of organizational competencies, which include better processes or innovations to product lines. Innovations are piloted and their effectiveness is measured in proof-of-concept studies before large scale adoption.

Individuals are seen to make personal commitments to the process of learning and sharing in both formal and informal forums. A good percentage of the workforce appears to be highly geared to assume frontline responsibilities. A natural outcome of solid mentoring relationships is the creation of multiple chains of leadership. Transitioning of individuals into critical roles appears seamless. A whole generation of well-groomed managers and leaders are grown to assume responsibilities starting from the CEO down. It is natural to expect an organization with highly capable mentoring practices to demonstrate organizational growth in leaps and bounds. The notion of incubation of projects and hiving off of separate organizations based on successful seeding and maturing of ideas of individuals is a manifestation of mentoring practice. Mentoring in its highly capable form is to cultivate, grow, and nurture positive organizational values and value systems. Those having mentoring responsibilities pride over their work responsibility and job description. Being an expert is a matter of theme and pattern recognition and applying insights from such recognition. Before advice is offered, coaches understand how they learnt it themselves and what their key experiences were. What were the first items they would teach as keys to help the person form notions about the learning events? [Lombardo]

> *Sequence 4*
>
> *Communication and coordination* ▶ *Participatory culture* ▶ ***Mentoring***
>
> ***Related Process Areas***
>
> *Level 2: Communication and coordination*
>
> *Level 3: Participatory culture*

Organizational Competency Management (Version 1.0)

Refer: Competency analysis, competency development, and competency-based practices at level 3

AND

Refer: Competency integration and competency-based assets at level 4

Organizational Performance Alignment

Refer: Chapter 7

Interpreting the Level 5 Process Areas

Level 5 Process Characteristics

THE PRIMARY OBJECTIVES at level 5 are to continuously improve and optimize workforce practices that have been established. There is an implicit assumption that individuals have a mechanism of expressing their personal innovations to the operating processes and aligning them with the unit's or organization's business objectives. Regardless of the kind of work assigned to an individual there is another added dimension. Not only does every person think about his/her work, but also about how well he/she does his/her work. If someone thinks she/he has a better way of doing something, she/he is empowered to use the process improvement framework to make the change and evaluate the results. Operational process descriptions established at the organizational level are tailored and institutionalized as personal software process. Knowing fully that having the right systems in place is only a necessary but not sufficient condition for operating at high levels of process maturity, the key lessons learnt at this maturity level are the following.

LESSON 1

Quality in a product is impossible without adequate quality in the process. And quality in the process is impossible without the right people and the right management leadership that is committed to excellence.

> ### LESSON 2
>
> *Even if you have all the right systems in place, it is not an assurance that you will be operating at high process maturity.*

Individuals in such an empowered work culture display a greater degree of employee satisfaction while guaranteeing customer satisfaction and delivering upon commitments which are attributed to the process improvement programme. And when these changes are incorporated into the process, their effectiveness is measured within a short three-month period. If it works they get the word out, so that every project within the organization can gain from the experiences and results. If it does not work, they let everybody else know about it as well so that the organization gains from such experiences as well. It is at this stage when people issues and people-based practices are linked to improvement with the software process that one can state confidently that the level 5 process has integrated lessons learnt into the very process itself.

The focus of practices at the level 5 is towards ensuring the highest level of professional empowerment at the individual level—where individuals make the day-to-day changes for optimal performance. The institutionalization goal of all of the level 5 process areas is at the individual level. If every individual has an ability to demonstrate a personal practice that supports either a tailored version of the organizational process definitions or makes use of these definitions as is, then there is a greater degree of confidence to ensure that these practices are supported within the organization.

At this level of organizational maturity, the sense for identifying and growing competencies is so high that individuals focus on continuous process improvement. Needless to emphasize, continuous process improvement cannot happen in isolation; there has to be a structured mechanism to experiment newer technologies and newer process manifestations as a result of a proactive engagement of the workforce with organizational practices—the defined process.

Personal Competency Development

- Refer: Continuous capability improvement

Coaching

- Refer: Mentoring

Continuous Capability Improvement

How does the continuous capability improvement process area look from one level below?

Processes are highly individualistic and have a tendency to be limited by individual capability to learn. There is no direction offered to individuals with respect to the pace of learning or providing an understanding for how individual capabilities translate to workgroup capability. Often individual learning is misdirected and is due to reactive planning. Individuals who have a particular skill-set are not provided adequate opportunities to fully exploit their capability. Based on perceived market or customer demand, individuals are retooled mindlessly in technologies and domains, which are not the mainstay of either the organization or aligned to individual capabilities and objectives. A lot of money is wasted in training programmes, which have no relevance to individual priorities and career objectives. People are found asking, for example, 'How was the training provided to us on *Supply Chain Management* useful?' or 'Of what use was the training provided to us in the area of m-commerce (mobile commerce) in the hope that we will have a project?' It is very likely that skills are acquired without honing them and would serve no practical use.

How does continuous capability improvement look at the level it belongs when institutionalized?

Everybody in the organization talks of commitment to quality in true letter and spirit. They talk about quality goals and objectives in numbers and are committed to improving workforce capability of the organization they serve.

> **DEFINITION: WORKFORCE CAPABILITY**
>
> *Workforce capability is defined in the People CMM as the level of knowledge, skills, and process abilities available for performing the organization's business activities*

Knowing what is important from an organizational perspective about the processes in use, individuals establish a personal commitment to enhance and improve the state of practice by continuously improving the process based on experiences with it. The internal dialogue among individuals is normally to evoke a response to 'Is this really the way I want to contribute and manage my work responsibilities? Is this best for my customer, my company, and for me?' While the well-documented Team Software Process or TSP [Humphrey 2000] can be used to establish workgroup operating processes, Personal Software Process or the PSP [Humphrey 1997] can be used very effectively to enhance personal work processes. Individuals are seen building common special interest groups and brain-trusts to quickly find resolutions to challenges facing them. With proliferation of applications based on Internet technology and modern-day work practices of 24 by 7 by 365, it is a lot easier to enable capability and performance improvement with good return on investment. A simple Help Desk application that is deployed on the Web and runs on every desktop within the enterprise is an example of how to find quick resolutions to technical problems. Individuals can pose their problems along with the context onto the Help Desk, which will flag itself off on every desktop upon submission within the enterprise. Experts in the subject matter, available in some part of the globe belonging to the enterprise, who know the solution can then send their solutions. Organizations provide an effective work environment and a framework to support such collaborative effort. With such a community approach to performance improvement, members belonging to special interest groups or brain-trusts are seen to provide greater ability for individuals to reach out to get quick access to solutions.

Focus groups or vision teams which are called by different names such as software process review team, metrics council, software engineering council, and so on are established within the organization to update the organization on the changes to the competitive environment and for strategic management. Feedback on practices employed is provided to projects based on project retrospectives and end-of-phase post-mortems at regular intervals. Such feedback mechanisms serve as valuable sources of quantitative data on process and product quality for analysis. One of the most useful processes in such a work environment would be peer reviews for all in-process verification activities and post-mortems or project retrospectives for post-delivery validation. Individuals who are trained on statistical methods perform analysis of execution outcomes by running causal analysis reports through an understanding of special and common causes of variation. Process capability baselines are established for key processes by establishing measures for design review effectiveness, code walkthrough effectiveness, peer review efficiency, first-pass yield for unit testing, and defect density measures for release data using customer feedback as an important input.

The capability of the workforce is kept current and fresh by institutionalizing competency development centres or learning centres comprising individuals who take responsibility to forecast and predict trends in technology and retool the organizational workforce with changes to competencies.

It is more than likely that process improvement initiative is organization-wide with full participation. Individuals participate in process improvement programmes voluntarily and such programmes are perceived as organizational key initiatives. Process improvement programmes and organizational learning become core competencies. Individuals are sensitive to causal analysis and such data is used to convert personal inadequacies to strengths through time-bound personal competency development programmes.

Individuals maintain detailed engineering records of what was accomplished and ensure that results align with organizational goals and objectives. Periodic assessments are made to individual and team contributions to the organizational process programme and the defined process is continuously renewed by capturing lessons learnt.

How does continuous capability improvement transform itself when the transition to the next level is made?

Does the organization know enough about how to sustain gains made with capabilities developed? Obviously, it costs extra money to ensure that individuals perform at the cutting edge all the time. It is also likely that organizations must pay particular attention to the fact that publishing a high maturity outlook is an easy way to fall prey to poaching from the competition! A delicate balance is necessary to ensure that the organization insulates itself from such a possibility. As is well said: 'Your organizational assets walk 'out' of the door each evening', and therefore there must be enough compelling reasons for them to walk back 'in' each morning. It is possible for organizations to sustain this high capability and make incredible progress if every individual is made to feel that they are an important part of the big picture and are allowed to bloom and grow their capabilities through self-renewal. Most high maturity organizations provide an avenue for such intellectual exchanges. Motorola, Inc., for instance, has a very popular and well-supported initiative called the Motorola Software Engineering Symposium and the Motorola Tools Fair. Such annual company conclaves, where professionals from all over the globe converge to discuss technical problems and strike common ground, is the best-known technique for personal renewal and quality revival.

Organizations having stable development and oversight processes engage in making them more capable through targeted capability improvements to process areas having the highest pay-off or return on investment. Within the scope of the CMMI^{SM} [CMMI 2002] organizations mature the rigour of individual process areas by profiling process area capability and advancing the state of practice through quantitative techniques and elimination of root causes of problems causing process variation.

To study the effectiveness of continuous capability improvement, it is therefore useful to draw the attention of the organization to the verification and validation or peer review activities. Most high-capability processes take data from verification activities for causal analysis and maintain a list of special causes and common causes of variation along with specific measures to minimize their impact in peer-review closure action reports.

It is useful to note that practices of causal analysis and quantitative management of project activities have a measurable influence and impact on the organizational process to sustain continuous capability improvement.

Sequence 1

Training and development ▸ *Workgroup development, competency development, competency analysis* ▸ *Competency-based assets, competency integration* ▸ **Continuous capability improvement**, *continuous workforce innovation*

Related Process Areas

Training and development

Workgroup development, competency development, competency analysis competency-based assets, competency integration

Continuous workforce innovation

Continuous Workforce Innovation

How does the continuous workforce innovation process area look from one level below?

Within continuous workforce innovation, improvements to basic workforce practices address aspects of technology and process change management. When this process area is not fully deployed, a majority of the improvements appear to be opportunistic without addressing the root cause of process variation or the critical-to-quality characteristics. Since improvements are not normally scheduled into an organizational process improvement calendar, there is very little evidence of ownership to this initiative resulting from an imbalanced SEPG or CDG team. There is even a tendency to observe deterioration in the quality of composition of the SEPG or CDG team over time. When organizations have not moved beyond level 3 in a while, there is a great tendency to display a low leverage process improvement programme. This can be observed by looking at the types of process and technology improvement suggestions. These suggestions most definitely do not display a breakthrough type of a characteristic. Improvements are mostly superficial and will include suggestions for changes to templates, forms, or guidelines.

There is also a possibility for process improvement to take on a highly localized view with some projects doing a more than reasonable job with tailoring their process and technologies to fit project-based critical-to-quality characteristics and others totally unconscious and insensitive to process improvements. The natural fallout of such impulsive or opportunistic deployment of improvements without adequate proof of trials at the organizational level is that management sponsorship for innovation is without direction. There is a good tendency for individuals to lose interest in the improvement programme with a yo-yo effect becoming visible, based on who the leader of the SEPG or CDG team was in a particular period.

Feedback to individuals in the organization on practices incorporating improvements and results from pilots is seldom visible. Status updates on the suggestions made by individuals to the process or technology are not made available to them. As a result, individuals are seen complaining during interviews with typical statements such as 'My team suggested half a dozen changes to the SEPG, which required creation of basic tools. But no action has been taken on them till date. We were told at least thrice that the management is looking at creating a separate technology management group which will address them, but in the last one year we have not seen a single idea being implemented. So, we have stopped sensitizing the SEPG and the management to improvement suggestions.' It is obvious from this excerpt (from a real assessment) that the organization is often reactive and individuals begin the blame game.

How does continuous workforce innovation look at the level it belongs when institutionalized?

Deep reflection and self-analysis is necessary for innovation. Organizations provide a framework for operations to reflect, study their products, services, and customer feedback, and generate strategies for measurable improvements. An effective self-critiquing forum to surface best practices and innovations is identified after studying lessons learnt from past successes and failures. Accepted best practices are then piloted and deployed on a larger scale across the different operations. The most important factor which has to be considered for continuous innovation is to stay close to the customer by proactively understanding customer priorities. Customer feedback and a quantitative understanding of both process and product quality is a key enabler for effective decision-making. In-process audit reports and work-product peer-review records along with action plans, based on an inventory of 'what worked' and 'what did not work', are useful process implementation indicators for continuous workforce innovation. Besides quantitative data, qualitative descriptions, which cover people (size of team by programme management, development, testing, product management and the like, number of work days), the product (languages used, platform and total lines of executable code produced), schedule (actual versus planned dates for milestones and shipment), and process (tools used, issues concerning development methods employed, interdependencies) are also maintained.

Organizations that are successful in re-inventing themselves take post-mortems and project retrospectives very seriously. Two types of repositories are maintained. One, for capturing the best practices and another, for capturing the worst practices. Instead of asking what went wrong, these sessions are used to understand why something went wrong for collective learning.

How does continuous workforce innovation transform itself when the transition to the next level is made?

Post-mortems, process audits, and product peer reviews are programmed into every individual's brain. A noteworthy qualitative attribute of a high-capability post-mortem exercise is the high degree of 'positivity' surrounding team self-talks while introspecting upon the failures. Most people in the organization understand their value and ensure that there is a certain sense of process coercion placed as an organizational demand on new recruits. It is my belief that gentle and persistent coercion is the only sure-shot formula for building a culture of continuous workforce innovation leading to process improvement. Organizations, which truly have practices to support a continuous workforce innovation outlook, have internal benchmarks for key metrics on process, product, and critical-to-quality parameters that indicate early warning signs and leading indicators if a project is getting itself into trouble or not. They also have process performance standards and process capability baselines, which include data from the SEI besides customer satisfaction reports. Needless to emphasize, it takes persistence and constant working at it to make sure that every individual in the workforce becomes a contributing member to the organization. It begins at the very beginning through effective screening and careful selection of talent, where individuals are selected for their intelligence, skills, business acumen, and core competency orientation.

Sequence 1

Training and development ▸ *Workgroup development, competency development, competency analysis* ▸ *Competency-based assets, competency integration* ▸ *Continuous capability improvement,* **continuous workforce innovation**

Related Process Areas

Training and development

Workgroup development, competency development, competency analysis competency-based assets, competency integration

Continuous workforce innovation

Organizational Performance Alignment

How does the organizational performance alignment process area look from one level below?

The organization may have adequate processes that address performance management at the workgroup and the individual level through effective process management. But what might be lacking is an alignment of goals and cascading objectives down through some form of an earned value analysis or a balanced scorecard. Initiatives and goals may have a high degree of coherence within units but run the risk from suboptimizing intergroup interfaces with low leverage. It is more than likely that best practices and improvements are reinvented all the time with no solid sense for a central repository that archives outcomes from such initiatives through knowledge management and knowledge sharing. Entities belonging to the same organization are not even aware of the development and improvements to core competencies. This is particularly visible in larger organizations, where improvement cycles are repeated more as a ritual.

Instead of hiving best practices into a central repository maintained by an organizational team, successful responses are normally kept as closely guarded secrets. Demonstrations of capability and organizational performance are mostly verbal with very little supporting documentation. Individuals get into turf-guarding exercises.

How does organizational performance alignment look at the level it belongs when institutionalized?

Cross-group sharing of best practices and cross-pollination of lessons learnt as a practice helps to make sure that interdependent work involving all aspects of development, testing, and marketing becomes truly integrated. When organizational performance alignment takes on an 'enterprise-view' with sharing of lessons learnt and innovations between geographically separate entities, seamless integration of competencies becomes possible. Communities of excellence are set up in such a manner that the best group always offers timely solutions in true collaboration. For example, while dealing with the development process, the requirements elicitation team uses best-in-class techniques such as joint application development sessions and what-if scenarios to elicit customer requirements. After a baseline of the system or product requirements is established, the design champions, who are part of the design community of excellence, develop the system or product design and perform a hand-off of the design after a perspective-based review to the implementation champions, who are experts in rendering the design into code. After unit testing and code walkthrough is complete, software reliability engineering experts conduct a verification and validation of the system or product to ensure compliance. Practices demonstrate a high degree of individual commitment and sensitivity to productivity improvement and cycle time reduction. Organizational measurement and process infrastructure is sensitized to collecting and improving factors that directly assist productivity with a good control on overall product quality. Feedback from expert reviews is immediate and therefore the feed-forward into the development process ensures intermediate work-products which have a 'zero-known' defects characteristic.

How does organizational performance alignment transform itself when the transition to the next level is made?

The key distinction about having a development process, which is assisted by an effective oversight process is, 'How quickly do we come to know about the corrections that are necessary?' Besides keeping the reaction time to the necessary corrections very small, the essential hallmark of a highly capable organizational performance alignment process area is that answers to these three questions on competency is known in clear terms—'Do we know what our core competencies are? Do we know how to leverage value from these core competencies? And, do we know how to sustain them and make money by selling on these competencies?'

Individuals display a high degree of innovation quotient by creating tools and infrastructure that assist in development and support activities enabling improvements to productivity and cycle time reduction. In general, individuals display a high degree of self-actualization with personal competency development measures that align individual career objectives to the unit needs and whereby to the overall business goals. Performance excellence, always the ultimate objective behind change management initiative dealing with improving organizational competencies eventually becomes possible when most individuals in the organization demonstrate a personal commitment to meeting organizational and business goals.

Sequence 3

Performance management ▸ *Competency-based practices, career development* ▸ *Organizational capability management, quantitative performance management* ▸ **Organizational performance alignment**

Related Process Areas

Level 2: *Performance management*

Level 3: *Competency-based practices, career development*

Level 4: *Organizational capability management, quantitative performance management*

Limitations of the People CMM

IT IS USEFUL to know where the People CMM practices cannot help. They cannot help you if you have problems arising out of lack of loyalty, deeply entrenched complacency, missing competitive spirit and excellence orientation, general apathy toward proactive change management, lack of a learning orientation or learning disability, poor organizational sense of belonging and bonding, lack of purposeful individuals, and lack of pride of association.

Before we go on, let us do a pop quiz. Imagine yourself, as a contributor to the organizational well-being, and as a person who wants to give your best performance. List down the inhibitors, which impact your performance adversely and as a consequence, negatively impact your productivity and motivation.

After working with the People CMM model for a while, I have a feeling that the underlying problems related to productivity and performance lie not only with what the People CMM practices addresses but also somewhere else! Though qualitative in nature, these factors are what are actually eating away at the foundations of an organization and causing large-scale organizational decay. While the People CMM focuses its attention to the more quantitative factors that improve productivity, and for the right reasons so as to establish an objective sense for measurement, I would conclude that it is worth the while to document and explore the list of the qualitative attributes that impact productivity and explore within the limitation imposed by the size of this book, what the probable solutions could be. Though this list is endless, a few of these qualitative stumbling blocks that I have personally observed are described here.

Fundamental Lack of Pride in One's Work

Unfortunately, very few projects in the knowledge-intensive field of IT have a component that would inspire breakthrough performance. It would not be too much of an understatement to say that on the whole, job satisfaction is a very difficult emotion to find in IT. There are many reasons for this. A few critical ones are these. Nobody knows exactly what the big picture is and how the solution that is being developed fits into it. Positive feedback, if any, on the successful completion of a work product is often a project closure dinner with a supporting statement of customer satisfaction—one never gets to see his work product in use! With large development teams, it is so easy to make a mistake and not get noticed! If the mistake gets noticed, feedback is oftentimes too late without adequate reaction time.

Periodic project retrospectives and post-mortems driven by well-defined project objectives are a good place to begin. Now, the thing that can fix this problem to a large degree is to also enable a highly structured development environment using the SW-CMM or the CMMI [CMMI 2002] with adequate management by oversight practices such as peer reviews and validations. With appropriate team orientation from 'do-what-is-needed' to a 'know-what-is-needed', it is possible to improve shared vision on projects, which will help to build ownership—one of the most important reasons for an individual to display a sense of pride in workmanship.

Lack of Customer Orientation and a Learning Disability to Walk Away from the Wrong Business

Most low maturity organizations don't have a management system for collecting periodic customer satisfaction reports. To a very great degree, this is exacerbated by a rather inept management style of singing the 'we will do whatever you want' tune to the customer! Such a management stance clearly shows that the organization is on a survival mode and is only interested in grabbing a piece of the business pie. When business propositions are explored more for quick profits without studying relevance to developing and growing core competencies, it is very likely that such decisions push everyone in the organization to the wall by forcing them to learn or pick up 'stuff' that matters only in the short term. Project initiatives, which do not evaluate the impact they will have on building organizational competencies, are doomed to fossilize existing talent. One of the reasons for the high churn rate of high calibre individuals is that competent individuals look at this management attitude as an abuse of their existing skills, which were the very reason why they were hired in the first place and begin to leave. Among the more geared knowledge workers, there is a greater degree of emphasis on professional loyalty than employer loyalty.

Project evaluation before project kick-off for a competency fitment within the profile or portfolio of organizational competencies is a much-desired practice.

Inability to Take Instructions from Knowledgeable Peers and a Know-it-All Vanity

When individuals think it *infra dig* to say the three golden words 'I don't know', there is yet another opportunity for learning lost. This know-it-all vanity displayed by some individuals comes with additional interpersonal issues resulting from an overbearing attitude. This may be one of the reasons why other knowledgeable peers tend to leave the group or unit keeping their own self-interests in mind.

There have to be enough mechanisms, such as counsellors or mentors internal to the organization, who will have to deal with inappropriate behaviour. Behaviour that is rewarded invariably gets repeated. Mature organizations make it a point to reinforce company values and organizational culture at periodic intervals. People, who have never obeyed, cannot command; so as a rule some successful organizations believe in promotions from within. It is extremely rare to find them recruiting individuals from the outside to fill in critical job positions.

Too Much Hangover from Past Memory

There is a tendency among managers and supervisors to bring in their pet work cultures through the 'in my previous organization we used to…' reasoning. While this might also seed some best practices, there is a greater risk of diluting the reasons surrounding current context. Let us suppose process improvements were a failure in the previous organization and the manager or supervisor of a work unit feels that is a waste of time and brings this perspective by challenging the process programme in current environment; chances are that the change management programme is set up for failure.

General Organizational Tendency to Favour Conformists and Look at Rebels with Contempt

Now this is the second face of the earlier problem. While process rebel may be a strong word, best innovations are possible only when a certain degree of self-critiquing of the process is ensured. A process is most definitely not an organizational icon that should be cast in stone and set on a pedestal at the reception so that every individual offers his/her respects to it before entering the organization.

Low Goals, No Goals, or Out-of-Sight Goals Coupled with Lack of Achievement Motivation

This is a situation that a majority of the individuals in the organization seem to drift into, especially when there is no conscious effort by the organization to provide enough encouragement to highly enthusiastic new recruits. When individuals come on board, they are most ineffective but highly enthusiastic and motivated to learn. Without proper guidance and mentoring mechanisms that offer an avenue to channel this energy, individuals soon become ineffective and demotivated. This is also a problem that is most often confounded when there is a massive restructuring programme on the anvil or when the organization drops enough hints at lay-offs when the guess-game begins.

*Unit managers and supervisors must set SMART goals for individuals—**S**pecific, **M**easurable, **A**chievable, **R**ealistic, and **T**ime-bound. Goals that are out of reach are motivating; goals that are out of sight are demotivating.*

No Sense of Belonging to the Establishment that is Providing the Basic Job Security

Organizational sense of belonging and loyalty are far-fetched emotions that only a symbolic identity such as "we work for a level 5 company" or "we know what the strategic competency framework is, and how our contribution is helping us achieve it" can afford to ignite. People will do things for money, more for a good leader, but the most for a belief. And belief is one of the greatest motivator anywhere in the world. Unless individuals believe that the work they produce is in harmony with their personal value systems, it is very difficult to expect individuals to display a sense of belonging.

I have however learnt from two opposite cultural settings—one from the East and the other from the West—as to the miraculous impact a simple lapel-pin can have on building a sense of belonging. In fact, even after I have left these illustrious companies, the only things I still treasure are the lapel-pins I was awarded! And, I mostly speak highly positively about these organizations!

Lack of Self-esteem and an Ability to Positively React to Critiquing

This is basically a culture thing. Self-esteem is not thinking less of oneself but it is thinking more of the others.

Context Switches between Work and Family that may be Counter-productive to Bring out the Best Performance

I have now come to conclude that two context switches basically consume our entire day. The first switch, from a family setting to the work setting and the second context switch from the work setting back into the family setting. And as human beings, most of us are extremely lousy in doing a good job with context switching. We take work life into the family and family life into the work and which one is the cause of ruin of the other is something that I would like the reader to introspect! To quote Plato, "An unexamined life is not worth living." My view today is that having to change your life when you arrive at work each morning is coming close to wearing golden handcuffs. Much of this problem is serious and often self-created by giving too much importance to our job titles or positions of authority, which we seem to take into our family lives as well.

Limitations Arising Out of Job Descriptions and Labels

This is by far the scariest limitation that most organizations begin to impose on the individual. Individuals are seen doing things—just enough to justify their titles or job descriptions. To this extent in the knowledge society, titles and job descriptions actually obscure the full range of contributions that individuals are able to offer. And most people don't realize how trivial job titles are in a knowledge society, especially where there is a high churn rate. Nobody cares who you really are; what matters most is how indispensable is the knowledge or capability you bring to the table! It all boils down to the commitment you make to yourself to know more and learn more. Ability opens the doors to get you up there, but competency keeps you up there. You cannot extrinsically motivate human greatness. It must be compelled from within. You have to light that drive for top achievement from within. That is the essence of the *Bhagavad Gita* [Vyasa BC].

Incompetent Bosses Who are Retired On the Job

These bosses are by far the toughest to deal with! They neither let go of you nor let you leave. These bosses often get recognized by the amount of hangover they have from past memory with such oft-repeated statements as 'Let's do it the good old way' or 'When I worked on the Mother Hen project...'

High Degree of Job Security

Naturally builds a lot of complacence.

Lack of Empowerment Arising Out of Deeply-entrenched Beliefs of Hierarchy

Being highly leader-dependent, decisions are normally of the command style [Refer Chapter 5 for details].

Poor Spirit of Teamwork and Empathy or Poor Social Factors

The unfortunate problem with the way teams are set up while executing software projects is that a team leader decides who belongs to it. There is more of personal chemistry than technology interests that dictate how well teams work. Teams unfortunately don't jell when there is a strict hierarchy of sorts since it works at its best when it is set up as a network of virtual peers.

Mistaking the Word 'Improvement' for 'Perfection'

The two words 'improvement' and 'perfection' do not mean the same! An obsession for 'perfection' can lead to grievous mistakes. Expecting perfect work from imperfect human beings is even worse! Improvements can never happen if individuals don't make mistakes. What is required of a good process improvement framework is a 'mistake recognition and mistake proofing system'. A few words from Jesus CEO summarize it best. 'Jesus had an astonishing ability to create what he needed from something that was already there. Jesus was keenly aware of his resources.' [Jones 1995]

Uncontrolled Access to Information on Other Individual's Compensation Package and Comparisons Arising out of such Gossip

Needs no further explanation!

Gossip Itself

Hello! We are human!

Chapter

9

Best Practices in People CMM Assessments

BEST PRACTICES RESULTING from the use of the family of different CAF-compliant methods such as CMM-Based Appraisal for Internal Process Improvement (CBAIPI), People CMM Assessment, and Standard CMMI Appraisal Method for Process Improvement (SCAMPI) is presented in what follows. This is definitely not exhaustive since it is limited by the size of the book.

Conducting a Class B Assessment at Least Three to Six Months Prior to a Formal Class A

Problem

Most Class A assessments are done without a Class B assessment since formal registration of results from Class B assessment is not required. This only means that 'continuity of purpose' behind process improvement is established only as a gut reaction from the assessment team.

Proposition

Class B assessment must occur three to six months prior to a formal Class A assessment. And further, results from such a Class B assessment can be examined by the assessment team during a Class A to prove beyond reasonable doubt that 'strengths' remain 'strengths' and weaknesses, if any, have been addressed using appropriate action plans. Without this measure, People CMM assessments will become more of level-chasing exercises with only a 'me-first' intent. Real intent behind a People CMM assessment should be to make sure that the process culture leading towards core competency development and the right process orientation is institutionalized into the guts of the organization based on a study of how well organizational process assets sustain and behave over 'elapsed time'. And it should be more than adequate to keep this elapsed time to be between three to six months. It is very important to make People CMM assessments take the view of being a 'process capability diagnostic tool' rather than a level awarding exercise. Currently, it is a level awarding exercise since sanctity to how well the process behaves and endures over 'elapsed time' is not even considered.

What Should be the Rigour of a Class B Assessment?

Use the SITARA's People CMM ASQ in Appendix B for a Class B Assessment

Problem

Most respondents to the full-length People CMM assessment questionnaire feel that the survey is too long and does not hold the respondent's interest. This feeling is best appreciated since most individuals who respond to the survey are neither trained on the model nor on the jargon used in the People CMM framework. Often, we even see that there is a big enough standard deviation on the responses received even though the average supports the practice as a strength. The average may be indicative of strength, but based on the large standard deviation (since such perception is not uniform) it might as well be a clear indication of a weakness. Assessment teams that use the survey analysis would therefore not have a strong indicator to base their initial perceptions of the site's process capability. We have even seen People CMM questionnaire being abandoned mid-way by about 40% of the respondents. The general feedback is that a 'crisp' survey-based rather than the People CMM model-based questionnaire is more useful.

Proposition

Questions from SITARA's People CMM Assessment Survey Questionnaire (Appendix B), used on mini-assessments conducted by SITARA have been included from the SITARA Process Jewelbox™ in Chapter 3 at the end of each process area. It uses descriptive types of questions to probe the organizational pulse on the interpretation of the process. This may be used for conducting a Class B assessment. This survey restricts the number of questions to at most two to five questions per process area of the People CMM. Depending upon the scope of the assessment, the questionnaire has been designed to ensure that total time to answer it should not exceed 1.5 hours with a level 5 scope. Surveys which are longer than 1.5 hours are not of much use since answers tend to be vague and seem to be given more out of frustration just to complete the survey. Since the proposed Class B assessment is driven more by a survey, it does not bog down individuals with having to set aside time for detailed interviews. Even in high maturity assessments, it becomes difficult for the right individuals to be scheduled into an interview. For more information on the People CMM survey, please contact SITARA Technologies from the wordinatex available on <http://www.SITARATECH.com>.

Script Questions Based on SITARA's People CMM ASQ Survey Analysis

Problem

Not using Class B assessment results to understand site practices before a formal Class A assessment restricts factual understanding of the process.

Proposition

It would be very useful to examine results from the Class B assessment and feed them as inputs to script questions for the formal Class A assessment. Since SITARA's People CMM ASQ is not of an objective type, but actually requires individuals to write descriptive answers, it permits a good visibility into the state of practice. The Class B does not require much face time with the respondents since much of the data will be available in the survey. Face time, if any, would be required from the process owners and from individuals only if additional clarifications are necessary.

Document review

Problem

Currently, the role of document review is to be inclusive of all projects in the organization since there is no guideline from the SEI. It also includes all of the process documents available in the organizational process asset library.

Proposition

For a Class B assessment, it is better to probe 'a couple of projects' chosen randomly 'in depth' for both process implementation indicators and with specific use of process tailoring. And, the remainder of the projects can be probed to span the complete life cycle followed in the organization based on the life cycle that is being executed by the project. If projects in the organization have different project life cycles, then all such projects must go through an 'in depth' examination of both process implementation indicators and specific use of process tailoring. Scripted questions should now orient the assessment team to understanding from the practitioners how specific aspects of the practice implementation indicators and the process have been found to be useful rather than merely for 'corroboration' of facts as having seen once and heard twice.

Since the intent behind a Class B is not to obtain coverage on the People CMM there could be a reason for having insufficient information to rate the goals. Class B must ensure 'institutionalization' of practices is consistent. At least, all institutionalization practices must have a clear understanding in the organization and must be visible as practice implementation indicators supported by process assets.

Focus on Weaknesses

Problem

Scope of conducting a Class B is not defined.

Proposition

Class B assessments have to be formalized from a point of view of ensuring that the ensuing Class A assessment establishes the degree of satisfaction of institutionalization practices. If done with the help of the proposed SITARA's People CMM ASQ, it is more than likely that key issues with the process can be highlighted as weaknesses or opportunities for improvement. Class B assessment results can then be used as inputs for the more formal Class A assessment to identify how the follow-on action programme works in the organization.

Selecting Interviewees and Structuring Interviews for the Class A Assessment

Interviews

Proposition

For a Class A assessment, a good rule of thumb is to interview at least 30–40% of the organization to get a practitioner's view of the process. Class A must ensure that the site offers at least 25% of the assessment participants who have not participated earlier in the Class B appraisal or assessment. What is very useful is, to front load the assessment with interview sessions. Having at least 4 interviews on the first day and 3 interviews on the second day is a good way to ensure that there is a very good likelihood for corroboration. We will explore this likelihood, next.

Exploration of Alternative Practices

On assessments, if a practice directly does not hurt a goal, then it should be supported by either an alternative practice or a system that is resilient to "changes to process owners" for a fulfilment of a level.

How to Know if a Practice is an Effective Alternative Practice

Alternative practices are those which may not fulfil the People CMM practices *in toto*. Normally, such practices can be rated either as, strength or as weakness. If a certain sense of rigidity is associated with alternative practices, then such practices are ideal candidates to be categorized into the 'Points to Ponder' and it would be in the best interests of the assessed entity that such rigid postures of the process become highlighted as a qualitative judgement of the assessment team.

Or, there could be a limited context within which they may become applicable and therefore the alternative practice can indeed be treated effectively as strength. If the site does not even understand the reasons surrounding the rigidity of practices, and the site cannot relate them as strengths from experiences with such institutionalization, they should be categorized as a weakness.

For illustration of this idea, we will use an example: practice 2 of Training and Development reads as—'Training needed in critical skills is identified for each individual'.

Since this practice calls for having a plan for each individual to develop his/her critical skills based on individual assessments of critical skills, it can definitely overwhelm the implementation. Many times, it can be both a daunting and an impossible task.

An effective alternative practice could be that the site ensures a policy which states and supports only those individuals who have served the organizational well and have enough team responsibilities to be the affected stakeholders on this People CMM practice. This also means that, the policy can make explicit mention that those who are on probation or temporary staff or contactors are exempt from this practice. Under such circumstances it is more than reasonable to conclude that the alternative practice is effectively, a strength.

This example proves that considerable tailoring of the People CMM practices is to be exercised in order to make them applicable and effective.

How to Rule Process Areas as not Applicable

Rating of practices can be considered as not applicable if and only if, there is very clear evidence that supports their not being applicable within the site's context. If all of the practices within a process area are to be treated as not applicable along with supporting justifications which the team and assessment team leader can accept, then the process area itself is ruled as not applicable. For an assessment with a level 5 scope competency integration at level 4 is by far the only process area that could probably be ruled as not applicable.

In larger organizations (excess of 300 people), there is yet another possibility when a Class A assessment is supported by evidence resulting from a structured Class B assessment. The process area might itself be applicable within a limited context of the organization. And, within this limited context all of the practices may be supported adequately and followed to the tee. In which case, it might be useful to examine reasons for their not being applicable within the rest of the organization and use the People CMM assessment principles to award the maturity rating.

What is the Best Way to Rate Practices to Confirm Goal Accomplishment on the Process Area

One of the available techniques is, to examine practice-by-practice and check if the findings considered holistically ensure that the goal is satisfied. And this is normally done using a thumbs up or thumbs down approach where the assessment team establishes consensus based on their recall of the assessment. This technique works only if we have an experienced assessment team which has a powerful ability to recall the discussions and bring the right context. Not a bullet proof technique! And, even with an experienced assessment team, this is a long and a dreary process.

A better way is to tag every observation from the People CMM assessment which will be used to develop the findings after establishing corroboration from at least two independent sources, to indicate whether it is a strength or a weakness.

After these findings are identified as a strength or a weakness, it is now important to tag these practices to the People CMM framework. Tagging involves identifying the practices of the particular process area of the People CMM that will be impacted either as strength or as weakness.

The assessment team can now take each finding which is a weakness *only* and examine the degree to which the goals of the process area are hurt. If the practices have a significant negative impact on the goal fulfilment, then the process area itself can be rated as 'not satisfied'. Many times, such a focused assessment of the weaknesses reveal an interesting observation that permits an exploration of the 'alternative practices' since the weakness may have a limited negative consequence.

Once consensus is achieved on evaluation of all of the weaknesses, then it is easy to establish the same on the strengths.

The above technique is a quick and easy method that establishes team consensus without losing time—one of the most important commodities which is often in short supply during assessments!

Have a Detailed Plan and Work the Plan

Sample Plan

Project start date: Monday, 1 March 1999

Project finish date: Wednesday, 31 May 2000

Table 9.1   *People CMM Implementation and Assessment Plan*

ID	Task Name	Duration	Start Date	Finish Date
1	**HOUSEKEEPING TASKS**	89 days	Tue 9/11/99	Fri 10/3/00
2	Change Agent Training Program on People CMM Model	3 days	Mon 6/12/99	Wed 8/12/99
3	Examine documentation vis-à-vis PA	23 days	Tue 9/11/99	Thu 9/12/99
4	Mock Process Appraisals	45 days	Mon 10/1/00	Fri 10/3/00
5	Class B Appraisal 1 – Raincheck for Level X	5 days	Mon 10/1/00	Fri 14/1/00
6	Class B Appraisal 2 – Raincheck for Level Y	5 days	Mon 6/3/00	Fri 10/3/00
7	**PREPARING PHASE**	65 days	Mon 3/1/00	Fri 31/3/00
8	P1 –Secure improvement sponsor	16 days	Mon 3/1/00	Mon 24/1/00
9	P2 – Determine assessment scope	11 days	Fri 14/1/00	Fri 28/1/00
10	P3 – Obtain organizational commitment	16 days	Thu 20/1/00	Thu 10/2/00
11	P4 – Define improvement infrastructure	16 days	Thu 20/1/00	Thu 10/2/00
12	P5 – Plan assessment details	16 days	Thu 27/1/00	Thu 17/2/00
13	P6 – Train assessment team on People CMM and Assessment method	7 days	Thu 17/2/00	Fri 25/2/00
14	P7 – Arrange assessment logistics	40 days	Mon 7/2/00	Fri 31/3/00
15	**SURVEYING PHASE**	42 days	Thu 3/2/00	Fri 31/3/00
16	S1– Select People CMM Survey sample	6 days	Thu 3/2/00	Thu 10/2/00
17	S2 – Prepare survey logistics	7 days	Mon 7/2/00	Tue 15/2/00
18	S3 – Administer and score People CMM Surveys	11 days	Tue 15/2/00	Tue 29/2/00
19	S4 – Analyse People CMM Survey Results (TeraQuest)	24 days	Tue 29/2/00	Fri 31/3/00
20	**ASSESSING PHASE**	5 days	Mon 17/4/00	Fri 21/4/00
21	A1– Organize assessment team	1 day	Mon 17/4/00	Mon 17/4/00
22	A2 – Brief assessment participants	1 day	Mon 17/4/00	Mon 17/4/00
23	A3 – Analyse People CMM Survey results	1 day	Mon 17/4/00	Mon 17/4/00
24	A4 – Review documents	1 day	Mon 17/4/00	Mon 17/4/00
25	A5 – Script interviews	1 day	Mon 17/4/00	Mon 17/4/00
26	A6 – Interview process owners	1 day	Tue 18/4/00	Tue 18/4/00
27	A7 – Consolidate process owner data	1 day	Tue 18/4/00	Tue 18/4/00
28	A8 – Perform follow-up interviews	1 day	Tue 18/4/00	Tue 18/4/00
29	A9 – Interview managers	1 day	Tue 18/4/00	Tue 18/4/00
30	A10 – Consolidate manager data	1 day	Tue 18/4/00	Tue 18/4/00
31	A11 –Workforce discussions	1 day	Wed 19/4/00	Wed 19/4/00
32	A12 – Consolidate workforce data	1 day	Wed 19/4/00	Wed 19/4/00

(Contd.)

(*Contd.*)

33	A13 – Develop preliminary assessment findings	I day	Wed 19/4/00	Wed 19/4/00
34	A14 – Prepare preliminary findings briefing	I day	Wed 19/4/00	Wed 19/4/00
35	A15 – Review preliminary findings with legal unit	I day	Thu 20/4/00	Thu 20/4/00
36	A16 – Review preliminary findings with process owners	I day	Thu 20/4/00	Thu 20/4/00
37	A17 – Review preliminary findings with managers	I day	Thu 20/4/00	Thu 20/4/00
38	A18 – Review preliminary findings with workforce	I day	Thu 20/4/00	Thu 20/4/00
39	A19 – Revise final findings and rate maturity	I day	Thu 20/4/00	Thu 20/4/00
40	A20 – Complete final findings briefing	I day	Thu 20/4/00	Thu 20/4/00
41	A21 – Present final findings	I day	Fri 21/4/00	Fri 21/4/00
42	A22 – Debrief sponsor	I day	Fri 21/4/00	Fri 21/4/00
43	A23 – Wrap-up assessment	I day	Fri 21/4/00	Fri 21/4/00
44	**REPORTING PHASE**	23 days	Mon 1/5/00	Wed 31/5/00
45	R1– Complete final People CMM assessment report	11 days	Mon 1/5/00	Mon 15/5/00
46	R2 – Report data to the People CMM Assessment Repository	13 days	Mon 15/5/00	Wed 31/5/00

Source: Adapted from SITARA Process JewelBox™ ©2002 with permission

How to Ensure Bullet-proof Corroboration

One of the most useful techniques is to ensure that there are at least 4 interviews each lasting about 1.5 hours on day 1. The key process areas that are in scope for investigation must be explored in such a way that at least two interviewees will get an opportunity to address practices of the same key process area. This is an effective way to ensure that enough insights on the site's practices can be obtained with an excellent chance for obtaining corroboration—to hear about practices from at least two independent data gathering sessions or sources.

After the interviews are concluded, use the first day's data consolidation session to identify both, process discontinuities and potential areas to probe further. And the assessment team should now script these questions for the second day's interviews. This is by far the best way to ensure that the assessment scripts are kept live and relevant on the assessment. Keeping a static script of questions developed at the very beginning of the assessment is a very ineffective way to approach the assessment. Such a method strips meaning of the assessment away from considering realities on ground and focuses only on ensuring compliance to the practices of the People CMM model. In my opinion, such a view of the assessment or appraisal which is concerned more to ensure compliance to the People CMM practices and not to ground realities which might highlight alternative practices is a text book style of conducting an appraisal. Offering real value and meaning to the business from an appraisal is possible only if the scripts can go after information obtained from practitioners. Normally, scripts are based on initial document reviews and maturity questionnaire assessment, which are performed as pre-onsite activities.

The same strategy can be applied on the second day where at least 3 interviews each lasting about 1.5 hours can be planned. This time around the key process areas which were not addressed adequately on the first day can become the focus for the interviews. This is again the only best known technique to ensure that corroboration of assessment information is made possible.

When such a strategy is used to facilitate and enable corroboration, it is very unlikely that there is ever a need for a follow-up interview session or that there will even be an occasion for a need to explore the 'information needed list or INLs' as they are referred to.

It is needless to emphasise the need for effective mentoring and steering of the appraisal by the assessment team leader using the above strategy, in order to make the process of establishing corroboration bullet-proof.

Have a Detailed Checklist to Guide Logistics and Pre-onsite Activities

Table 9.2 *Logistics and pre-onsite checklist*

Requirement	Assigned to	Status
■ One large room for all the functional are representatives (FAR) discussions with adequate security ■ One large table and enough chairs to be arranged around the table to seat assessment participants scheduled for the interview		
Secure the room and make sure that you have enough duplicate keys available when needed. Each room that is used by assessment team members must have a lock and a key to secure access to them		
Block/reserve two separate conference rooms, preferably adjacent, during the assessment week for discussions		
Arrange one large table in the interview room to keep enough copies of the People CMM book, observation sheets, white papers, and writing material that will be used during the interviews		
Arrange a large box for confidential item trash in the interview room		
Extension cords for power with enough power outlets.		

(Contd.)

(Contd.)

OFFICE SUPPLIES

Paper for printers: at least 2000 sheets of paper

Paper for copier: at least 5000 sheets of paper

Paper for note-taking

Sufficient sets of observation sheets for each assessment team member.

Stationery

1 or 2 sets per assessment team member

Yellow Post-its

Sufficient 5" by 3" stickies and 3" by 3" stickies to tag each document received (about 200)

Miscellaneous Supplies

Stapler and extra staples, tape with dispenser, couple of pairs of scissors or box cutters

Others

Analog Phone Line (Number is only given to assessment team)

At least 2 copies of the Model description (People CMM) OR have each ATM bring his/her own copy

If English is not the primary language, a translation dictionary along with a couple of individuals who are versatile in English and native languages

Dedicated access to a high-speed printer connected to a high-speed PC with everyone in the team knowledgeable about how to get support if required

Copier or access to a copy machine whenever required; additional assistance may become necessary to replace toner, etc.

Shredder

Blank out any glass doors/windows with opaque cover

COMPUTING INFRASTRUCTURE

Make 2 high-speed PCs available within a Local Area Network and on the Internet. The PC must be Intel Pentium 3 or higher with mouse and at least 4 MB Memory, a 3½ inch floppy drive, 10 MB hard disk space at a minimum

Make available a backup laptop with similar capabilities for making presentations compatibility to presentation software used on PCs

Floppy disks: 20 blank pre-formatted floppy disks whichever size fits the supplied hardware with labels for floppy disks

Overhead projector for direct computer display; recommend SVGA or better

(Contd.)

(*Contd.*)

FOOD AND BEVERAGES

NOTE: Whatever the assessment team eats or drinks during the interviews, the same must be offered to the interviewees.

For the interview room

Beverages available during the day for both the assessment team members and the interviewees: coffee, tea, bottled water, juice, soda, etc. and a table to hold them

Lunches

Lunches should be available so that the team can eat and resume work in 45 minutes. Lunches can either be brought into the interview room or the assessment team can go to the cafeteria (provided it is reasonably close)

Dinners

On nights, if the team works past 8.00 P.M., this would apply. Should be available so that team can resume work in 45 minutes

Snacks

Enough supply so that assessment team must be able to offer whatever they are eating or drinking to the participants as well. Best to avoid eating/drinking during the conduct of the interview

Should an accident result from food spills, know where to get help with cleaning without losing time. Or have enough tissue paper

Check the speed on printer to make sure it is 8/12 pages per minute

Check from the team members on whether they have to commute long distances and whether they need hotel accommodations to be made closer to the venue of the assessment

Complete the People CMM assessment forms with available information and keep it ready before assessment. Update it as an when more information becomes available

Have a dedicated configuration management repository and responsibility during the assessment to maintain updates to People CMM assessment work products

Schedule of the assessment week to be maintained and updated by onsite coordinator and the lead assessor

If there are any changes to the assessment week schedule, the onsite coordinator must ensure that everyone on the team and the lead assessor are consulted and modified after consensus

Check to read the softcopies that come along with the People CMM assessment kit

Make assignment of process areas to team members prior to the commencement of assessment-related activities

Script assessment questions before the commencement of the interviews based on a Class B assessment and document review

(Contd.)

COMMUNICATION EQUIPMENT

Telephone: Telephone number for messages, which may be sent to the assessment team

If assessment involves interactions with a remote site, facsimile

- Telephone number for fax, which may be sent to the assessment team
- Delivery of any fax received to the assessment team

MEETING WITH SPONSOR

- Before the commencement of the assessment activities, it is useful to set up a meeting with the assessment team leader and the site sponsor to ensure that there is good understanding of the sponsor's requirements and commitment for a follow-on action programme
- Assess readiness of the site for the assessment and sponsor's disposition to the assessment report
- Prepare sponsor for the assessment and for any possible timely interventions that might become necessary.

Source: Adapted from SITARA Process JewelBox™ © 2002 with permission.

Have a Detailed Checklist and a Guideline for Chartering the Necessary Infrastructure

Table 9.3   *Infrastructure checklist*

Presentation for all participants on first day during opening meeting or assessment participants briefing session

- This room should be large enough to comfortably seat everyone who will be interviewed
- A few additional chairs in the front for assessment team use
- All necessary projection mechanisms to present the assessment participants briefing presentation
- Everyone attending this meeting needs to be informed about both the time and the location and the logistics coordinator must ensure that everyone is seated at least 10 minutes prior to the start of the presentation
- Access to a spare projector should a situation warrant quick replacement of the projector
- Reserve the same room used for this meeting, for the FAR feedback and the final findings report sessions

Draft findings feedback to process owners, project leaders, and middle managers

- Reserve the same room we used for the interviews or the larger conference room used for assessment participants briefing session
- The assessment team will sit at the front of the room facing the participants and must have chairs that enable note-taking
- All necessary projection mechanisms to present the draft findings presentation

---

(Contd.)

(Contd.)

Draft findings feedback to all FARs
- Reserve the same room used for presentation to everyone on the first day or for the assessment participant briefings
- The Assessment team will sit at the front of the room facing the participants and must have chairs that enable note-taking
- All necessary projection mechanisms to present the draft findings presentation

Final findings presentation
- Reserve the same room used for presentation to everyone on the first day or for the assessment participant briefings
- All necessary projection mechanisms to present the final findings presentation
- The assessment team will sit at the front of the room facing the interviewees

Executing briefing
- Usually this is done in either the interview room or the senior manager's conference room. This room needs to be sufficiently large to accommodate the team and all of the people senior management invites
- All necessary projection mechanisms to present the draft findings presentation

Source: Adapted from SITARA Process JewelBox™ © 2002 with permission

Interleaving Draft Findings Finalization and Follow-up Interview Schedule

Having a draft findings finalization step in the assessment or appraisal is a SITARA innovation to the assessment process.

This is by far the most useful technique found to ensure that follow-up interviews are actually based on ensuring the assessment or appraisal actually clarifies the assessment team's understanding of the assessment or appraisal. Interleaving draft findings finalization step before any follow-up data collection sessions ensures that the site is given adequate opportunity to actually arrive at consensus beyond reasonable doubt as to what the merits and demerits of the practices are.

The draft findings finalization step requires a new set of site specific scripts to be generated by the assessment team that will focus only on process discontinuities which have been observed by the assessment team. This new best practice being reported in this book from SITARA has tremendous advantages at actually ensuring a truly collaborative approach to the People CMM appraisal, particularly when the scope of the appraisal is a high maturity.

If there are no significant process discontinuities requiring a follow up, then the outcome of the draft findings finalization step can actually lead very effectively into the actual preparation of the draft findings in the draft findings consolidation step of the appraisal or the assessment.

Have a Solid Plan for the Assessment Week—Failing to Plan is Planning to Fail!

Table 9.4 *Assessment week schedule*

	Monday, DDMMYY	Tuesday, DDMMYY	Wednesday, DDMMYY	Thursday, DDMMYY	Friday, DDMMYY
9:30 9:45 10:00 10:15 10:30 10:45 11:00 11:15	Interview 1 9:30–11:00	Interview 5 9:30–11:00	Interview 9 9:30–11:00	Draft Findings Presentation for Process Owners, Middle managers 9:30–11:00	Debriefing of the Assessment Team 9:30–11:00
11:30 11:45 12:00 12:15 12:30 12:45 1:00	Interview 2 11:15–12:45	Interview 6 11:15–12:45	**Draft findings finalization [SITARA's new best practice]**	Draft Findings Presentation to FAR Group Participants 11:15–12:45	FINAL FINDINGS PRESENTATION Executive Session
1:30 1:45 2:00 2:15 2:30 2:45 3:00 3:15	LUNCH Interview 3 13:30–15:00	LUNCH Interview 7 13:30–15:00	LUNCH **Draft findings finalization [SITARA's new best practice]**	LUNCH Draft Findings Presentation to Practice Heads & SEPG or CDG 13:30–15:00	LUNCH Wrap-up Appraisal
3:30 3:45 4:00 4:15 4:30 4:45 5:00	Interview 4 15:15–17:00	Interview 8 15:15–17:00	FOLLOW UP FOLLOW UP FOLLOW UP FOLLOW UP FOLLOW UP FOLLOW UP FOLLOW UP	Final Findings Consolidation & Rating	
UNTIL WORK IS COMPLETE	Day 1 Information Consolidation	Day 2 Information Consolidation	Day 3 Draft Findings Consolidation		

Source: Adapted from SITARA Process JewelBox™ © 2002 with permission.

Epilogue

What is the Real Meaning of Process Maturity?

BEFORE A DEFINITIVE answer on what process maturity is could be attempted, let us take a look at whether we should define operating processes at all in the first place! If initiatives involve an active collaboration of individuals, it goes without saying that teamwork and building a shared vision or a shared meaning of the execution objectives among the team is significantly important. The process is nothing more than an articulation of these execution objectives using a formal language that can be understood by all relevant stakeholders.

Most software initiatives have the following process components—management, development, verification–validation and support, and continuous improvement. Needless to say, the overall process maturity is governed and dictated by the maturity of all four components. Management processes include both external and internal customer interfaces. Development processes include the practices used to decompose the problem and develop a solution space that addresses the problem. Verification–validation and support include the processes that are necessary for identifying the mechanisms to establish correctness, completeness, consistency, and testability of the solution. Continuous improvement deals with exploring and building organizational core competencies by having both capable and enduring processes that provide lasting value.

It is therefore natural to think in terms of best practices that address all the above process components. The degree of detail to which these components are addressed decides the process maturity. And, this degree of detail must be based on valid business and strategic objectives. Most important of all is the ability to look through the customer's eye. And this ability to look through the customer's eye is in my opinion the real meaning of process maturity.

Looking through the Customer's Eye

A process is only a means to the end. And, therefore having a process is only a 'necessary' but 'not sufficient' condition to operate at high process capability. The sufficiency conditions are normally underemphasized and, as a consequence, overlooked. But, it is the sufficiency conditions, such as the following, which dictate whether the customer is a happy customer or not.

- Highly talented and empowered leadership at all levels
- Teams of people who live by a "can-do" attitude and are all quality champions
- Organizational sponsorship, which is supportive of proactive growth
- Individuals pursuing continuous personal competency development and personal mastery
- Strong visionary leadership council, which evaluates workforce competencies

Fortunately, it is your people-power that can offer a solution to the above sufficiency conditions with the right competency orientation! If a high process maturity organization cannot be flexible enough to accommodate changing customer priorities, then it is worthless! Since high process maturity does not necessarily provide cost-effective solutions, the only prudent thing to expect from such a process is to derisk the tendencies of a lower process maturity customer. If such derisking is not direct fallout of having high process maturity, then its applicability is suspect. Irrespective of how robust the definition of the process in the four categories of management, development, verification–validation and support processes, in order to accommodate the vision through the customer's eye, there is need for articulating one more process–competency management process.

In order to sustain the gains of a change initiative by useful application of the people-power, we now come to conclude that we must work to change the relationship styles, attitudes, and self-esteem of the people who are expected to live out these changes. A strong blend of both technical and people skills are needed for a successful management of a change initiative. Whatever an organization is doing now, no matter how bizarre or dysfunctional it might appear it was at one time a successful response to the reasons surrounding the exhibited behaviour. The People CMM framework helps an organization to continually clarify and explore whether the exhibited response is still a valid response, or should the organization do something different with the changes to the circumstances. The People CMM framework is an evolutionary approach to managing the circumstances that surround organizational competency development.

Some key areas addressed by the People CMM framework include career development, compensation, competency development, culture development, performance management, training, team building, workforce management, and personal competency development. When viewed as a staged model, at level 2 (the *repeatable level*), issues that keep people from being able to perform their work responsibilities are addressed by building a foundation of basic workforce practices to create a *culture of commitment*. At level 3 (the *defined level*), any inconsistencies in workforce practices are removed by analysing skills required by its workforce to execute the business functions by identifying best practices and tailoring mechanism in its own workforce activities to create a *culture of professionalism*. At level 4 (the *managed level*), the experience of the organizational workforce is effectively leveraged to provide strong mentoring and alignment of individual performance to the team, unit, and organizational goals by creating a *culture of competencies*. At level 5 (the *optimizing level*), continuous clarification of individual competencies by finding innovative ways to improve workforce capability by providing an environment of perpetual improvement and growth of competencies using effective coaching programs to build a *culture of continuous improvement and empowerment* is established.

If the end objective of any change management initiative using the People CMM framework is to grow core competencies and make the organization's response time to change as minimal as possible, then Peter Senge's *The Fifth Discipline* [Senge 1990], can be explored as an effective leverage tool to exploit the benefits from implementing the People CMM framework. In order to create and sustain a successful process culture, it is important to exploit the synergy resulting from the People CMM and concepts such as systems thinking, personal mastery, mental models, shared vision, and team building to accomplish larger organizational objectives.

The central message of *The Fifth Discipline* is that organizations work the way they work, because of how people and other constituencies in it think and interact. Only by improving this collective thought can we change deeply-embedded policies and practices for the better. And, only by improving the interaction among all constituencies can shared vision and shared understandings, with new capacities for coordinated action, be established. This notion is pretty new for most of us.

The People CMM framework provides ample scope to define the stakes in the ground while providing for a boundary to operate. It is challenging to think that while we redesign the manifest processes of our organizations, we must consider business objectives. This also requires a redesign of the internal structures of our mental models. But anything less will fall short of the changes required. "Companies that have reengineered themselves around horizontal processes often discover that they have little or no experience in actually operating in such an environment," says Michael Hammer. "Radical change in how work is done inevitably leads to the definition of new jobs with new skill requirements, which in turn demand new kinds of people." [Hammer 1993]

Knowledge is represented as two components in Chinese Kanji characters. The first pictogram depicts a child standing under the roof of a school—the learning component. The second pictogram depicts a baby bird struggling to fly out of its nest for the first time—the practice component. So, in order to leverage, one needs to learn first. In order to sustain the practice component, I have also come to conclude that the following sufficiency conditions must exist.

A strong process improvement mindset and orientation in all activities at all times

While making process improvements is an ongoing change management process, having the right thinking in place is very essential. The process must allow problems to surface—early and effectively. And when they do, it must permit solutions to be rendered to fix them immediately so that they do not reappear. If the problem surfaces more than once, then it is obvious that there is a problem with the process improvement process. Encouraging problems to be surfaced and finding a solution for them is one of the most important sufficiency conditions.

Strongly humanistic to improve the way employees are treated, included, and inspired in a software process improvement initiative

Along with a strong emphasis on improving competencies and the software process, there ought to be robust plans to improve the people-related processes as well. The People CMM is an excellent compilation of the 'what-is-needed'. And this book can supplement and serve the 'how-to-do-it' keeping the right rigour of practice in place.

It must be applied holistically so that the principles of process improvement, policies, and practices reach every nook and cranny of the organization.

The process only sets a framework within which individuals are required to function. But they must have the freedom to do what they were trained to do. And freedom to do what they want to do the way it is done best. They also must have the freedom to use their knowledge and experience to their best possible capabilities.

Empowerment at all levels, especially at the frontline

The organization must be able to state without hesitation: 'we are a fully empowered work force'. For everything that needs to get done, empowering individuals with the support of adequate information to do it, is necessary. And, when the individual does something different from expectations after the necessary inputs are provided managers must display the necessary sensitivity that the individual did so for the right reason after exercising professional judgement. However, for empowerment to work, it is necessary to have a progress review based on trust—Management by Exception.

Any organization can be at level 5 for just five minutes. It is my belief that only an empowered workforce can make the day-to-day changes that are required to operate and keep a level 5 process at level 5 for more than five minutes.

A rich and satisfying work life is everyone's birthright. I hope the information presented to you has broadened your perspective and has offered you a range of choices to make. But before you take the next measured step to implement the People CMM, check if your organizational circumstances or the context have changed!

Frequently Asked Questions

Q. Is the People CMM to be looked at as a certification process or does it provide guidance on how to enhance people practices?

A. The People CMM is most definitely not a certification process. The People CMM is a framework, which when effectively deployed, determines the extent to which an organization is versatile in managing its workforce competencies. While building core competencies requires conscious effort and determination from an organization, the People CMM framework highlights practices that help to retain, grow, and nurture competent individuals.

Q. Does a company have to be assessed for each level before being assessed for the next one or can it take two steps at a time?

A. There is no rule that an organization has to progress one step at a time. Our belief within SITARA Technologies is that evolutionary change happens only in revolutionary steps. The only lasting representation of change in our opinion, based on a number of years of in-the-trenches experience with change management, is that slow and steady loses the race! Dynamism is best at work when aggressive targets are set and behaviour change is mandated. I read an interesting anecdote that tells it best. An industry, which was planning to adopt a pension scheme, put up a proposal in the organization for a consensus decision. They said that they would move forward only when they had 100% consensus. But then, just one Johnny was totally opposed to it and so, the whole process came to a grinding halt much to the chagrin of other individuals. The CEO called up Johnny and told him, "Here is the paper and here is the pen, sign it or else you are fired!" Johnny immediately complied by signing his consent to the pension scheme. When the CEO later asked Johnny, why he had not done so voluntarily? Johnny replied, "Nobody explained to me the consequences of not signing so very clearly!" So you see consensus-based 'change management' may not work in practice all the time. It is theoretically a nice thing to say that we will go after consensus. Champions of the People CMM programme should decide how they are going to lead the team and where they want to be ... and the rest should march ahead to reach that goal.

Q. Can one quantify the contribution of adopting best people practices to the bottom line?

A. Of course, when done correctly, there are both tangible and intangible benefits. The intrinsic worth, which is the true worth of a company, goes up. The books of accounts may not capture this information, and this may not reflect in a company's stock prices. It shows up as the several much-wanted intangibles—pride in individuals, pride in their work, a high sense of self-esteem, courage and discipline, a value-based and purposeful existence, and so on. The thing that is significantly lacking is not best practices in organizations. It is an attitude to best practices that is lacking. SITARA's Universal Excellence Framework is all about 'cultivating and nurturing this attitude' to best practices.

Q. How long does it take for an organization to evolve from level 1 to 5?

A. Anywhere between one year to forever! It all depends upon where the motivation for change is coming from. Is it intrinsic or extrinsic? If it is intrinsic, how many of the people in the organization share the vision and value system?.

Q. Is personal competency development related to work alone or to other spheres of an individual's life, which are likely to affect and impact performance at work?

A. SITARA firmly believes in what is attributed to Mahatma Gandhi: 'One cannot excel in one department of life, while the others are found wanting'. We believe that personal competency development operates fundamentally on multiple dimensions. It is not just how good a professional you are, it is also about how good a family person you are, how good a citizen you are, how good a human being you are, and so on. Mind you, all of these are competencies. By good I mean, dependable. As Shiv Khera puts it so well: "Ability without dependability is a liability." That to me, sums up the People CMM better than anything else! Any organization can be a People CMM level 5 for just five minutes! Having just an ability to grow core competencies does not mean a thing until organizations have nurtured the abilities within individuals to be self-directed and empowered to make the day-to-day changes that are so very necessary to keep the People CMM level 5 at level 5 for more than just five minutes!

Q. Is there a similar process for non-IT companies?

A. The People CMM is nothing but a framework of best practices—distilled common sense. You can also think of the People CMM framework as a generic management paradigm that can be applied to both IT and non-IT companies to accomplish the same business purpose of organizational development.

Also refer to

📖 http://www.SITARATECH.com/QnAPCMM.htm

Appendix A

Suggested Reading List

[Aguayo 1990] Aguayo, R "Dr Deming—The American Who Taught the Japanese About Quality", *Fireside Book*, 1990.

[Basili 1984] Basili, V R, and D M Weiss, "A Methodology for Collecting Valid Software Engineering Data", *IEEE Transactions on Software Engineering*, Vol. SE-10, 1984, pp. 728–738.

[Brown 1992] Mark Graham Brown. *Baldrige Award Winning Quality, How to Interpret the Malcolm Baldrige Award Criteria*, ASQC Quality Press. 1992.

[CMMI 2002] CMMISM for Systems Engineering/Software Engineering/Integrated Product and Process Development, Supplier Selection, Version 1.1, Staged & Continuous Representations (*CMMI-SE/SW/IPPD/SS V1.1*) *Technical Report CMU/SEI-2002-TR-012*), Pittsburgh, PA: Software Engineering Institute, Carnegie Mellon University, March 2002.

[Constantine 1993] Constantine, L Larry, "Work Organization Paradigms for Project Management and Organization", *Communications of the ACM* October 1993/Vol. 36 No. 10: 35–43.

[Coutu 2002] Coutu, L Diane. "The Anxiety of Learning", *Harvard Business Review*, March 2002.

[Creech 1994] Creech, Bill. *The Five Pillars of TQM*, Truman Talley Books/Plume, New York. 1994.

[Curtis 1995] Curtis, Bill *et al. People Capability Maturity Model*, CMU/SEI-95-MM-02, Overview of the People Capability Maturity Model® Version 1.0, CMU/SEI 95-MM-01 Pittsburgh, PA: Software Engineering Institute, Carnegie Mellon University, September 1995.

[Curtis 2002] Curtis, Bill *et al. The People Capability Maturity Model*, Addison-Wesley, Pearson Education, Inc. 2002.

[DeMarco 1985] DeMarco, T and Lister, T. "Programmer Performance and the Effects of the Workplace", *Proceedings of the 8th International Conference on Software Engineering*, London. 1985, pp. 269–72.

[Hammel 2000] Hammel, Gary. *Leading the Revolution*, Harvard Business School Press. 2000.

[Hammel 1994] Hammel, Gary and Prahalad C K. *Competing for the Future*, Harvard Business School Press. 1994.

[Hammer 1993] Hammer, M, Champy, J. *Reengineering the Corporation*, Harper Business, 1993.

[Humphrey 1997] Humphrey, W S. *Introduction to the Personal Software Process*^{SM}, Reading, MA: Addison-Wesley, 1997.

[Humphrey 2000] Humphrey, W S. *Introduction to the Team Software Process*^{SM}, Boston: Addison-Wesley, 2000.

[Intelligroup 2000] PR Newswire, *Intelligroup Global Development Center Achieves SEI Certification for Continuous Improvement of Software and People Development*. New York, 2000.

[James 1991], Harrington, H James, *Business Process Improvement*, McGraw-Hill, Inc., 1991.

[Jones 1995] Jones, Beth Laurie, *Jesus CEO*, Laurie Beth Jones, New York. 1995.

[Kaplan 1992] Kaplan, R S and Norton, D P. "The Balanced Scorecard—Measures that Drive Performance", *Harvard Business Review* 70, 1 (1992): 71–79.

[Kirkpatrick 1998] Kirkpatrick, D L. *Evaluating Training Programs* (2nd Ed). San Francisco: Berrett-Koehler, 1998.

[Lombardo] Lombardo, Michael M and Eichinger, Robert W. *The Career Architect Development Planner*, Lominger Limited, Inc. Minneapolis, MN ISBN 0-9655712-1-1.

[Nandyal 2001], Nandyal, R S, "A Practitioner's View of the CBA-IPI", *Asian SEPG Conference*, 2001 New Delhi.

[Nandyal 2002] Nandyal, R S and Nandyal, S R. "Do you really have a software development strategy?" *7th Annual European SEPG Conference*, 2002.

[Prahlad 1990] Prahlad, C K and Hamel, G. "The Core Competency of the Corporation". *Harvard Business Review* 68, 3 (1990): 79–91.

[Rothwell 1994] Rothwell, W J and Kazanas, H C. *Human resource development: a strategic approach.* pp. 484–486. Amherst, MA: HRD Press, Inc. 1994.

[Grover 1991] Andrews, Grover A. (1991) *A practical handbook for assessing learning outcomes in continuing education and training.* Washington, D.C.: International Association for Continuing Education and Training.

[Satir 1991] Satir, Virginia. *The Satir Model*, Science & Behavior Books, 1991.

[Senge 1990] Senge, Peter M. *The Fifth Discipline*, Century Business, 1990.

[SITARA 2000a] *SITARA's People CMM Assessment Survey Questionnaire* (People CASQ) released from SITARA Process JewelBox™ with permission from SITARA Technologies Pvt. Ltd.

[SITARA 2000b] *SITARA Process JewelBox*™, Repository of best practices conceived and compiled from years of research and study of global companies using SITARA's Universal Excellence Framework (UEF).

[SITARA 2001] SITARA 10W5D Competency Hierarchy Model and SITARA Domain Competency Sandwich Model released from *SITARA Process JewelBox*™ with permission from SITARA Technologies Pvt. Ltd.

[SITARA SE/JUNE 2001] <http://www.SITARATECH.com/innovations.htm>, [*SITARA Technical Report*], SITARA Technologies Pvt. Ltd.

[Vyasa BC] Maharshi Vyasa, Veda. *The Bhagavad Gita.*

Recommended Reading List

[Albrecht 1992] Albrecht, K. *The Only Thing That Matters*, Harper Business, 1992.

[CMU 1995] Carnegie Mellon University, Software Engineering Institute. Paulk, M et al. *Capability Maturity Model: Guidelines for Improving the Software Process*, Addison-Wesley, 1995.

[Covey 1990] Covey, S. *Principle Centered Leadership*, Simon & Schuster, New York, 1990.

[Constantine 1993] Constantine, L. "Work Organization: Paradigms for Project Management and Organization", *Communications of the ACM*, October 1993 Vol. 36 No. 10 pp. 35–43.

[Gibson 1997] Gibson, R. *Rethinking the Future*, Nicholas Brealey Publishing, London, 1997.

[Humphrey 1997] Humphrey, W. *Managing Technical People*, Addison Wesley Longman, Inc., 1997.

[Kan 1995] Kan, S H. *Metrics and Models in Software Quality Engineering*, Addison-Wesley Publishing Company, 1995.

[Kelley 2001] Kelley, T. *The Art of Innovation*, Doubleday New York, 2001.

[Khera 1998] Khera, S, *You Can Win*, Macmillan, 1998.

[Pande 2000] Pande, P S *et al*. *The Six Sigma Way: How GE, Motorola, and Other Top Companies are Honing Their Performance*, New York: McGraw-Hill, 2000.

[Scholtes 1998] Scholtes, P. *The Team Handbook*, Joiner Associates, Inc. 1988.

Appendix B

SITARA's People CMM Assessment Survey Questionnaire

Instructions

- Answer only those questions, which are applicable to you.

- Please list your answers and provide elaborations, where necessary.

ROLE (MANDATORY):

UNIT (MANDATORY):

NAME (OPTIONAL):

PROJECT (OPTIONAL):

Level 2

Work Environment

- How does the organization ensure safe working conditions?

- How adequate are the resources, space, and infrastructure provided to you to perform your work effectively?

- How are environmental factors and distractions affecting your performance identified and how does the organization resolve them?

- Who is responsible for assisting and advising you on work-environment-related activities?

Communication and Coordination

- How are organizational policies, events, and practices communicated?

- What mechanisms are in place for you to maintain ongoing communication within your unit to effectively perform your role?

- How are poor interpersonal relationships handled?

- How often is your opinion sought regarding your working conditions?

Staffing

- How are individuals selected to work in your unit?

- How are open positions staffed, and what is the criteria used to transition individuals on their assignments within the unit?

Performance Management

- How are individual performance objectives determined in your group?

- How frequently do you receive communication about your performance at work?

- How is unsatisfactory performance of individuals handled within your group?

- How is outstanding work performance recognized or rewarded?

Training and Development

- How are training opportunities identified to support you in your work assignments?

- How do you maintain ongoing awareness of your job performance and development opportunities?

- How are you made aware of your capabilities?

Compensation

- What is the basis on which your compensation was determined?

- Under what conditions are adjustments made to your compensation and how is equity ensured?

Level 3

Knowledge and Skills Analysis

- How does the organization determine the knowledge, skills, and abilities required for use with its current and anticipated needs?

- How are such assessments used to provide competency orientation to units?

- How frequently does your organization reevaluate the knowledge and skills required to perform its business functions?

Workforce Planning

- How are the unit's tactical and strategic competency needs established?

- How do units determine and assess the growth in workforce competencies?

- What is the frequency between such assessments and how do corrective actions ensure that unit competency objectives are fulfilled?

Competency Development

- How are workforce competencies defined and how are individual aspirations aligned to the organizational competency development?

- How frequently are individual competency plans reviewed and how are they assessed for effectiveness?

- What measures are taken to ensure that growth of workforce competencies is established as an internal capability?

Competency-Based Practices

- What is the role of staffing on the growth of workforce competencies?

- How do you become aware of the best practices within your identified competencies?

- How has the work assignments helped you to develop knowledge and skills needed for your professional and career advancement?

- How frequently do you receive performance feedback and how does it align with the organization's competency assessment?

Career Development

- How are career advancement opportunities identified?

- What is the preparation you receive prior to a career transition?

- How is the personal competency development plan used to align with your overall career objectives?

Participatory Culture

- How is information about business activities and performance communicated?

- How are decisions on the day-to-day business engagements made?

- How is your opinion sought and used on decisions that impact your work?

- What are the training opportunities provided to you and what are the available support mechanisms that assist you to make decisions best made by you?

Workgroup Development

- How are team charters established and used for envisioning interdependent work?

- How is the organizational standard tailored to fit your workgroup needs?

- How are ongoing assessments made to determine the progress made by your workgroup?

- How does the organization ensure growth in workforce competencies?

Level 4

Mentoring

- How do you identify mentors who can help you with your personal development plan?

- How frequently do you get to share your development opportunities with your identified mentors?

- How are assessments made to establish progress with respect to your personal growth objectives?

Team Building

- How is collaborative work facilitated in your organization?

- How does the organization ensure that individuals leverage complementary skills?

- How is project-specific tailoring of workforce practices facilitated?

- How are you made aware of internal resources that may help you with your competency development?

- How are team-based objectives established for competency development?

Team Based Practices

- How are teams formed and how is ongoing communication among team members maintained?

- How is team performance assessed and how is teamwork recognized and rewarded?

- How does the organization support and promote team-based activities?

Organizational Competency Management

- How are individual competency profiles established?

- How are individual competencies assessed to ensure alignment with overall organizational goals for competency development?

- How are competency assets identified and used?

- How are workforce competencies requiring complementary skills integrated?

Organizational Capability Management

- How are target capability profiles established for the identified workforce competencies?

- How are the results of quantitative analyses concerning the organization's capability in its workforce competencies used?

- How does the organization establish quantitative goals for capability development in its critical competency-based processes?

Organizational Performance Alignment

- How are performance goals established and aligned for individuals across units?

- How is 'cross-group sharing of lessons' learnt and best practices enabled?

- What is the feedback mechanism that helps in timely corrective and preventive actions?

- What are the performance measures used to understand organizational workforce competencies?

- In interdependent and collaborative work, how are competencies leveraged to offer the best competency alignment?

Competency Integration

- How does the organization leverage value from multidisciplinary work?

- What are the project management activities and organizational infrastructure supporting collaborative work?

- How is a common shared vision for competency development and integration of complementary team competencies established?

- How does the organizational process repository enable integration of competencies?

Empowered Workgroups

- How are teams assisted and supported with decision making that is best made by them?

- How are practices tailored to support project-based activities?

- How are individuals and teams supported by knowledgeable experts within the organization?

Competency-Based Assets

- Where are the lessons learnt and best practices captured and how are they used on projects?

- How are competency assets identified and kept current with the changing organizational capability profile?

- How often is the asset library assessed and how is the assessment result used?

Quantitative Performance Management

- How is feedback provided on project performance with respect to the identified critical-to-quality measures?

- How are process capability baselines established?

- How is sub-process variation stabilized and how are corrective actions rendered?

- How is the impact due to special and common causes of process variation determined and minimized?

Level 5

Personal Competency Development

- How are training opportunities ensured to enable individual's competency development objectives?

- How are personal competency development plans established?

- What are supporting infrastructural mechanisms available to individuals that help to capture individual learning?

- How are organizational development activities aligned to foster individual learning opportunities?

Continuous Capability Improvement

- How are causes of defects identified and minimized?

- How do you suggest improvements in your work processes?

- How have the self-improvement programmes, you have undertaken in the recent past, helped you to improve your performance?

Coaching

- How is coaching made available to you in order to improve your performance?

- How are coaches selected in your organization?

- What is the mechanism used to collaborate with your coach for setting quantitative goals for improvements in performance?

Continuous Workforce Innovation

- How are incremental and innovative improvements to the competency assets rendered?

- How frequently does your organization evaluate innovative workforce practices and technology?

- How are innovative workforce practices and technologies that prove beneficial in a trial implementation adopted in an orderly way across your organization?

Appendix C

SITARA ODER Paradigm

The need to identify workforce competencies in the field of IT has never been more relevant and vital to the success of a software initiative than it was a few years ago because today we see a lack of differentiation. The quickest way to differentiate until recently was to get a quality appraisal through a certification or an assessment process. For which, *having a capable and a mature development process* is a crucial component of a software development strategy. For purposes of illustration, we will explore SITARA ODER (Objective, Determinants, Enablers, and Realignment) paradigm as applied to the strategic need of *having a capable and mature development process.*

We have found applicability of using the ODER paradigm for identifying organizational workforce competencies using SITARA's 10W5D method which was described earlier in the book. We will look at the Determinants, which we believe are the *sufficiency conditions* that seldom exist. This is an experiential report and is based on observing the growth of IT within the context of the Indian subcontinent.

Introduction

What has been observed in a number of years is that, having a strategic intent often begins with the right focus—gain a label of quality consciousness and sensitivity through its myriad forms ISO, SEI-CMM, Malcolm Baldrige, Six Sigma initiatives, and the like. Organizations begin fixing their processes and go about earnestly in their quest for a capable process. Unfortunately, given the very objective *assessment techniques,* where you either have or don't have a process capability, even a quality assessment becomes a limitation very soon. Organizations are found doing things "for the sake of" an assessment, with no understanding of the real intrinsic worth these may have for the company. As a result, one finds numerous organizations announcing the same flavour of the month process maturity. And soon, this focus becomes one of getting your competitor's process capability on record if not in spirit. Since the industry has taken note of this phenomenon, a mere quality assessment or certification alone is no differentiator today because everybody seems to have an assessed process capability, which is theoretically a very good accomplishment. *But do these organizations really have a sound strategic intent for competency development behind their software development initiatives?*

This question gets amplified when something else also happens almost simultaneously. The finance controller begins to scream saying that 'productive dollars' are going down the drain through these so-called 'change initiatives'. The questioning is often based on a lopsided reasoning: "We have been successful in our business so far, why do we need to change?" The sponsor begins to take note of the fall in stock prices. The change management initiative, so very crucial for building a competency-oriented learning organization, gets the axe. And then the entire process is repeated cynically not understanding that financial controls are essential but a company does not sell only on its extrinsic worth. The financial books do not reveal the true worth of a company—the intrinsic worth which is due to a highly mature, consistently stable delivery process that puts quality services and products on the market shelves.

We would look at this 'waste' in a slightly different manner, giving the financial controller the benefit of doubt. We wonder how many of the so-called level 5 organizations, the highest rating for software engineering and management practices awarded on the Software CMM maturity framework are level 5 true to this day! And, assuming for the moment that most of them who have not re-assessed themselves in the last 12 months may not be operating at that level of maturity anymore because sustaining a level 5 process capability goes beyond having just the systems and processes in place—what could be the reason? Why are organizations seen to rust away so badly in mere six months after spending so many dollars and productive time of their brilliant talent on process initiatives, which easily last for a couple of years until they get to the level 5?

From our experience with CMM assessments, most organizations articulate their systems, processes, and methods—what we call the enablers—almost perfectly. They also have an impressive line-up of customers. Both these are essential to work the strategic intent. What is often found missing are the following 'sufficiency conditions' behind the strategic intent that should be the bedrock of any organization that wants to be a level 5 on a sustained basis. And the operative word is 'commitment'.

SITARA ODER Paradigm

SITARA ODER paradigm includes the following to exist for a sound strategic intent.

Objective: The strategic intent defining the purpose of the activities or practices

Enablers: Having the right systems, processes, and methods for coordinated action—the necessary conditions

Realignment: Evaluation of the what-if conditions and results to revalidate management commitment

What we find missing in the software development strategy is the D (determinants) or the sufficiency conditions.

Determinants: The sufficiency conditions that must exist for consistent demonstration of the strategic intent

Illustration of SITARA ODER Paradigm

Objective: The strategic intent defining the purpose of the activities or practices

Example: 'To have a capable and a mature development process'

Enablers: Having the right systems, processes and methods for coordinated action—the necessary conditions—to make sure that the objective is met. Since there are many well-defined prescriptions to choose from, we will not elaborate on these enablers beyond just making a mention of them here.

Example: Adopting the practices of SW-CMM or the People CMM or CMMI as a reference framework

Realignment: Evaluation of the what-if conditions and results to revalidate management commitment

Example: Depending upon the outcome of execution, redefine the objective for next iteration.

Determinants: The sufficiency conditions that must exist for consistent demonstration of the strategic intent, are explored in what follows.

Determinants

Commitment to Differentiate

While differentiation has to do with what is termed as the Unique Selling Point or the USP, it is unfortunately not as simplistic as it is made out to be. It requires chains of leadership to be able to question status quo relentlessly and be prepared to pioneer new ways of thinking by looking beyond the shoulders of their organization for inspiration and solutions. Effective differentiation happens only in counterintuitive ways of reasoning. To differentiate effectively, it is necessary to go beyond identification of industry-wide best practices to maybe 'enterprise-wide best practices'. To understand how to reduce defects and cycle time in software product development and customization initiatives, it might require that traditional methods be evaluated against a totally different industry, say from Domino's Pizza for instance. To reduce typographical errors in user manuals and software documentation, we may need to examine how it is done day-in and day-out with minimal errors by the print media that puts out newspapers on a daily basis. We have observed this practice in a South Korean company, which called it tear-down reengineering. In a recent software process design initiative we were involved with, the inspiration for the final process came from observing a machine drawing of the parts of an electric motor, which were rendered on different sheets of transparent paper. When superimposed upon each other, they took the final shape of an electric motor! What a great way to remove redundancies! We got a picture perfect process in a matter of a couple of months in what we called the operational process descriptions. Identification of core competencies is a very essential first step for effective differentiation. Differentiation using innovation is the need of the hour.

Commitment to Core Competencies

In our seminars on the People CMM, the question that often draws a blank response is, "What do you think are your core competencies?" When core competency is defined as a network of disciplines with which value generation becomes possible, answers still don't seem to be forthcoming. Organizations also seem to have difficulty in understanding that in order to succeed at software development, there is a need to have a portfolio of interdependent competencies upon which services and product offerings are based.

Committing to core competencies requires an organizational think-tank that has a view of the future based on current reality. Without current reality becoming the basis for this futuristic vision, flexibility, which is so very essential, will be missing from the strategic intent. There is also a need to understand that a 'network of competencies' is often necessary for full range, end-to-end solution offering. A general rule that should be adopted while identifying and defining competencies is 10 wide and 5 deep (10W5D). What the 10W5D means is that you need to have at least 10 different profiles of services, which all add up to the totality of your business. The 5 deep are what are in your mainstay and no matter what, the strategic intent behind these competencies will not change significantly. It is only after you have identified these lines of competencies, that a successful network of leverage becomes possible to render. Process improvement has to now ensure improvements to these systems. It is only when process improvement takes on a systemic view in true systems thinking approach, that you can nurture and breed creativity. Strategic vision has to do with unearthing the competencies that matter most and defining a growth orientation in realizing value entitlement from a symbiotic and synergistic blend of this portfolio. For such thinking to take hold, what is extremely important for process improvements to address is to improve the 'context' and create the right context. Action is only secondary.

A good way to begin the 10W5D is to go after broad definitions of competencies—reliability engineering instead of testing; programming languages rather than C or C++; software engineering instead of object-oriented methods; and so on. The broader you can keep the list in the 10W, the better are the chances you will have with defining the 5D. Many times the 10W5D at one level will soon have a subset in itself.

Commitment to Create Chains of Leadership

If empowerment was the buzzword until recently, turned-on people are an even more important requirement today. Organizations, big and small, seem to have a problem dealing with inefficiencies and underutilization of talent. What is often mistaken for dead wood is actually wood that is rotting as well! Change is a first-principle thing—"Unless I change first, I cannot bring about change below my command." And, this must begin with the CEO. Leadership at all levels has to take note of the fact that decisions are best taken at the level they ought to be taken. What is more important in an empowered work culture is that when a decision is taken at a particular level, the rest of the organization stands by that decision. And, all remaining decisions surrounding it are made at the same level using a management process that we will term 'management by exception'. Management reviews happen to support decisions with a purpose of clarification and not exhortation. Organizations that are truly empowering are nurturing environments having the innate ability to draw forth the best out of individuals. One often finds even in a highly process capable organization, the most important ingredient for success—a sense of belonging—that is missing. Little wonder then that commitment is a superficial emotion. To build this sense of belonging and bonding, the best known observed practice from a leading multinational in South Korea is to transform the managerial style into one of 'parenting' which works perfectly well in this culture. The subordinates in the organization feel that the manager is like an extended parent who cares for their growth and well-being. Individual learning and personal competency development happens almost as an obsession leading to a culture of excellence.

Commitment to Excellence

Identifying the best practices and implementing them in the organization sounds very simplistic. From the many years we have been associated with organizations that are truly sensitive to employee suggestions to process improvement, what is extremely difficult is to stay in this proactive mode 'willfully'. Organizations that are committed to excellence seem to have mechanisms in place where individuals are encouraged to make recommendations to the day-to-day changes that are necessary for optimal performance. If the depth of the core competencies is lacking, what is observed is that the quality of suggestions seem to have only a superficial effect on the overall process effectiveness. Depth also connotes diversification and differentiation.

And like everything else, educational qualifications and training must also have an expiry date! It is only when this happens that individuals are geared towards continuous personal competency development—an essential hallmark for building a culture of innovation.

Commitment to Innovation

One of the best-known practices that encourage individuals to get into an innovative frame of mind is to have a handbook of practices. This handbook of practices is often updated based on engineering notebooks or records that individuals maintain on a day-to-day basis after trying out newer techniques or approaches to solving problems. A chronological record of such a nature will also help an individual keep track of the innovation and help to structure his thought. A recommendation for the truly level 5 organization that is committed to maintaining and excelling as an innovative organization is to institutionalize this practice of individual record keeping of engineering ideas. Technology and process change management issues are best addressed through this process of continuous renewal where individuals become sensitive to the needs of the organization they serve and consciously move the borders of innovation a step further each day through trials and pilots. Both, successes and failures from such trials or pilots are recorded and shared within the organization. A highly-beneficial outcome of such a system is openness and transparency to both failures and successes. This is a primary requirement to build a system of high self-esteem. An organization that is motivated into action through individuals with high self-esteem can very rarely go wrong or make a mistake. Even if there is a mistake, there is a learning process that automatically takes note of the changes that are necessary to insulate, isolate, and eliminate the mistake in the future. The hallmark of a learning organization is in its ability to ensure that such a mistake proofing mechanism is part of the strategic intent. Leveraging value from mistake proofing leads to an ability to differentiate services and products that invariably involves a competitive environment—which may be unfair.

Commitment to Excellence Despite a Lousy Competitor

Nothing destroys the competition more badly than a lousy competitor. Unfortunately, the watering down of true excellence is because of a lousy competitor. And it requires both a naïve customer and a lousy competitor to serve as catalysing forces to hasten the entropy of mediocrity and have a catastrophic impact on excellence and quality. Customers, who are only sensitive to 'spending', think in a very unconventional manner when it comes to initiatives with which they only have an affiliation to and not true sense of ownership. World-class quality never comes cheap and a lousy competitor will sell his wares at prices that can kill the entire system. Customers are seen buying on cost and not on value. Organizations that are truly committed to 'excellence' have learnt the tough art of walking away from the wrong business. 'Cheap and best' is often a figment of one's imagination in an industry such as software development, where the development process cannot be automated. The question that is essential to address in order to have a strategic intent is "cheap at what value?" and "best at what cost?" Unless this becomes explicit within the strategic sourcing of services from a customer's viewpoint and strategic intent within the delivery mechanism from a provider's viewpoint, blooming of the IT industry is based on 'assumptions' and 'false hopes'. No wonder we witness stalling and stagnation of investments because of underperformance due to an overhyped solution offering or an under-evaluated product. The only optimal solution lies in evaluating and assessing both the acquisition and outsourcing and the development and delivery sides of the system.

Commitment to Superior Performance

It is our conclusion after working with change initiatives for so long that dramatic improvement to results and great resilience to getting back to square one is possible only in revolutionary leaps. Evolutionary changes are not only slow but also not lasting. For an organization to outperform its competition every individual within the organization must be committed to superior performance with a sense of pride. And for this to happen, there must be an organizational sense of belonging and bonding.

The Bottom Line

The strategic intent behind software development must be to build an innovative learning organization. It is no wonder then that organizations that outperform the norm have an innate ability to do all of the above correctly, completely, and consistently. The probability of succeeding is high if the strategic intent is based on the above determinants—the commitments.

List of Abbreviations

Abbreviation	Expansion
HR	Human Resource(s)
CEO	Chief Executive Officer
CMM	Capability Maturity Model
IT	Information Technology
TQM	Total Quality Management
KPA	Key Process Area
CDG	Competency Development Group
SEPG	Software Engineering Process Group
IDEAL	Initiating, Diagnosing, Establishing, Acting, and Learning
PDCA	Plan–DO–Check–Act
SW-CMM	Software Capability Maturity Model
ISO	International Organization for Standardization
QMS	Quality Management System
CAF	CMM Appraisal Framework
AT	Assessment Team
PCAR	People CMM Assessment Repository Record Form
ODER	Objective, Determinants, Enabler and Realignment
GQM	Goal–Question–Metric
PCMM ASQ	People CMM Assessment Survey Questionnaire
CTD	Cumulative Trauma Disorder
IEEE	Institute of Electrical and Electronics Engineers, Inc.
CMMI	Capability Maturity Model Integration
SME	Subject Matter Expert
HRD	Human Resource Development
SWAT	Skilled with Advanced Technologies
TSP	Team Software Process
PSP	Personal Software Process
CBAIPI	CMM-Based Appraisal for Internal Process Improvement

SVGA	Super Video Graphic Array
PA	Process Area
FAR	Functional Area Representative
USP	Unique Selling Point

Index

About the Author

Raghav S Nandyal is the Founder and CEO of SITARA Technologies, a professional services company with core competencies in strategic management consulting, process assessment and web-based product development. He is among the very few authorized lead assessors by the Software Engineering Institute, Carnegie Mellon University, on the CMMI (SCAMPI Method), the Software CMM and the People CMM. He is authorized by the Software Engineering Institute to teach the Introduction to CMMI course. Raghav Nandyal has been a prime consultant, coach and an assessor on Software and People CMM based process improvement initiatives in leading multinationals, worldwide. He is on the international review panel for IEEE Software.

Raghav Nandyal held several software and management positions ranging from software engineer to Chief Process and Quality Officer with leading multinationals such as Motorola, NYNEX Science & Technology, LG Group and Intelligroup, Inc., before going into business for himself.

His current research interests in software management are in mitigating software risks and building self-sustaining software process improvement programs in development environments working on emerging technologies. He has published a number of technical papers in international conferences. He has a Master's degree in Electrical and Computer Engineering from the Illinois Institute of Technology, Chicago. He is a donor alumnus of Indian Institute of Science, Bangalore.